Faust!

Pocket Battleship p 3

Wehrmacht p 60

Gulag p 119

Russian Prison Camps p 117

U-BOAT ADVENTURES

U-BOAT ADVENTURES

FIRSTHAND ACCOUNTS FROM WORLD WAR II

Melanie Wiggins

NAVAL INSTITUTE PRESS

ANNAPOLIS, MARYLAND

Naval Institute Press
291 Wood Road
Annapolis, MD 21402

Library of Congress Cataloging-in-Publication Data
Wiggins, Melanie, 1934–
    U-boat adventures : firsthand accounts from World War II / Melanie
Wiggins.
        p. cm.
    Includes bibliographical references and index.
    ISBN 1-55750-950-6 (alk. paper)
    1. World War, 1939–1945—Naval operations, German. 2. World War,
1939–1945—Naval operations—Submarine. 3. World War, 1939–1945—
Personal narratives, German.   I. Title.
    D781.W55 1999
    940.54'5943—dc21   99-13892

Printed in the United States of America on acid-free paper ∞
06 05 04 03 02 01 00 99 9 8 7 6 5 4 3 2
First printing

Frontispiece: U-128 arrives at Lorient on 23 March 1942
after a second patrol. *Bundesarchiv, Koblenz*

Unless otherwise noted, the photographs in each chapter
were provided by the veterans themselves.

. . . on the sea it is difficult to find a man with gray hair.

Phalaecus

CONTENTS

ILLUSTRATIONS

FOREWORD

Historical writers for years have spotlighted the most noted U-boat commanders and their achievements in both world wars, leaving a great many crewmen's adventures untold. Melanie Wiggins' book presents fresh insight into submarine warfare as experienced by radiomen, helmsmen, watch officers, engineers, and petty officers, as well as some of the commanders who survived.

Wiggins' well-documented book about German U-boats, *Torpedoes in the Gulf: Galveston and the U-boats, 1942–1943,* was published in 1995, and her research for that project led to the discovery of many German submarine veterans who wanted to relate their stories. Wiggins' current work encompasses the adventures of twenty-one U-boatmen who came forth with diaries, letters, photographs, and interviews for this collection. Their dramatic accounts reveal every conceivable German U-boat situation from 1939 to the bitter end of World War II and include scenes in postwar prisoner of war camps.

One of the older U-boat captains, Jürgen Wattenberg, recalls his early navy career and the sinking of U-162 off the coast of Trinidad, plus his remarkable escape from a POW camp. Wattenberg's story is complemented by the experiences of Wolfgang von Bartenwerffer in U-536, sent into the Gulf of St. Lawrence to pick up Otto Kretschmer and other German submariners who were to break out of Camp Bowmanville in Canada. Kretschmer, top U-boat ace of the war, reminisces about his navy life, the sinking of his boat and his capture in 1941, and his years as a prisoner of war.

Some of the first missions into the North Atlantic are described—notably by Georg Högel, who went on the initial patrol of U-30, when she sank the British liner *Athenia* and was later attacked by aircraft of the carrier *Ark Royal* in September 1939. In July 1940 Ernst Göthling survived the sinking of his boat, U-26, by convoy escorts, only to be a POW for the next seven years.

In the Caribbean we have Hans Burck's secret diary of U-67's journey in February 1942 to Aruba in Operation Neuland, and Hermann Wien and Otto Dietz, crewmen on U-180, remember the time they transported Indian freedom fighter Subhas Chandra Bose and his aide to the Japanese submarine I-29 off Madagascar. From the Mediterranean the commander of U-616, Siegfried Koitschka, tells of his many successful patrols against the Allied invasion fleets off Sicily. Arctic adventures are related by Hans Georg Hess, skipper of U-995, and Walter Tegtmeier of U-997, who operated against Murmansk-bound convoys in 1944 and 1945.

Several stories chronicle the war's end, including an RAF attack on the German naval base at Horten, Norway, in December 1944, and Helmut Wehlte's account of U-903's evacuation of civilian refugees from East Prussia in 1945. Günther Thiemrodt tells of U-1205's participation in the rescue operation as well, and Commander Wolfgang Heibges recalls his last days on U-999 in Operation Regenbogen—the scuttling of U-boats on 4 May 1945 in Flensburg Bay. Peter Marl, who served on three U-boats for the entire war, experienced a thirty-five-day journey underwater from Bordeaux to Penang, with the final delivery of U-195 at Jakarta. Josef Matthes, in U-963, sailed off to Portugal after Germany's surrender rather than return home, and Walter Tegtmeier accompanied U-997 to Scotland in Operation Deadlight, where the Royal Navy sank the remaining German submarines.

We thank Melanie Wiggins for collecting the memories of such an outstanding group of former German submariners, with their wide-ranging experiences in all oceans during the great sea battles of World War II.

Jürgen Rohwer

PREFACE

In a submarine training school at Wilhelmshaven I noticed a large enclosed tank rocking back and forth, up, down, and side to side. Wondering what it was, I asked a U-boat veteran in our tour group to explain. "There are men inside, and they'll be there for several hours, to see if they can take the motion of a sub." I was shocked at what appeared to be a kind of torture, then realized that the rocking and pitching of a claustrophobic undersea vessel was only a minor part of a U-boat crewman's war experience. At that instant I gained added respect and admiration for every man who served on a German U-boat.

Each individual crew member had equal importance in his submarine; one error in his job could mean death for all. I have attempted to demonstrate the worth and historic value of these men's memories in this collection of U-boat stories by including experiences of every rank, from Able Seaman to Captain. Executive Officer Wolfgang von Bartenwerffer, for instance, served on U-536's mission to rescue Otto Kretschmer from a Canadian prison camp; Radioman Georg Högel witnessed U-30's sinking of the passenger liner *Athenia;* Fireman Second Class Josef Erben on U-128 told about his boat getting stuck on a huge rock; Hans Burck kept a secret diary about his voyage on U-67 and their attack on oil refineries at Aruba; and Battle Station Helmsman Hermann Frubrich recounted U-845's near-sinking of the *Queen Mary.*

In the often chaotic settings of attacks by the U-boats on merchant ships, there were times when commanders could not ascertain easily whether or not they had sunk a particular vessel, notably in convoys.

In those instances they attempted to report results as best they could, but history sometimes has proven them in error. German and U.S. naval historians have worked for over fifty years to piece together the facts, and these statistics can be read in books by Dr. Jürgen Rohwer. It was my intention to relate the individual commanders' and crew members' stories exactly as they remembered them, giving readers a feeling for the difficulties not only of making attacks, but of recording the precise results.

In searching for photographs for some of the stories, I browsed through the World War II U-boat collection at the Bundesarchiv in Koblenz, Germany. There, among others, I found a picture of three grinning crewmen displaying a big shark on their boat deck, sailors eating lunch as they sat on huge torpedoes in the bow room, and the crew of U-123 enjoying Christmas dinner as one man played the accordion. Taken in the first glory years of U-boat successes, hundreds of submarine scenes hinted at intriguing stories. Many showed the boats' victorious arrivals at French ports, with pennants flying, bands playing, commanders holding bouquets, and crews enjoying cold beers.

Photographers and reporters accompanied some of the missions to take 35-millimeter still photos or movies for Hitler's propaganda campaign. Of course the photos made excellent material for the newspapers and were widely published.

In mid-1943, when the subs' successes were rapidly diminishing and most were being sunk, Hitler's government abruptly stopped photographing the U-boats. One might say that the submarines, at that point, were relegated to oblivion in more ways than one. I have attempted, with my collection of individual U-boat stories and photographs, to give readers an experience similar to that of browsing through an old scrapbook, with glimpses into the strange world of submarines.

Such a high percentage of German submariners died in the war that the memories of the few who remain are, I believe, beyond price in world history. Each of the survivors who contributed to this collection has my profound gratitude, respect, and admiration. Every one of their anecdotes, stories, diaries, and photographs is invaluable, and thanks go to the following: Otto Kretschmer, Josef Matthes, Helmut Wehlte, Josef Erben, Ernst Göthling, Dr. Hans Georg Hess, Georg Högel, Dr. Siegfried Koitschka, Peter Petersen, Tom Poser, Walter Tegtmeier, Günther Thiemrodt, Jürgen Wattenberg, Walter Kozur, Johann Kremer, John Whiteley, Hermann Wien, Herbert Hermann, Robert Klaus, Fritz Lamprecht, R. E. N. Porrett, Wolfgang von Bartenwerffer, Hans Burck, Alfred Dietrich, Otto Dietz, Peter Marl, Wolfgang Heibges, and Hermann Frubrich.

Others are: The Görlitz U-boat Kameradschaft; the crew of U-682; Timothy Mulligan, U.S. National Archives; Heinz Kuhlmann; Hubert Hardt; Hans Hornkohl; Prof. Matthias Brünig; H. R. Rösing; Dr. Ralph Uhlig; Dr. Herbert Uhlig; Herbert Wodarz; Gerd Thäter; Chris Reuleaux; Hannes Esken; Erich Evers; and Horst Bredow of the U-Boot-Archiv in Cuxhaven.

In many places I visited in Germany the wives went out of their way to be hospitable, preparing delightful lunches or desserts and coffee. Frau Kretschmer, Frau Kremer, Frau Kozur, Frau Uhlig, Frau von Bartenwerffer, Frau Kuhlmann, Frau Brünig, and Frau Tegtmeier all have my affection and appreciation.

Since most of the material for this book was written or spoken in German, I was dependent upon the assistance of translators and inter-preters, who gave willing and enthusiastic assistance. Several friends helped me with interviews in Germany: Kurt Ludewig, Dirk Ohling, and Birgit Sfalinna. In addition, Peter Petersen spent untold hours converting dozens of letters, reports, and stories into English, adding brief explanations where needed. Tom Poser helped as well, as did Dr. Hans Georg Bone. We had a great deal of fun doing the work and attempted to put all technical terms into understandable language. Equivalents between U.S. and German naval ranks have been provided; however, it should be noted that German ranks reflected both the job title and the grade of the submariner.

Perhaps those who read these U-boat stories will be encouraged to search out and record as many as possible of those that are left untold. That is my hope.

U-BOAT ADVENTURES

1   Jürgen Wattenberg, U-162

■■

In the spring of 1995, former Commander Wattenberg, age ninety-four, consented to be interviewed in Hamburg, and when I first saw him, I was struck by his dark brown hair and fierce gaze. During our visit he recounted several of his many memorable experiences in the German navy and as a prisoner of war in Arizona. When we were about to part, he confided that he hoped to live to the age of a hundred so he could witness the year 2000. "Do you think I'll make it?" he asked. "Yes, I believe you will," I assured him and impulsively kissed him on the cheek. Seven months later I received notice that Wattenberg had died on 27 November 1995, just before his ninety-fifth birthday.

■■

"It was always sunny where my parents lived, in Lübeck," Wattenberg recalled. "My father played the flute and Mother played the piano. They made a lot of music in our home." Jürgen's father, a doctor of psychiatry and neurology, directed a large medical facility near the town. "The center was a very nice place between fields of corn, woods, and forests. It was lucky we had that."

Wattenberg, born in 1900, entered the Royal Prussian Cadet School at the age of fourteen. In June 1914 a school officer took some of the boys by train to Kiel to attend the renowned Kieler Sailing Week; when they arrived at the scene of the great boating event, they beheld an immense array of German battleships and cruisers anchored among

Jürgen Wattenberg

British Grand Fleet warships. "They were visiting us in 1914. We passed all these ships—a British one, a German one, then a British one. All of them were tied to buoys in the fjord."

Jürgen and his fellow cadets boarded a lightship so they could get a good view of the regatta. Leading the great armada of sailboats came Kaiser Wilhelm II's enormous yacht, the *Meteor*. "When he passed the lightship where we were standing, we shouted, 'Hooray, hooray, hooray!' and waved at him. He kindly waved back at us, laughing," Wattenberg went on. "This was a big point in my life, and I decided then to go into the navy. The sun was shining, the grand ships were there all gleaming, and the emperor sailed past the whole fleet. Every ship called, 'Hooray, hooray, hooray!' and we saw it all."

The race began, and at the moment the *Meteor* reached the first buoy, the majestic yacht turned and headed back toward the fjord with sails down and flags at half-mast. "We feared that the emperor was in trouble, and we could not think what was wrong." The regatta stopped, all the boats came sailing in, and hundreds of spectators watched, wondering what had happened.

A few hours later the cadets learned that Archduke Franz Ferdinand, the Austrian crown successor, had been assassinated in Sarajevo. The boys could not know that this would be the beginning of World War I.

"When the British ships sailed away from Kiel that day, the English admiral signaled to the German admiral, 'Friends forever,' and this was three months before the war. It was a remarkable event in my life."

In 1921 Jürgen Wattenberg entered the German navy and spent three enjoyable years as education officer, training young cadets on the sailship *Niobe* and cruisers *Emden* and *Karlsruhe*. "I went on three cruises—in 1923, 1930, and 1934—and have been around the whole world. Those were very interesting times with the training ships. I am sorry I didn't write down all those voyages in a book."[1]

When World War II exploded in 1939, Wattenberg was serving on the *Panzerschiff* (pocket battleship) *Admiral Graf Spee* as chief navigating officer under Captain Hans Langsdorff. Immediately after Great Britain and Germany went to war that September, Germany's two *Panzerschiffe*, the *Deutschland* and the *Graf Spee*, steamed out to attack enemy commerce vessels. Between 30 September and 7 December, Wattenberg's battleship sank nine British merchantmen.

The *Panzerschiff*'s successes came to an abrupt halt when Langsdorff encountered three British warships off the Brazilian coast: the heavy cruiser *Exeter* and two light cruisers, the *Ajax* and the *Achilles*. A rip-roaring naval battle ensued in which the *Graf Spee* inflicted serious damage on her opponents, but was in the process hit by twenty shells and had to seek shelter for repairs.[2]

"It was a jolly good fight—a fair and honourable battle. The last to be fought in the old tradition," remarked Sir Eugen Millington-Drake, British minister at Montevideo, Uruguay, at the time of the conflict. Years later Wattenberg commented, "We could have engaged the three ships in turn and destroyed them."[3]

Langsdorff anchored at Montevideo that night, knowing that as a belligerent warship the *Graf Spee* would be allowed to stay in the neutral harbor long enough to get fit for the trip back to Germany. Uruguayan government officials inspected the ship and gave him seventy-two hours to make repairs. "Langsdorff was of the opinion that we were not able to stand the rough North Atlantic in December," recalled Wattenberg, "and he wanted to have the ship seaworthy. And this was the wrong decision." The longer he stayed in port, the better chance the British had to amass defenses at the entry to the Atlantic.[4]

Seizing an unexpected opportunity, the British sent three more warships to trap the *Graf Spee* inside the estuary of the River Plate. Langsdorff had three choices: surrender, try to break through the blockade, or scuttle his ship. He reasoned that fighting his way to the open sea allowed no chance to damage the British vessels, and in a battle the *Graf Spee* could be sunk in the shallow estuary waters, allowing her to fall into enemy hands. The possibility of sacrificing his crewmen weighed heavily on his mind as well. "Then he decided to sink the ship himself," said his navigating officer, "with the permission of the High Command."[5]

On 17 December Langsdorff transferred seven hundred of his men to the German merchantman *Tacoma,* and a skeleton crew sailed the *Panzerschiff* out of Uruguayan territorial waters. Wondering what would ensue, British authorities in Montevideo watched her slowly leaving. On board the *Graf Spee,* forty-three men proceeded to carry out their plans as quickly as possible.

"It was a glorious sunny day," remembered Friedrich-Wilhelm Rasenack, *Graf Spee* officer. "All Montevideo was watching the spectacle. The docks were covered with people." Airplanes flew overhead to photograph the naval battle for American newspapers.[6]

Wattenberg and the others set dynamite charges in their doomed vessel, allowing twenty minutes to get away. Just before the time was up, five of the officers gathered with Langsdorff on the quarterdeck, saluted the flag and pennant as they were hauled down, then boarded a launch and made their way to a distance about a mile off.

Two tremendous explosions ripped the air, lifting the battleship and throwing wreckage into the sky. A few seconds later the magazine blew up with a massive boom, flames devoured the entire vessel, and the broken wreckage of the *Graf Spee* settled into the shallow waters. "It was a shattering sight," said Wattenberg.[7]

Langsdorff and his crew left hastily on an Argentinian boat to Buenos Aires where they hoped, as shipwrecked mariners, to avoid imprisonment. But on 19 December the government advised them that they were to be interned. At midnight the commander wrote letters to his wife, parents, and the German ambassador. "I am happy," he expressed to the ambassador, "to pay with my life to prevent any possible reflection on the honor of my flag." With the ensign of the *Graf Spee* laid across his writing table, Langsdorff fired a bullet through his temple. "He was a very good man," reminisced Wattenberg, "and I'm sorry I didn't say, 'Captain, you are making the wrong decision [delay for repairs].' But he was *so* capable."[8]

Officers of the *Graf Spee,* imprisoned in the naval arsenal in Montevideo, were allowed to go out for excursions, during which they contacted people in the German community. One of Wattenberg's friends smuggled civilian clothing to him, and he and others escaped, remaining in hiding for several weeks. By various means they crossed the Andes, met in Santiago, Chile, and from there flew on commercial airlines back to Germany, arriving in the spring of 1940.[9]

As the German U-boats succeeded in keeping the upper hand in the Battle of the Atlantic, Wattenberg returned to his homeland and entered submarine training, subsequently becoming commander of U-162. "I sank fourteen ships, eighty-six thousand tons in all." On one of his early patrols (May 1942 off Brazil), when U-boats had little or no opposition, he sank a 6,700-ton freighter, the *Parnahyba,* which broke in half, freeing a menagerie of chickens, turkeys, and pigs. Flying away from the sinking vessel, the chickens landed on drifting wreckage, and two pigs came swimming expertly through the waves. The crew captured this unexpected treasure and enjoyed excellent chicken soup and roast pork for several days.

Shortly afterward, in the same month, Wattenberg spotted a small coastal sailing vessel, the *Florence M. Douglas*. After firing a warning shot across her bow and allowing the crew to escape, U-162 sank the boat; one survivor turned out to be a black pig—the third they had encountered in a week. Because U-boatmen had heard stories about pigs bringing good luck, they decided to catch and keep the little animal, naming him Douglas in honor of his former home.

Aboard the U-boat, Douglas rode in the engine room, and the crew treated him like a prince. Just after stashing him on the boat, Wattenberg sank five more merchantmen, arrived back at Lorient in triumph, and presented Douglas to the flotilla commander, Victor Schütze.[10]

On his third patrol in September 1942—and still enjoying the "Happy Time" for U-boats—Wattenberg was cruising off the island of Tobago in the Caribbean. Traveling at periscope depth at about six in the evening, he spotted the tip of a mast. Crewman Alfred Dietrich said that the captain saw that the ship was a destroyer but did not notice two others a mile away. Wattenberg fired an electric torpedo that turned out to be defective—first traveling underwater, then coming to the top, "going up and down like a dolphin," explained Dietrich. The *Pathfinder* commander saw the torpedo coming and frantically turned his ship away from it, barely avoiding a hit. He headed full speed toward the submerging U-boat and dropped a spread of depth charges. Immediately, the two other British destroyers rushed in to attack, unleashing a barrage of canisters on U-162. "The first concussions caused water leaks inside the boat, and we went deeper and deeper. We were really afraid," Dietrich went on. "We could hear the *ping, ping, ping* of the sonar, and we knew that they were above us." The ear-shattering booms continued, and Wattenberg took the boat down farther. "And then we started to say our prayers." Alfred remembered that the worst part was having to sit silently, doing nothing.

"We had many problems: we were losing oil and heading to dangerous depths." Working the pumps as hard as possible in an attempt to bring the boat into balance, the engineer managed to get the water back to the opposite end of the boat; meanwhile, the air was growing scarcer and scarcer. At three hundred meters the chief told Wattenberg he could no longer hold the boat, leaving only two possibilities: to stay underwater and die or to surface and try to survive. Wattenberg ordered the boat to surface.

As soon as U-162 made it to the top, the commander ordered all hands overboard. "I jumped into the water wearing my life vest," said Dietrich. "It was evening, and I could see flares shooting through the sky." Groups of German sailors tied themselves together, and as they struggled in the waves, they could see the destroyers surrounding them.

Realizing his boat could be seized by the enemy, Wattenberg quickly ordered the sea valves opened to scuttle his vessel, and as it started to sink, he leaped into the sea—the last man to leave U-162. The *Pathfinder* picked up Wattenberg, and the two other destroyers, *Quentin* and *Vimy*, rescued the remaining sailors. Some months later the commander found himself united with captured fellow U-boat crew members in Papago Park prison camp near Scottsdale, Arizona.[11]

A little more than two years after his capture, Wattenberg participated in a well-organized escape on the night before Christmas Eve, 1944. "Why did we undertake this risky adventure only a few months before the end of the war? We wanted freedom from barbed wire, freedom at Christmastime, and a chance to go back to Germany."[12]

Twenty-five men conceived and executed the plan—several of them well-known captains: Friedrich Guggenberger, Horst Günther, Hans-Werner Kraus, Friedrich Horst, and forty-one-year-old Wattenberg, the oldest. Two of Wattenberg's crew members, Walter Kozur and Johann Kremer, had been put into the officers camp for refusing to pick cotton and were ready to help with the escape. As a cover for excavating an underground passage, they asked permission to build a *faustball* (type of volleyball) field and were given the go-ahead.

One of the camp overseers was to watch construction of the field, a second to provide a dirt source. But officer number two detested Germans and refused to give them a source, creating an opportunity for the prisoners to dig a tunnel. "The field officer thought we were getting it from the other officer, but if they had talked to each other, they would have found out what was going on," explained Johann Kremer.

The diggers located their tunnel entrance at the side of their bathhouse behind a large coal box, a place where tower guards could not observe them. Using a coal shovel and a pick, they mined in the direction of a canal outside the prison fence. "The tunnel was very small," recalled Wattenberg, "so that it was only possible to crawl. We had lighting by an electric bulb on a long wire." Every evening they had to return the pick to their guards, but they kept the coal scoops and excavated at night, placing the dirt on a pile at the *faustball* field. None of them had ever dug a tunnel before, and it zigged, zagged, and went up and down.[13]

Just before Christmas 1944, everything was ready for the great breakout. "I was head man of my group of three. Everybody had to decide by himself where he would go. Fifteen men wanted to travel southward in groups of twos or threes to reach the border of Mexico, which was 250 kilometers away," explained Wattenberg. The group of three under Commander Günther planned to go to the Gila River, having spotted it on a map as a blue line; they carried backpacks with parts of a canoe they could assemble to travel down the river to the Colorado and on to the Gulf of California.

Wattenberg had collected food supplies for four weeks, a can of water, cooking and eating utensils, a first aid kit, blanket, a map from an American newspaper, one passport, and a few dollars. In preparation for their adventure, Kozur and Kremer had been saving potato peelings and procured yeast from the kitchen to concoct a supply of schnapps. "We put it in a four-liter glass jug, hid it, and waited for several weeks for it to ferment. And we made fishing hooks out of some paper clips." Kozur, trained as a cook, saved a sack of bread crumbs, mixed it with raisins, and made a kind of soup.[14]

"I wanted to go . . . northward to the Colorado Plateau and hide for fourteen days," Wattenberg said. "There we could get a little food from a prearranged place [wrecked car], where some of the prisoners in the auto repair shop were to stash edibles."

On 23 December the exodus started. "It was raining, and in the petty officers barracks the men made a lot of racket so they could get the guards' attention. We left in small groups between nine and twelve o'clock in the evening, crept through the 178-foot tunnel, and emerged at the canal bank."

Wattenberg, Kozur, and Kremer scurried along the waterway, hidden by a levee, and, unseen by guards in the watchtowers, made it about five hundred yards to the south. "Then we waded across the canal. At the other side we dried ourselves, dressed, and ran across a field and hid in an orchard."

The next afternoon they heard the far-away wailing of sirens, and "that was very alarming for us." Believing it better to stay put, they remained in the orchard, and that night, 24 December, the POWs had a small Christmas celebration. "Hannes [Johann] played *Silent Night* on his harmonica, and we thought about the people at home, our friends and relatives."

Under cover of darkness the little band started off once more, headed northward toward the mountains. "My intention was to find a good hole, a living room of stones where there was no rain and nobody could see it, then leave it for the next escapees. After three nights we found a cave in a canyon in the mountains, which was very safe." The three built a fireplace of rocks and hauled in a cactus stump to use for a table. Every night two of the men slept while a third kept watch.

Wattenberg planned to use the cave as a central point from which to explore the region. "It was most important that we get food supplies. I wanted to contact a friendly American farmer and work for him to get money for our food, but I couldn't find such a man. I walked in all directions, and no one lived there. I met nobody."

Feeling homesick and nostalgic the night of 31 December, the three Germans walked to a secluded area near a small lake. There, with a bit of homemade schnapps, they drank a New Year's toast to their wives and to Germany. "Walter and Hannes looked very sad because they were thinking about their families in Cologne, which had been heavily bombed. We asked Hannes to play the national anthem, *Deutschlandlied*, on his harmonica, then we walked back to the cave."

"In the moonlight the cactus flowers were very nice, and we could see that in the higher mountains there was snow." To avoid leaving any footprints, they attempted to tread on top of rocks, avoiding the dirt. On that lonely New Year's Eve, "We were wondering where our escaped companions were."

The following night Wattenberg sent his two crewmen, each with a dollar in his pocket, to try to find some newspapers. "That was a lot of money, considering the small amount that we had, only a few dollars." At dawn the two returned with backpacks filled with fruit and a couple of newspapers. "Some POWs are Recaptured: Wattenberg Still at Large," read the headlines. One article announced: "Wholesale Nazi Escape Screened Bigshots' Flight." The cave dwellers learned that most of their comrades had been captured, and "that was sad," noted the commander. "It was probably easier to find their tracks in the desert sand."

One night, after four weeks, Kremer checked the wrecked auto where other prisoners had been stashing food for them and found only a few scraps to eat, some cigarettes, playing cards and matches. "We put a note in the car saying, 'Please, food only.' When we looked the next time there was an answer: 'This location is hazardous. Many Americans pass it every day.'" The three discussed the problem, and Hannes volunteered to sneak into a working prisoners camp and talk to them about a new hiding place. He left the cave, but after three days there was no sign of him.

"Walter wanted to do the same thing as Hannes, being very careful, but Walter did not come back either." Left alone, Wattenberg pondered his next move. "I decided to walk to Phoenix. I had eight dollars, and perhaps I would be able to buy some bread with it." Before leaving, he placed a note to the FBI in his cave, saying, "I am very far away from here. Good hunting! Yours, W."

Loaded with backpack, blanket, bathing supplies, cigarettes, sugar, salt, and schnapps, the last escapee set out in the direction of Phoenix. Upon arrival in town, he spotted a Chinese restaurant, entered, and ordered a fifty-cent dish. "It tasted exquisite. After eating I attempted to find a place to spend the night, but it was impossible to find a hotel room because it was a weekend and everything was full."[15]

At three-thirty in the morning, speaking somewhat accented English, the commander asked a street sweeper the way to the train station, and after being told, headed in that direction. The sweeper, Charles Cherry, suspicious that the stranger might be a German prisoner, hailed a passing police officer, Gilbert Brady. Brady caught up with Wattenberg in a couple of minutes.

"Excuse me, sir, where do you live?"

"I am a rancher in town for the weekend."

"Yes sir, but where do you live?"

"In Glendale."

"Glendale, California, or Glendale, Arizona?"

"Why, Glendale back East."

With that, Brady asked the "rancher" to show his Selective Service registration card, and, having none, Wattenberg gave himself up. "They did a body search and made an interrogation, but I did not say anything about the escape. Then I slept in the jail for one night, had a good breakfast, and was brought back to Papago Park. The camp commander greeted me with: 'Hello, Captain,' and shook my hand."[16]

"They gave us only bread and water for four weeks, but this was no problem, because we had had forty-five days of freedom, which was a wonderful experience."[17]

Many years afterward, on a crisp January morning in 1985, the former U-boat commander and nine other ex-prisoners of war attended ceremonies at Papago Park, scene of their adventurous getaway. The governor of Arizona proclaimed 5 January "Papago Park POW Camp Commemoration Day," and the local newspaper declared, "Warm Welcome Waits Former German Prisoners of War."

Local host Lloyd Clark accompanied former commanders Horst Günther and Jürgen Wattenberg on a tour of their old escape trails. "First we followed the tunnel route to the canal," recalled Wattenberg, "then to the Gila River, where Günther's group had discovered that the riverbed was dry and that they could not use their canoe to flee on the water. We went on to Sun City and tried to find the cave we called 'Cave Group Wattenberg,' now in the neighborhood of Squaw Peak, but we could not get to the exact place where it was."

After several days of sightseeing, ceremonies, and reminiscing, the German visitors said farewell to their American hosts. With flags flying and bands playing, the old enemies saluted each other—now friends forever.[18]

"I have had a lucky life," smiled Wattenberg.

2   Georg Högel, U-30, U-110

■ ■

If you observe Georg, you will notice that he incessantly studies people, gazes at buildings, or ponders scenic views. He travels everywhere with sketchpad and pencil, making quick portraits, small landscapes, or architectural drawings. Early in his naval career Georg drew a whimsical cartoon of Schnurzl, Commander Fritz-Julius Lemp's tousled mutt, who faithfully awaited the arrival of his master's U-boat at the Wilhelmshaven dock and clamped his teeth on the first line thrown ashore. Georg's cartoon of the little dog became U-30's emblem, and throughout the war the young artist continued to practice his creative talents, producing hundreds of watercolors, charcoals, and oil paintings in a Canadian prison camp. To watch him quietly sketching, one would never guess he played a role in some of the most remarkable submarine adventures of World War II.

■ ■

"On 14 September 1939 our U-boat was positioned west of Northern Ireland, and from the east we saw steamer smoke a long way off. The ship was zigzagging as we moved toward her, but she saw us coming and tried to escape, sending SOS signals," wrote radio operator Högel. U-30 charged forward and blasted a shot in front of the freighter's bow, stopping her, and in a few minutes the freighter's crew members climbed down into lifeboats.

Great Britain had declared war on Germany eleven days earlier,

Georg Högel

and Hitler, determined to break the English naval blockade before the admiralty had time to organize a convoy system, sent out eighteen U-boats to do the job. One of these, U-30, under the command of *Kapitänleutnant* (Lieutenant-Commander) Fritz-Julius Lemp, immediately sank two vessels: passenger liner *Athenia* (believed to be a warship) on 3 September and the freighter *Blairlogie* eight days later. "Lemp made us swear to keep the *Athenia* sinking a secret," admitted Högel, and the incident, of course, shook the world.

Unaware of the consequences of the British liner sinking, Högel felt sure that U-30 could demolish enemy ship number three without much effort, but this was not to be.

"We towed the lifeboats about a mile away from the British freighter and told the crew that we would come back and help them, but first

Fritz-Julius Lemp on U-30. The Schnurzl emblem is on the tower.

we had to board the ship." To save costly torpedoes, the captain decided to destroy the *Fanad Head* with explosives, but the first order of business was "to see if there was any bread on board." U-30's men had eaten all the *Kommissbrot* (fresh bread) in their storage hammocks; when they looked for the canned variety, all they found was milk, milk, and more milk. "We thought the periscope casing was filled with bread, but no, it too turned out to be tins of milk. The provisions manager had checked off the wrong can number in ordering food for the trip."

For a German submarine crew, this was terrible. They were eighteen days out to sea, without a single loaf of bread. "We expected to be gone for six weeks, so we were now forced to eat milk with raisins, milk with dried potatoes or eggs, and I don't remember what else. It was unthinkable to have sliced cold meat and cheese without bread, and what could we put our butter and jam on?"

Lemp observes *Fanad Head*, British freighter, with the idea of obtaining food supplies.

With a loaded freighter in hand, the men, with visions of delicious foods from the ship's stores, made ready to board her.

First Watch Officer Hinsch and Otto Ohse rowed their dinghy to the freighter and climbed the rope ladder. Shortly afterward, they rowed back, loaded with white and whole wheat bread, ham, grapefruit marmalade, tobacco, newspapers, and magazines. "The supplies were wonderful and improved our mood considerably."

As Högel listened to radio messages directed to the doomed ship, he picked up continuous calls from other vessels. "I became a bit nervous, but we were far away from Northern Ireland, where no planes could reach us." Or so they thought. The hour was approaching noon.

Commander Lemp ordered several floorboards opened in front of the radio room for procuring explosives and grenades, and sent two more men to the *Fanad Head* to blow up the engine room and sink the ship. About this time Högel's radio officer asked him if he wanted to see what was going on, so Georg eagerly climbed to the bridge. "Just in front of me was a fifty-two-hundred-ton ship; we knew the

U-30 crewmen passing food garnered from *Fanad Head* to deck hands.

size from *Lloyd's Register*. We had rigged a rope from the bow of the U-boat to the steamer so that we could pull the dinghy over without having to row it. Ten men stood on our deck and hauled it to and from the ship." Georg said that many of the crew were standing on the bridge enjoying the goings-on, but that no one on watch was surveying the horizon.

"Suddenly one of our men on the ship started waving at us and pointing. I saw a plane about three thousand yards away, but it was not heading toward us. At first I thought it might be an airline because they were still flying then, but suddenly I heard the alarm." All the men on the bridge scrambled down into the hatch, taking what seemed an interminable time. As U-30 started to catapult into the depths, the crew heard thumps like someone jumping up and down on the outside of the hatch. Nothing could be done but to hope that the unfortunate crewman made it to safety.

With tremendous jolts the depth charges erupted around them. "Those were the first explosions we had felt since the war started," remembered Högel. "We tried to go deeper, but we were too close to the ship and could have hit our tower."

"Double full power back!" shouted Lemp, and the boat's engines strained to reverse, bringing U-30 up to twenty meters.

Five crew members were missing: *Oberbootsmaat* (Petty Officer Second Class) Hanisch, who was on the tower when the boat dived, First Watch Officer Hinsch, Otto Ohse, *Obermaschinist* (Chief Petty Officer) Büsgen, and *Maschinenmaat* (Petty Officer, Engineering) Schmidt. "We thought that the first four, who had rowed to the ship, were safe, and Hanisch would perhaps be able to swim, if he had not been hit by the blasts. But we couldn't shoot torpedoes at the ship because our men were on it."

As they were deliberating the problem, another detonation thundered above them. Lemp gave the order to go to thirty meters and at that level started circling the freighter, hoping the plane would run out of fuel. As the U-boat went around and around, another charge erupted near the tower. "Could it be that we were not deep enough to be out of the plane's sight?" they all wondered. "Go to forty meters," Lemp ordered.

A few more minutes passed, then another jarring blast. "It was completely impossible at this depth for a pilot to see us; therefore, something else was giving away our position." Possibly they were losing oil or perhaps air. To find out what was happening, Lemp was forced to go to periscope depth. "Everyone was nervous, because we were being bombed, and so we had absolute quiet in the boat. We put up the periscope, and from the radio room I heard the commander swearing."

To his astonishment, Lemp saw that the long dinghy line was tangled around the net deflector, and that the small boat had been trailing U-30 on the surface, making a conspicuous target for the plane. "Even a blind pilot would have noticed that an empty dinghy could not be circling a freighter."

One of the crewmen grabbed a kitchen knife and whacked off the telltale appendage, but as he did so, the watch spotted a plane coming straight toward them. Machine-gun fire burst out, clattering against the tower: apparently the aircraft had run out of bombs. U-30 hurdled downward again; as they went below, the crew realized they had to act fast to rescue their five comrades before enemy warships appeared.

Lemp brought U-30 to the surface on the lee side of the *Fanad Head,* but as soon as he did so, a plane roared in, ejecting a stream of machine-gun shells and letting loose a bomb. "We managed to dive again before the thing exploded, but where had the second plane come from?" An air attack so early in the war and so far from land seemed incomprehensible.

They had stayed close to the freighter since noon, and now it was six o'clock in the evening. Lemp tried to get into rescue position once more, and as he did so more planes appeared in the distance. As U-30 neared the lee side of the *Fanad Head,* the U-boat was rocked by a thunderous crash. "Everyone was thrown against walls, machines, and everywhere." Lemp ordered, "Air in all tanks," to bring the boat up. They had collided with the ship, which had shifted forward because of a high, rolling swell. "Any water in the boat?" the captain yelled. Högel then heard voices from the bridge: "They are coming, they are coming." He heard steps on the bridge, then the hatch was closed, and U-30 headed for the basement again.

Högel had asked a crew member to replace the missing floorboards by the radio room, and a few minutes after this was done, a man fell down the passageway. Had he plunged into the open storage pit, he would have been killed. "I did not know who he was," said Högel. "He was not one of our men. He had ripped his trousers up one side, and he had such a deep wound that you could see the bone and muscles." Right away the unknown man (a British pilot) was taken to a bed for treatment.

After picking up the missing crew members, U-30, using her stern tubes, fired one torpedo. Soon Lemp announced, "We hit it in the middle, and it's breaking in half and sinking." Högel then learned that the five men from U-30 had jumped off the *Fanad Head* right after the collision and were hauled onto the U-boat. The sailors later said that when the first airplane appeared, one yelled a warning to the others, who were in the ship's engine room placing explosives. It was too late to get off the ship, and as they stood on deck, the crewmen could see the plane dropping bombs on the U-boat. Shrapnel flew out, hitting them on the arms, backs, and heads, and they fled into the ship's interior to bandage each others' wounds. *Fanad Head* sailors, witnessing the attack on the U-boat, whistled and cheered in the distance.

Hoping that Lemp would make another attempt to rescue them, the five submariners waited and watched. Then one of them noticed a body hanging in the water, motionless. "Otto secured himself with a rope around his waist, jumped in and swam back with a badly burned man, who was wearing leather clothing and a microphone. At first Otto believed he was a crew member of our boat, but he saw from the microphone that he was an English pilot." They later learned that the pilot was Lieutenant Thursden from the British aircraft carrier *Ark Royal*. Moments afterward, the pilot of a second aircraft from the *Ark*, Lieutenant Gus Griffiths, climbed aboard the freighter and was startled to see one of his compatriots already there.

When U-30 crashed into the freighter, the wounded U-boatmen, who were tied together in pairs, leaped from the deck into the sea, and were in turn helped aboard their submarine. "But the two Englishmen were still standing there," said Högel, "unsure whether to jump." Lemp shouted to them: "Come on, you idiots, this ship will be sunk!" The pilots immediately dropped into the waves and were hoisted onto the U-boat moments before it hurdled below. At that point U-30 torpedoed the freighter, and as it was sinking Lemp spied two destroyers bearing down on them, already close. He screamed, "Go deeper!"

"Only the depths could save us. We rushed down to seventy, eighty, ninety meters, and at a hundred meters there was a warning mark, but we kept going to 120. Terrible explosions shook the U-boat, and we were thrown in all directions, but compared to these depth charges, the airplanes' bombs were nothing." Shattering booms echoed again and again.

While the attack continued, one of U-30's radio operators, trained in first aid, took care of the wounded as best he could. Adolph Schmidt had severely injured his right arm jumping on board; three others suffered with shrapnel punctures. Hanisch was the only one intact. He had been standing on the tower when the boat went into its dive. He attempted to hang onto the periscope, but soon found himself swimming. He made it to the *Fanad Head* and climbed up the ladder to join the four other crew members. Both British pilots, Griffiths and Thursden, had flown too low while dropping submarine bombs and had blown up their planes, during which they were burned critically and thrown into the Atlantic. Thursden had ripped open his leg jumping off the *Fanad Head* into rough seas, as well, and was the one Högel saw falling into U-30's passageway.

As depth charges lashed and whipped the submarine, the overwhelming pressure caused several water leaks, and the crew rushed to repair them. Högel went on: "In my earphones, I could hear the bombs coming and warned everyone before they exploded. The two-second wait caused my heart to stop."

The two destroyers were hunting them hard. "My job was to listen to their propellers, and I gave their positions to the bridge. I could also hear the creaks and groans of the freighter sinking. An awful noise."

As the destroyer relentlessly blasted the submarine, the electric engine room reported water leaks, and the bilges started to fill, causing the boat to slope toward the stern. One pump could not do the job, and a second was started. "We were sinking—100 meters, 110 meters, 120—and then the needle stopped. At some point the U-boat would not withstand the pressure, and we would all die. U-30 was an old boat, built in 1935."

Lemp ordered all available men to line up, grab every container they could find, and start bailing. "We passed water from the back of the boat to the front, and since it was some meters deeper at the stern than at the bow, there was danger that water would get into the electric engines and ruin them. Without power, this would be the end."

Sweating and silent, they bailed and shuttled water from back to front for interminable hours. A couple of times they were forced to pause to clean the pump filter, and in those few minutes they could hear ominous cracking noises in the hull. At 11:00 P.M. the explosions ceased, allowing U-30 to rise to a safer depth. "To be sure that the enemy had gone, I had to listen to every little noise. We knew that one destroyer was at thirty-seven degrees, but where was the other? The men kept asking, 'Have you heard anything?' as the boat slowly rose." Everyone had taken off their shoes and wrapped their feet in towels to stay as quiet as possible. Electric heating was turned off, as were all unnecessary lights, for the batteries were almost depleted. "It was very cold, and we were freezing. We knew that our batteries would last one-and-a-half hours more, but what if at the end of that the destroyers were still there?"

The submarine silently and cautiously climbed to thirty meters, where it started to rock from side to side, swayed by the motions of storm swells. Lemp cut the engines to listen, then brought the boat to the surface. He opened the hatch and went out to have a look. No destroyers in sight.

U-30 was apparently safe in the rainy darkness. Fresh air and oxygen flowed into all the compartments, giving new life to the men, and tension vanished. Then someone thought they saw a spotlight on the waves, but it was a false alarm. Lemp gave orders to get the boat underway, and U-30 started her voyage. "The diesel engines whined, charging the batteries, and the compressed air tanks were refilled. In short, everything went fine, but the next day we found out that our compass had been destroyed."

As they headed toward Iceland, U-30 attempted to sink a freighter and failed because of the defective compass. Bad weather prevented using stars for navigation, and they were two days past schedule reaching Reykjavik. "We were worried about Adolf Schmidt's life. We had stopped the bleeding in his forearm with a tourniquet, and we kept opening it, but his hand was already black and the bandage filled with blood." At Reykjavik, a neutral harbor, German Consul General Gerlach, who was also a physician, arrived in a motorboat and took Schmidt and the other wounded men to the hospital. The doctor dispensed some medicines for U-30's first aid cabinet, and several German merchant ships in the harbor contributed supplies of bread, meat, and other provisions.

Though Iceland maintained neutrality at that time, the Danish population heard about U-30's unexpected visit and raised their voices about interning the boat and crew. "We disappeared as fast as we could," declared Högel, "and headed back to Germany." At one point they almost ran into a German mine in the North Sea because their compass was still out of order. At the mouth of the Weser River they waited for an escort, which soon appeared and accompanied them into Wilhelmshaven, home of the 2. U-Flotilla.

"Just before we reached the pier, we brought out the live turkey we had taken aboard in Iceland. He was named 'Alfonse,' and we tied him to the cannon. All the people standing on the warships and wharf stared at him with surprise, and the next day the cook prepared turkey soup for us—a great treat."[1]

As soon as the boat touched the docks, Lemp reported to the flotilla chief, where he discussed the *Athenia* disaster. Immediately afterward, he called Georg into a private office and said, "I want you to change my war diary." Totally astounded, the young seaman did as he was instructed, retyping the two pages to eliminate all references to the passenger liner sinking. Following that, Lemp summoned all his men and made them swear an oath of secrecy a second time, as well as demanding that they keep a straight face if the subject of the *Athenia* were brought up. "That was really hard to do," said Georg, "and we had to continue this act until the end of the war."[2]

Regarding U-30's exploits, local newspapers published an article proclaiming that the U-boat had shot down two British planes and taken the pilots prisoner. (The two pilots were those who flew too low and blew themselves up.)

Subsequent to his ordeals on U-30, Högel rejoined Lemp on U-110 and experienced a second hair-raising patrol. In early May 1941 Lemp had sunk two merchantmen in an enormous British convoy when he came under heavy attack by the destroyers *Bulldog* and *Broadway*. Severely damaged, the submarine sought shelter far into the depths, causing the hull to begin popping, floorboards to buckle, and oxygen to reach near depletion. "The depth charge explosions were so strong, we thought the end had come. We were in a cage and could not escape."

With death staring them in the face, Lemp was ready to give the order to surface, but a broken pressurized air distributor caused the boat to rise of its own accord. When U-110 breached the surface, *Bulldog* commander Baker-Cresswell made a sudden decision to ram the U-boat and ordered full speed ahead. Lemp glimpsed the destroyer bearing down and yelled for the men to scuttle the boat and abandon ship as fast as possible. Baker-Cresswell, watching them jump out of the conning tower, suddenly realized that he might have a chance to capture the U-boat and swung his ship to avoid hitting the sub. Believing that he spied some of the Germans manning their guns, he gave the order to fire. A barrage of bullets and shells burst from the destroyer as he realized the crewmen were simply abandoning ship; he then ordered a cease-fire, stopped the *Bulldog,* and made ready to board U-110. At the same moment, Baker-Cresswell noticed the *Broadway* rushing straight for the submarine, apparently intent upon ramming.

Broadway's commander Taylor did not see Baker-Cresswell's flashing signals to keep clear, so he kept coming. With that, Baker-Cresswell shouted into his megaphone: "DO NOT RAM!" but to no effect. Intending to throw two depth charges under the U-boat, Taylor accidentally collided with U-110, tore a large gash in *Broadway*'s bow, and knocked off a propeller. He immediately withdrew, allowing Baker-Cresswell to continue his boarding activities.

After the shooting stopped, Högel and his mates tried to stay afloat until they could be rescued, but some of the crewmen had been killed trying to get off the boat or while swimming, and Lemp disappeared. Thirty-four of the crew were picked up by the corvette *Aubrietia* and ushered into a closed compartment below decks so that they could not observe what happened next.

Baker-Cresswell's flash of genius had succeeded. His boarding party rowed over to U-110, gingerly entered the sub (expecting armed crew members to be inside trying to scuttle her), and found in it only eerie silence and a priceless treasure: German secret code books and an apparatus that looked like a typewriter—the Enigma machine. Their momentous capture of these key tables and cipher device, together with code information from two German weather ships, enabled the British to decipher encrypted radio messages to and from the U-boats, giving the Allies a crucial advantage in the deadly battles at sea.

Ironically, Georg Högel and his U-boat friends had no idea that their boat had been captured. The *Bulldog* towed it for a while, and then U-110 mysteriously sank, but the English sailors kept quiet about their unexpected prize, and no one in the world knew about it until the British Admiralty told the story in 1958. "We fixed it so it would sink," testified Högel.[3]

At the end of World War II the Russian army seized German navy records from Berlin headquarters and discovered the *Athenia* secret. After a quick search they located three survivors of U-30 in a Canadian prison camp and requested an inquiry be held. "I was one of the three," said Georg, "and they asked us a lot of questions, but I did not tell them anything. One of us finally did, and that's how it became known."

In April 1998 Georg and his wife traveled to Thunder Bay, Canada, for the opening of a special art show at the Thunder Bay Military Museum, featuring 315 magnificent watercolors, drawings, and oil paintings by radioman Högel, painted during his prison camp days in northern Ontario. Georg donated them to the museum in gratitude for the Canadians' humane treatment of him and his crewmates during those long, dreary war years.

"Luck was always with me," mused the Münich sailor-artist, "and fate decreed that I live, but I feel a great sadness for my good comrades, who are long since gone."

3   Otto Kretschmer, U-35, U-23, U-99

■ ■

Cool and elegant in a pale yellow corduroy shirt and tan slacks, the renowned commander sat reminiscing on his back porch, while motorboats hummed along the nearby canal and bicyclists pedaled to and fro down distant paths. In this peaceful Saturday scene Otto talked about his exploits during the war, chuckling frequently and thoroughly enjoying the whole thing. We were interrupted occasionally by a chaffinch loudly warbling on the roof or the Kretschmers' terrier, Biggi, barking at a duck. When my two-day visit was over, I regretfully parted with Otto and his wife Lieselotte, feeling that they had become dear friends.

■ ■

In the ancient German kingdom of Bohemia (now part of the Czech Republic), Otto Kretschmer's Protestant ancestor, Johannes von Kretschmer zu Sachwitz und Laskowitz, lost everything in the Thirty Years' War and was forced by the Catholic League to begin life anew. The aristocratic family, driven into Silesia, managed to survive but again was forced out of their home at the end of World War II, when Silesia became part of Poland. Otto emerged from seven years' imprisonment in 1947 with "nothing but a hundred pounds of luggage. That's all that was left."

Otto's father, director of a school, had managed to support his family and even sent Otto to Exeter College in England to study math-

Otto Kretschmer, recipient of Knight's Cross, in August 1940, at Lorient, France. The photo was later retouched, adding Oak Leaves and Crossed Swords.

ematics, chemistry, and English for two terms. Already yearning for the sea life at age sixteen, Otto signed up with the German navy, to begin service a month before his eighteenth birthday. With some time to spend before entering a military career, he decided to study at the Sorbonne in Paris, but the lure of the city compelled him to put off scholastic activities, and Otto spent two months enjoying the sights.

Before returning to Germany, the young traveler continued his tour to Milan, Genoa, Pisa, and Rome. With almost no money left, Otto went to the bank to pick up funds from his father but was told that in order to obtain them, he would have to pay a "fee." When further argument availed nothing, Otto announced he would go to the German embassy for help; hearing this, the Italian banker promptly handed over the money. At age seventeen Otto was showing signs of future talents as a brilliant strategist.

In 1930 the German navy consisted of fifteen thousand men and some old pre–World War I ships—no submarines. Otto's first experience at sea came on the *Emden,* a cruiser built after 1918, which, because it was the most up-to-date, was used as a training ship for cadets. After a one-year cruise around the world, the youthful seaman sharpened his skills at various schools, including the Flensburg Naval Academy, learning gunnery, torpedoes, mines, and communications. As a midshipman Otto sailed the seas on the *Panzerschiff Deutschland* and cruiser *Köln* in the gunnery division, and after four years' service was elected to officer status, which made him an ensign.

"Then I was put in the torpedo department, but I didn't want to go, because I liked gunnery better. It was more modernized, and our torpedo weapon department was still like World War I." In 1935, by the German-British Naval Treaty, Germany was allowed to have submarines once again, and new ones were built for training purposes. Small (250 tons), with no deck guns and no compartmentalized interiors, the new boats were promptly dubbed *Einbäume* (canoes).

"I was a lieutenant on U-35, in the second submarine flotilla, and together with U-28, we were the first to go into the Atlantic, to Ponta Delgada in the Azores. As was customary, the boat went out for practice maneuvers in the Bay of Lübeck before departure." After continuous ups and downs on that cold December day, Kretschmer and the captain went up on the conning tower, where Otto lit up a cigar to indicate that the crew needed a rest. "I thought maybe he would let me smoke it to the end, but I looked at his eyes and thought, 'No, he will not.'" To delay any more dives, Otto announced he was going down onto the deck to get the water out of the gun and promptly descended the ladder, with cigar still clamped between his teeth.

"I was on the foredeck, adjusting the gun, when PSSSSSSH he was diving. Then up came the green sea, and I ran to the conning tower and tried to climb the periscope, hoping that I could be seen in the optics. But of course it was too oily, and I couldn't get up." Still clinging to the periscope, Otto surged downward with U-35. "When the water was dark green I let loose and popped up again."

In the impending darkness, without a life vest, Otto began to think he could not long survive in the frigid water. "It was December, and I had on heavy clothing—my leather suit with rubber at wrists and ankles—so it kept in some air to help me float. Also I had seaboots, and they held air, but in the end I had to paddle like a dog because the air was disappearing."

As Kretschmer wondered whether he could hold out, U-35 came from nowhere and threw Otto a life ring, but he was so numb with cold he could not climb aboard. "They pulled me out, pushed me up onto the conning tower, and then I said to the captain, 'Reporting back on board, sir.' He said, 'Thank you, thank you very much. Please go down.' No apology."

"When I got down I took off all my wet things and drank a good deal of rum—you see, there was no heating in the boat. I lay down on the bunk and vigorously exercised my arms and legs, and then I asked for hot water bottles to put on myself so I could get warm again. Otherwise I would have died there on the bunk."

Were it not for the captain looking through the periscope as U-35 dived, noting as he did that something was "funny"—that perhaps someone was out there—Otto Kretschmer soon would have disappeared. When the boat arrived in port, someone told a reporter about the incident, and an article appeared in a local paper that Kretschmer had survived a near-fatal accident in the Baltic with a cigar in his mouth. "Obviously the cigar part was not true," smiled Otto. (He has given up smoking.)

Before U-35 set out for southern waters, the captain informed Otto, who was in charge of provisions: "Rule number one is to feed the crew. If the crew is well fed, everything will work." Otto followed instructions to allow everyone access to the food stores for twenty-four hours a day, letting each sailor take what he liked. Unfortunately, at the end of the trip the consumption had gone way over the budget, and Otto was held accountable.

"I was going to have to pay for all that myself, so I told the authorities that I had only followed the commander's instructions. But the commander denied knowing anything about it, and even though I said I would swear to it and that others had witnessed, I still had to make it good." The naval staff explained that he could cut back somewhere and credit would be applied to his debt, so Kretschmer told the crew that from then on, since they had eaten so much, they could have their usual late meal of bread and butter, but with nothing on top except tinned fish. "The fish cost ten pfennigs only, but this saved us a lot of money. It was the only way." And it worked.

Otto continued his duties on U-35, with a mission to Spain as part of an international force involved in the Spanish Civil War. Four U-boats were assigned to guard the borders of Spain against Soviet and other reinforcements, and "we had two lines to protect—one at the French border in the Bay of Biscay. We were at El Ferrol, then at Cádiz and then Tangier, Morocco. The intention was to keep the civil war inside Spain."

Better prospects lay ahead for newly promoted Kretschmer, now commander of his own boat—U-23, a small coastal craft. "With a canoe in wartime, my range of operations was in the North Sea, not the Atlantic, and this meant only a few targets—just a few small ships— but also very bad torpedoes. They missed the target and they didn't explode. The results would have been double if we had had good torpedoes."

Nonetheless, by the time Otto had completed nine missions he had succeeded in laying a number of mines, searched for the British Home Fleet, and sunk seven merchant ships and one destroyer. His skill and daring were becoming obvious, resulting in the Iron Cross Second and First Classes, as well as command of a new five-hundred-ton boat —the U-99.[1]

With his gleaming new vessel Kretschmer sallied forth in May 1940 for convoy attack practice in the Baltic. One night, while surfaced, he succeeded in dashing between two escorts and gaining access to the ships, a feat that convinced him he could manage this brazen maneuver under enemy conditions. This was to become Kretschmer's great claim to fame. When U-99 finished practice attacks and weighed anchor, a crewman discovered an old horseshoe hanging from one of the flanges. Then a second horseshoe was found, and with this, the sailor suggested to Otto that they adopt a horseshoe insignia for the boat. Kretschmer immediately agreed, and the crew painted a shiny

gold horseshoe on each side of the conning tower, the open part downward as German farmers hung horseshoes in their barns.[2]

Early on the morning of 17 June U-99 departed Kiel on her way to
the Atlantic, where Otto Kretschmer now had plenty of targets and
an excellent boat. He was bound to succeed—but for less than one
year, when he was stopped. In the beginning, after leaving port for an
assigned area of operations, "I quickly tried to get into the line of
approaching single ships coming from Argentina, Australia, or wher-
ever they were coming from, approaching the North Channel. This, I
found out, was on a forty-degree course. So, getting out of Lorient, I
followed this course, with one engine slow speed, telling the lookouts,
'We will be overtaken by large, fast, single ships, and if they come,
they will be armed. We must not be seen, and I will overtake and sink
them at night.'" Kretschmer closed on the ships to about six hundred
yards or so; he had been trained this was the best and safest distance
for firing torpedoes to be sure they hit the target. "And of course this
was done while approaching with a narrow silhouette so I couldn't be
seen. I aimed for the middle of the ship, under the central keel plate."
By the time Otto had reached the assigned convoy, he had spent half
his twelve torpedoes, each for a separate merchantman. In cases where
the freighter or tanker failed to go down, he used gunfire to finish the
job. Otto firmly believed one torpedo should be enough for one ship.

Returning from his first patrol, Kretschmer received orders to proceed to the French port of Lorient; upon arrival he discovered no
clean uniforms were available. "We had no base, no nothing, and our
things had to be washed. What could we wear?" Otto was told that he
could use some battledress left in a warehouse by English troops. "This
was summer wear, very light. It was wonderful." Attired in enemy
clothes, the U-boatmen attempted to avoid suspicion by tacking their
shoulder straps and collar bands onto the British khakis.

In successive war patrols on U-99 Kretschmer electrified the naval
world with his tactics against convoys. No one had dared take a U-boat
inside the great mass of merchant ships—guarded front, sides, and back
by destroyer escorts—but Otto did, always at night and on the surface. "This was something new," wrote Admiral Sir George Creasy.
"But I remember, too, that I considered that the maneuver was so

risky that he had done it by mistake." For Otto it was simple: "While maneuvering in the lanes of the convoy, I looked for the biggest ships. My intent was to sink as many tankers as possible, to cut off the British oil supplies. There was plenty of space [in the convoys], and I could change from one lane to another—'look, there's a big one, and over there another big one, and so on.'" (Recently a German historian informed Otto that he had sunk more tankers than any other commander in World War II, aside from sinking the highest tonnage. Kretschmer averaged 1,218 gross tons per day for his one year of duty.)[3]

Each success spurred the commander to greater achievements, not only to win the war but to outdo his fellow sub captains. "The High Command was issuing daily radio reports, giving names of submarine captains who, on returning from patrol, had surpassed forty thousand tons of shipping. I always wanted to exceed them." In short order, Otto's tonnage rose like a rocket, bringing him fame and decorations —so much so that the German navy ordered him to take an Italian submarine commander along for instruction purposes on his next three-week mission.

"He was a *Korvettenkapitän* [Lieutenant Commander]—a very nice officer named Longobardo. I had learned Italian but had had no practice, and he had not practiced German, so we talked English, the language of our common enemy." After a slight diving mishap and a serious depth charge attack, Kretschmer fired three successive torpedoes that went out of control, two hitting the wrong ships in the convoy. Following these embarrassing incidents the ace U-boat commander attempted to finish a ship with gunfire, failed, then watched as the dinghy he sent out with men and explosives capsized. "Then there was no other way—I would have to spend another torpedo. Ha!"

Following his apprenticeship for Atlantic warfare with Otto Kretschmer, Longobardo went out on his Italian boat, *Torelli*, in January 1941 and sank four freighters. No further news was reported of his activities.[4]

On 22 February U-99 departed Lorient for what was to be her last war patrol. Günther Prien had already left in U-47 and Joachim Schepke in U-100 followed, all three aces heading for a designated convoy. On 7 March Kretschmer, once within the convoy, destroyed a huge whaling ship and a tanker; on the 16th he decimated five more tankers in a second convoy, plus one more on the 17th. Like a fox in the henhouse, he wreaked havoc, demolishing eight ships in eleven days.

Headed homeward with empty torpedo tubes, Kretschmer and his officers were totaling up tonnage sunk when the alarm bell startled them, and U-99 plunged below. "The bridge watch were surprised by a destroyer, and it was very close. I had given standing orders that if we were surprised by a warship by night, we would get away on the surface, showing them the stern, and they were to call me up to the bridge, where I would do the rest. But *never* dive." Much later Otto decided that recent changes in his crew had contributed to the disaster of U-99.

Two destroyers from the last convoy, the *Vanoc* and the *Walker,* had seen U-100 leaving the area; following, they had rammed the surfaced boat amidships, killing Joachim Schepke and some of his crew. Then they saw Kretschmer and went after him, but he heard them coming and dived to three hundred feet. Explosions, the closest Kretschmer had ever experienced, lashed the boat, knocking out the lights and glass dials on instruments, and creating a nightmare of noise. As the barrage continued, water came hissing into the control room and the depth gauges, except for one in the forward torpedo room, ceased to function as U-99 began to drop even deeper. Otto checked the depth and found they had sunk to six hundred feet, where at any second they could be crushed to death. "I had to blow the ballast tanks and head to the surface." After making some urgent adjustments, U-99 shot up to the top, out of control.

Kretschmer rushed to the bridge, and "I saw a destroyer [*Vanoc*] right in front, broad silhouette (a wonderful target for torpedoes!), taking up survivors of another submarine. Then I saw another, the *Walker.*" With useless engines and no torpedoes, U-99 waited helplessly as the destroyers opened fire, sending shells over Otto's conning tower. "I couldn't man my gun or the machine gun on the conning tower, because I was covered with tracers, but I had a list on the starboard side, and because the conning tower was leaning, I ordered my men to come up and stay in the lee of the tower. The men started coming up, and the destroyers stopped firing. I told the men to get back down again and put on some warm clothing, because they would have to swim in icy water." Again the crew emerged, this time with leather clothing and life vests, and assembled on the afterdeck.

"I just waited to see what would happen. Two officers were down below attempting to destroy the secret papers and the coding machine, when the stern suddenly went down, and all the men on the afterdeck were washed overboard except the boatswain, who quickly closed one of the deck hatches. The engineer hastily blew the ballast tanks again, so the stern came back up somewhat." Still inside were the engineer and the first lieutenant, and the stern was still so far down in the sea that water was coming into the tower hatch. Otto shouted, "Come up, come up quickly!" First an arm appeared through the onrushing water and Otto grabbed it and pulled the engineer out, then the second man scrambled up.

From the bridge Kretschmer could see his crewmen floating, but the two destroyers were drifting away into the night, probably to avoid a torpedo attack. "I said to my second lieutenant, 'Now call the destroyer.' At my instructions he signaled a message with the Morse lamp to the destroyer saying, 'Please rescue my men, drifting in your direction. I am sinking.'" After each word was given, the *Walker* light flashed back in verification, until the message was complete.

Looking through his binoculars, Kretschmer watched as the destroyer approached the floating crew, turned on the signal search-light, located the men's heads, threw out scrambling nets, and helped them climb aboard. "They were all safe—all who had been washed overboard. I could see them." Then Otto observed the destroyer attempting to lower a dinghy and guessed that they might be coming over to board his sub to confiscate secret material. Not knowing exactly when his boat would sink, Otto decided the time had come for scuttling. "So I said to my officers: 'I am going to sink the boat, but I want to know if you have any other opinion.' [War orders stated that in case of scuttling, the captain was supposed to get the opinion of his officers first.] There was no other opinion, but I did that any-way, for fun."

"I told the engineer, who had volunteered for the job, to go down and open the stern ballast tank just a bit, so he could get out again. And he went in there, but suddenly the stern sank, so I shouted, 'Quickly, quickly!' I never saw him again."

As the U-boat fell into the ocean depths, Kretschmer, still on the bridge, found himself afloat and immediately paddled toward the rest of the crew, who were scrambling as best they could up the destroyer's nets. "As captain, I could not go on board until everyone had been taken on board, and so I looked around, and no heads to be seen. Just as I grabbed the nets, the ship started to move forward. A big swell surged against my body, my boots were full of water, and I was so weak I could not climb up." Once more Otto Kretschmer felt that it was all over, but he heard the boatswain's voice shout, "There's the captain!" He and a British sailor came down the nets to help Kretschmer make it to safety.

"Well, once on deck I was still wearing my binoculars, and there was no time to take them off and throw them overboard [they were under his life vest], so they were taken from me. They gave me a bit of rum, dry clothes, and led me to the captain's cabin, and there I noticed that he also had a horseshoe insignia, but his was placed with the open part at the top." After a two-hour nap in a big leather armchair, Kretschmer awoke at the entry of Commander Donald Macintyre. When Otto thanked him for saving his men, the two shook hands, and Macintyre commented that Otto's boat emblem was turned the wrong way: "Luck can get into mine, but for yours, luck is falling out." Otto told him, "You did have good luck, because I had no torpedoes left," and at that moment the two became good friends.

The next evening, a group of merchant navy masters, whose ships had been sunk, came to see Otto, introduced themselves, and explained they needed a fourth for bridge and wondered if Otto played. "So we played bridge. It was nice, very nice."

When the destroyer docked at Liverpool two days later, Otto insisted he be given his leather uniform, which had been drying on the ship somewhere. "I said I would stay aboard as long as I did not have my trousers, and in ten minutes, here they came." Dressed in original submarine outfit with peaked cap, Otto Kretschmer marched off the

Walker after the British officers had exited. From there the renowned U-boat commander was taken to Cockfosters Camp and later to a secret meeting at the apartment of Captain George Creasy, director of antisubmarine warfare in the British Admiralty.

"Silent Otto" gave him no information but was astonished to learn that the British navy was informed completely about U-boats. "They knew everything about Dönitz, our top personnel, the submarine captains, everything. We didn't know anything about them except that they were the enemy." Soon after Otto Kretschmer landed in England, a story appeared in British newspapers that his boat had been sunk and he had been captured.

"When I was in British captivity, the Crossed Swords to the Oak Leaves did not exist. I was the first in the navy who got it." When this prestigious German decoration arrived for Otto via the International Red Cross, the Canadian camp commandant expressed a desire to present it, but the decision was made that this would not be appropriate. Instead, "A German general presented it to me, and this was also published in *The Times*."

After a year or so in British prison camp, Otto was sent to Bowmanville Camp in Ontario, Canada, arriving there in May 1942. Using freely distributed magazines and newspapers, the German prisoners learned vital facts about American war production and passed the information back to Dönitz by way of coded letters. Kretschmer, his first officer, and two other commanders began to plan an escape as well, and notified Dönitz that they thought he should send a U-boat to the east coast of Canada to pick them up. Once the admiral had approved the plan, Kretschmer's team started work on a tunnel, piling the dirt into the attic of their spacious quarters. All was proceeding apace, when the heavy soil crashed through the ceiling, and that was the end of the escape plan.

Another commander, Wolfgang Heyda, then volunteered to sneak out of camp by climbing a power pole and pulling himself across the wires on a "boatswain's chair" he had rigged up. He actually succeeded in getting out, but three days later was detained by a patrol and sent to another camp. Meanwhile, U-536, under the command of Rolf Schauenburg, made an arduous journey across the Atlantic in

September 1943, found no one, and barely escaped a Canadian trap when departing. As Kretschmer put it: "The Royal Navy had known about the code we used since World War I days."

In 1946 Kretschmer and his men sailed to England and were put into prison camps there. "We were subdivided into categories: white for nondangerous, gray for undetermined, and black for dangerous. I was black. I don't know why." Finally, on 31 December 1947, Otto Kretschmer received his freedom, but because of his classification he was not allowed to "use his brain." After being reclassified, the captain of U-99 entered Kiel University, studied law, and married a lovely blonde physician named Louise-Charlotte. From 1955 to 1970 Otto served in the German navy, attaining the rank of admiral.

In 1955, on the occasion of the publication of Terence Robertson's book about Kretschmer, entitled *Night Raider of the Atlantic* (in England: *The Golden Horseshoe*), Otto and his wife traveled to London for the ceremony. One of the guests, Donald Macintyre, former commander of the destroyer *Walker,* astonished Otto by presenting him with the Zeiss binoculars that Macintyre had taken from him when he was captured. Macintyre had been using them on hunting trips for fourteen years and must have regretted giving them up; however, he placed a small silver plaque on the glasses reading: "Returned to Otto Kretschmer, A Gallant Foe. Donald Macintyre, Captain R.N., October 24th, 1955."[5]

Otto Kretschmer died on 5 August 1998.

4   Josef Erben, U-128

■■

"I was a member of the crew of U-128 from the beginning until the dead end, and I lived through all the heights and depths of it," wrote Josef. In response to my request to some of the German U-boat club leaders to describe their patrols, Seaman Second Class Erben sent reports, letters, and memories of U-128 that he had saved for half a century. He was especially glad that a woman was writing about U-boats, because, as he said, "A female always sees many things that happened during the span of many years from a different side. She will emphasize the human aspect."

■■

In May 1941, as the great convoy battles against England progressed, U-128 finished the usual sea trials, torpedo firing practice, and final overhaul. Then on 23 July 1941 she embarked from Horten, Norway, for diving practice. "It was beautiful sunny weather, and we were going to do the last exercises before going out for frontline action. Early in the morning we were on course to the given location in the [Oslo] fjord when suddenly we felt a very strong hit, and the boat kept grinding against something very hard. At the same time, the bow rose out of the water, exposing the torpedo tubes with the torpedoes in them."

The boat had rumbled to a halt on top of a rock, unmarked on the sea charts. The submarine was positioned so that the water depth beneath the ten-centimeter artillery cannon in front was four feet, but

Josef Erben

in the stern the depth was about ninety feet. The men ran to the deck to see what had happened, and as they looked around they noticed that the weather was turning bad. A little later, as daylight faded, a thick fog began creeping in. "The light cruiser *Leipzig*, on the way to Oslo, happened to pass close by, saw us, and interrupted her trip to help us. The captain took off most of our crew, leaving only a few men on watch, who stayed aboard to see that nothing else happened to the boat."

Unable to get the submarine off the rock under her own power, Commander Heyse radioed the navy base at Horten for help, and two days later a depot ship and two heavy tugs arrived. "At first they tried to get us off sideways, but that didn't succeed, so they stopped and started all over again the next day with more tugboats and other powerful boats. Finally, on the twenty-fourth of July, the strongest tugboats of the North German Lloyd, passenger ships, and smaller tugboats worked on the submarine." With an ominous crackling noise, the iron cables between the U-boat and the tug started to split, but still the sub did not move. On 25 July the crew of U-128 started to lighten their vessel by removing ballast and some of the fuel, putting it into tanks and transferring the tanks to nearby ships. "With great hopes we started again the next morning. We thought the lightening would be the answer, but by three in the afternoon we still had made no progress."

At this point Engineer Johann Engelkes started the diesel engines and "gave her everything we had, to get lift for the boat while we were being pulled. After two tries we suddenly were lucky, and the boat came free of the rock." As soon as all the cables were taken off, U-128 sailed into the Horten dockyard, where a thorough inspection revealed she had minor damage and could still travel.

U-128 proceeded to Kiel, Germany, spent many months getting repairs, then journeyed to her home base at Lorient. The boat made the entire trip on the surface, even through the Bay of Biscay, observing no enemy aircraft. They entered the bay at noon, where a minesweeper met them, and U-128 made a safe four-hour passage through the minefields to the base, arriving on Christmas Eve 1941.

As part of the first lightning-like attacks on U.S. shipping, on her second patrol U-128 crossed the Atlantic and stationed herself off the Florida coast in the Bahama Channel, southeast of Cape Canaveral. "We were so close to shore that we could see all the activity going on there," remembered Erben. "This was at a time that there was no danger—no one was around to check on us and there were no ships against us, so we could stay on the surface without any problem and see what was going on."

They sank the *Cities Service Empire* and the *O. A. Knudsen* in February 1942, then returned to Lorient. On her next trip U-128 sank five ships and damaged one in the French Guiana–Trinidad area. Early in July the U-boat went to a quick rendezvous with a supply U-tanker and collected a small store of food and some fuel oil. The fueling operation took place as both boats lay motionless in a parallel heading, about 165 feet apart. A long hose, supported by eight or ten floats, held the line on the surface as the diesel oil was pumped through. Food and other essentials were rowed across in a dinghy.

U-128 arrives at Lorient on 23 March 1942 after a second patrol.
Bundesarchiv, Koblenz

As usual, a physician from the supply boat went aboard U-128 and checked the crew members. U-boats carried no doctors at this stage of the war; there was very little need for them, and each vessel had a pharmacist's mate, trained in first aid, who took care of minor medical problems. Later, when the Allies were inflicting heavy damage on U-boats and sinking scores of them, the German navy forced doctors to go on patrols and many were killed.

The first week of September 1942, U-128 went out to test a new radar detection device called a German Search Receiver. Five technicians went along, and they traveled around the Bay of Biscay, where Allied air surveillance had increased dramatically.

The equipment, a receiver and a crude wooden cross with aerial (called the Biscay Cross) gave a loud *pinging* when radar hit it. Using enemy planes to try out the new equipment, U-128's crew discovered they now had plenty of time to dive at each warning, but there was one difficulty: having to grab the contraption and bring it inside before they headed down. All German U-boats were then given the new equipment, and losses in the Bay of Biscay immediately decreased.

Supplies being transferred to a U-boat from U-459, one of the supply U-boats, or "milkcows." *Bundesarchiv, Koblenz*

Up to this time, German submarine commanders had been unable to understand how Allied planes were finding them in the dark, beaming searchlights down on them, and attacking. U-128 was the first to use this useful new tool, called Metox.[1]

U-128's fifth patrol began in September 1942 and lasted four months. Such an unusually long voyage could be accomplished with the help of "milkcows," or supply U-boats, operating without the knowledge of the Allies at secret rendezvous points in the Atlantic.

The big subs had everything they needed on board and operated beyond the reach of Allied planes until May 1943, carrying fuel oil, fresh bread, food, medications, torpedoes, tools, mail from home, and everything else required for U-boat war operations.

In the first few days before departing, Heyse and crew carried out test diving practice, but in three instances the officers in charge failed to close the conning tower hatch correctly, thoroughly drenching the men in the tower. The captain made the three officers practice opening and closing the hatches, much to the amusement of the crew.

U-128 arrives at Lorient after successfully testing new Metox (radar detection) equipment. Note the emblem of a white plow horse and City of Ulm coat of arms on tower. *Bundesarchiv, Koblenz*

On 10 November, after sinking two ships, U-128 went to a meeting with milkcow U-461, whose usual contact point was west of the Cape Verde Islands (off Africa). A second German submarine, U-161, arrived and started the transfer of diesel oil while U-128 motored around awaiting her turn. Suddenly the announcement came from U-128's engine room that a ship was heading toward them, so the supply boat and U-161 hastened away on the surface, and U-128 took off in hot pursuit of the merchantman. Heyse fired two torpedoes, dispatching the British freighter *Start Point* with no trouble, then brought on board the first officer and chief engineer as prisoners—an unusual event. The captain had gone down with his vessel. Early that afternoon Commander Heyse met the U-tanker again and transferred the two officers to it.

Heyse requested two torpedoes, but Commander Stiebler told him he would have to take four. Two of these were stored in the forward compartment and two in the aft section of U-461, and they were transferred onto the deck, where the crew wrapped ten life preservers around each one. They lowered the wrapped, twenty-one-feet-long torpedoes into the water one at a time and towed them with a dinghy over to U-128. The other crew, using a small collapsible crane (stored under the deck grating), hauled the huge missiles onto the partially submerged forward section of the U-boat, placing each onto the torpedo loading dolly. After leveling the dolly, they pushed it into the designated torpedo hatch. The transfer of one torpedo took about two hours, and refueling lasted around four hours.

Heyse then continued his patrol in the waters off the bulge of Brazil, where he sank a British freighter, the *Teesbank.* "We attacked them as they were having their midday snooze," noted Erben, "so they were surprised when they were suddenly blown up." The captain, sitting on deck in his pajamas, was thrown into the ocean, and he and a few of his crew were taken from their lifeboats onto the German submarine. "We brought them aboard and gave the captain special quarters in the officers mess and a khaki uniform so he would have something to wear. All our crew liked him very much because he was similar to a nice old father." Heyse was friendly with the quiet older man, who made very little comment about the sinking of his ship, and the commander allowed Captain Brown to stay with him and the watch officer on the bridge. A few days later the U-boat transferred Brown and his men to a nearby supply submarine, where they were to be taken to France.

About twelve days later U-128 rendezvoused again with U-461, and the meeting took on the aspect of a party. A group of seven or eight U-boats gathered to receive supplies, including U-126, U-172, U-161, U-174, probably U-508, and two others. The commanders hopped from boat to boat greeting each other, sharing the latest news, and generally enjoying a rare chance to communicate. (At sea they could send and receive messages only through headquarters, referred to as *BdU*, or *Befehlshaber der Unterseeboote.*)

"*Kapitänleutnant* Sühren came on board to visit with us. We had stopped next to his boat, and he came on over. This was an unusual occasion, not often done." Commanders Witte and Emmerman arrived as well, and one of U-128's crew members went over to the supply boat to get some dental treatment. The submarines spent that afternoon, the night, and most of the next day getting resupplied, doing sundry chores, and having a pleasant break.

U-128 then started home. When they reached the Bay of Biscay a fierce gale was blowing, and one of the men on watch was almost washed overboard when his safety line broke in heavy seas. Other than the weather, U-128 had no problem getting back to Lorient and saw no Allied planes. The boat arrived about noon on 15 January 1943, a time when the submarines as yet had the upper hand on the seas.

The crew soon discovered that a bombing raid had devastated large parts of the U-boat base the previous night, and their barracks building next to the pier was a smoldering ruin with no roof. However, shortly after arrival, they enjoyed the customary welcoming reception with music, speeches, beer, champagne, and fifty French girls. Early that evening the crew members rode on busses to a newer camouflaged barracks building nine miles from town.

Around ten o'clock three of the men, worried about a warning the French girls had given them about a second air raid that night, returned to the pier where U-128 was tied up. There they joined the four men on watch duty and, just as predicted, at 11:00 P.M. the first drone of planes could be heard, then the explosions of bombs on the submarine base, the first of many in a massive air attack.

The bombs, falling all around U-128, set fire to the pier where she was tied up. One of the crew members raced to the officers club to tell the commander or first officer that U-128 was in extreme danger. He could find neither, so he ran back to the boat. Flames had already ignited some of the pennants on the conning tower, so the crew quickly decided they must try to move the submarine away from the burning dock. Because they were so few, they now faced a serious problem but proceeded to do the best they could. The seven men, including the engineer, a midshipman, and a chief petty officer, moved the sub away from shore, but the inexperienced midshipman, who knew nothing about the electric motor compartment, accidentally burned out the clutches.

After struggling for an hour they managed to maneuver the boat to a buoy in the middle of the river, arriving at midnight. There they made the boat fast and remained the rest of that night. "Early in the morning of January seventeenth the whole crew went down into the burning city of Lorient on a bus. At the edge of town we got out and went by foot to the place where our boat was tied up. It was gone, and no one around there could tell us what had happened or where it was." Erben and the officers and crew members went out in a navy craft, and after a quick search found U-128 tied to the buoy. Upon a hasty inspection of the vessel, they were relieved to find it had very little damage, so they proceeded to tow the submarine into a bunker, "where it was very safe," said Josef. "We were glad it turned out that way, after such a long voyage—and nobody killed or wounded."

One month later the German Navy transferred *Kapitänleutnant* Ulrich Heyse to a shore job and sent Executive Officer Heinz Hungershausen to the U-boat commanders school at Memel. The crew members regretted the loss of their captain, because they felt he was a friend to them. Often on long cruises he had sat down with the kitchen detail, pulled out his pocketknife to help them peel potatoes, and talked about anything they were interested in. On shore he sometimes joined them for a glass or two of beer. Everyone agreed Heyse should have been on U-128's next patrol, because with him in command, they thought, she would have escaped disaster.

Some of the men had a premonition of bad luck when U-128 put out to sea again on 6 April 1943, carrying twenty-three torpedoes and accompanied by U-154, skippered by Oskar Kusch. A month later, they were patrolling ten miles off Bahia, Brazil at night, and so close to shore they could see the city lights. The British, who had just decrypted a message from U-128 to Berlin, dispatched search aircraft, but the boats spotted it and crash-dived. One plane dropped some depth charges just as U-128 went under, but no damage occurred, and the next morning the sub set out in pursuit of a convoy. Captain Steinert had not ordered the crew to put up the Metox antenna, believing that patrolling airplanes had no need of radar in clear weather. However, another plane spotted U-128 on her radar screen from eighteen miles away, but the sub watch officer saw it coming. Their crash dive failed because of a malfunction; a few minutes later the boat finally started to go under, at which point the plane dropped six depth charges set at twenty-five feet. One explosion blew a hole in the pressure hull near the forward torpedo tubes, a flood of seawater gushed in from a four-inch hole from the galley hatch, and the electric motors and gyro compass were completely knocked out.[2]

As the boat plummeted toward the bottom at a terrifying rate, the crew scrambled to the aft section of the boat to try to get it in trim. Steinert stopped the dive, and ordered them to surface, realizing that remaining submerged would endanger the crew. Once on top, the U-boat made full speed toward the direction of the South American coast, with the antiaircraft guns manned. A second plane saw the submarine surging through the water, flew down to one hundred feet, and blasted them with six bombs, causing more damage to the crippled boat. As the plane started a series of strafing runs, U-128 floated helplessly, unable to fight back. On the conning tower the second officer and another crewman lay badly wounded, so Steinert courageously crawled onto the bridge to administer morphine to them.

As the shots rained down like hail, none of the men could get out to the bridge, and the commander, who had made it back inside, was forced to steer by looking through the periscope. The crew, assembled in the control room, felt that only a miracle could save them. Several crew members were ordered to go onto the deck behind the conning tower and surrender the boat. One made it topside and waved his arms to signal the airplane that was shooting at them, but either the pilot did not see him or failed to recognize his motions. Another crewman frantically searched the boat for a white sheet to wave but could not find one. (The U-boats all used blue-and-white checked sheets.)

At this point the two remaining deck lookouts saw a pair of American destroyers, the USS *Moffett* and USS *Jouett,* approaching on the horizon, and Steinert gave the order to abandon ship and carry out scuttling. Most of the crew jumped off the boat, but the destroyers, seeing no white flag, opened fire on the submarine, using the plane as a spotter. In a heavy barrage, they scored four direct hits, and in a short time U-128 disappeared under the waves. The captain, one of the last to leave, had stayed aboard to carry out scuttling procedures. Later, the first officer remarked that he was surprised that neither of the two destroyers tried to close in and board the U-boat.

The *Moffett* rescued fifty-one crewmen, but four died on U-128, one from chlorine poisoning. "After our sinking we were transported to the United States, to New York. From there the trip continued by train to Stringtown, Oklahoma, and then to Papago Park in Phoenix, Arizona." Josef said that he and his mates looked forward to the end of "that terrible war in Europe." In prison camp he earned a little money by washing clothes for his friends, and after Germany surrendered, Erben worked for a year at the Phoenix Waterworks.

In 1946 Josef was shipped to Liverpool, England, and spent another year there stuck in a work camp before he returned to his country. "Then the worst part of our lives started. Everywhere in Germany we saw rubble and ashes and poor people without places to live, scratching hard to earn their daily bread." He said the crewmen only hoped that they could find employment and that their loved ones were still alive and happy. "I, personally, had good luck, for eventually I qualified as a train engineer, and after serving for forty years, I retired in 1987."

Josef's collection of photographs of U-128 was burned in a bomb attack on his home in Koblenz in 1944. "The pictures would have been very interesting for the world," he wrote, "but that's the way it was."[3]

5   Hans Burck, U-67

■■

One of three survivors of the sinking of U-67 on 13 April 1943, Ober-bootsmaat *Johann Burck was shipped to a prisoner of war camp in Phoenix, Arizona, where he spent three-and-a-half years. An inveterate communicator, Hans wrote many letters to his mother, but the censors, unable to read Sütherlin German, refused to mail them. Hans learned to correspond in standard German, and eight months later his mother finally learned what had happened to him. In early 1942, on one of his first missions, Petty Officer Burck kept a secret journal of his trip to South America and it survived intact, written with pencil on small scraps of paper. The complete account is presented here, edited slightly for clarity.*

■■

THE DIARY

17 JANUARY 1942. "We depart from Lorient at 6:00 P.M., and at 11:00 the escort leaves us. We are traveling under war conditions [everyone extra alert and ready to dive at any minute, with the boat running submerged during daylight hours].

18 JANUARY. Nothing special all day. At night we sail on the surface.

19 JANUARY. I hope we will be leaving the Bay of Biscay soon. [Heavily mined, the bay had become extremely hazardous for U-boats.]

Hans Burck (center). After war patrols crewmen had bushy beards, as they were unable to shave on U-boats.

20 JANUARY. We are traveling underwater, and progress is very slow. Finally, at night we surface again and run southward with high speed.

21 JANUARY. Thank the Lord, this is our last day underwater, and we are out of the danger zone. At dark we surface.

22 JANUARY. We are at last in the free Atlantic, off the Spanish coast, and we do a practice alarm dive so that new crew members will get used to it.

23 JANUARY. Again we are cruising with war conditions, but nothing happens as we pass Gibraltar.

24 JANUARY. Another practice crash dive, and now we are sighting [ships'] smoke on the horizon, but we avoid it because we don't want to be seen.

25 JANUARY. We are marching right along, and toward evening we see the Azores. The sea is very calm, and there is a full moon.

26 JANUARY. At dawn the last lights of the Azores fade away. From now on we are forbidden to shoot at anything but battleships and air-

craft carriers [to keep a low profile and accomplish the mission]. The weather is getting hotter.

27 JANUARY. When morning comes we sight the tip of a mast, so we change course. Probably a Portuguese fishing boat. We move along toward the southwest.

28 JANUARY. The Azores disease is noticeable in the whole crew, and the climate is changing rapidly. [After vacationing onshore, crew members felt a kind of depression when leaving for war again, and the Azores were their last sight of friendly land.]

29 JANUARY. Another practice dive, and this time we stay underwater for an hour. For the first time, we go on deck without our shirts, because the noon sun is nice and warm.

30 JANUARY. We are still traveling on a southerly course, but we still do not know where we are going.

31 JANUARY. It is slowly getting to be boring, just marching along.

1 FEBRUARY. We are already in our third week at sea. Where you are it is probably snowing, but here we are getting a suntan on the deck. [This message was intended for his mother.]

2 FEBRUARY. Today we practice gunnery, shooting with all calibers, and the new crew people are a little slow, but they are soon up to speed.

3 FEBRUARY. Still cruising on a southwest course, which will bring us to America, but we don't know where. Otherwise nothing special today.

4 FEBRUARY. Again, it is a beautiful day with a light wind breezing about our ears. Now we are used to the climate, and the Azores sickness has disappeared like magic.

5 FEBRUARY. We practice several alarm dives. We are getting better and better and are almost satisfied with ourselves. [Top commanders could get a boat down in twenty seconds.]

6 FEBRUARY. The mood is somewhat happier, the wind is blowing, and the boat jumps around quite a bit. The new men are somewhat subdued, but there are no incidents.

7 FEBRUARY. The sea is quiet and visibility is good, but the sun is gradually getting unbearable. Temperature on the deck is 48° [118°F], and inside the boat 65° [149°F]. The first sunburns are visible.

8 FEBRUARY. We are traveling at the same pace, same weather as yesterday. Great numbers of porpoises are following us, and many flying fish are here.

9 FEBRUARY. Since noon only two off-duty men are allowed on the bridge. At 6:00 we sight an airplane far away, and when it comes closer, we can see that it is a white American land plane. We dive, and everything goes nicely, just like our practice. After an hour we surface again, and the plane is gone. They did not see us.

10 FEBRUARY. Today we have extra lookouts and are extra alert, because we are close to the Lesser Antilles. At 4:00 we see land, a small British island, Sombrero, and as night falls we see navigation lights near shore, just like in peacetime. We do not know whether we have been detected or not, but we are very close to the island. At night we travel through the Anegada Channel.

11 FEBRUARY. We are now in the Caribbean, and at 1:00 A.M. I see an airplane with its navigation lights on. We get the impression they have no idea that German submarines are anywhere near, and we consider the Americans still beginners as far as war is concerned.

12 FEBRUARY. This morning Commander Müller-Stöckheim tells us our destination. We are going to Curaçao, an important island for America because it has the biggest oil company in the world. [Their target: Royal Dutch Shell, second largest.] Our orders are to create a disturbance at Curaçao. At noon we see the first [ship's] smoke, but it is a neutral freighter.

13 FEBRUARY. It is a wonderful day today, and flying fish fall onto our deck. At noon one of our pith helmets is blown into the water, and we jump in to get it and have a nice swim. I am the first to be in American waters, and the swim feels really good.

14 FEBRUARY. The heat is still increasing, and inside our sub it is 65° [149°F], on deck 54°[129.2°F]. In the afternoon we sight our goal, Curaçao. We go closer and closer to see what is happening there.

15 FEBRUARY. During the day we stay submerged to keep from being spotted. When dark comes we are amazed to see that there are so many tankers, one more beautiful than the other, but as yet we cannot shoot. We are all looking forward to the action, and at three hours before daybreak we start. The long-awaited hour is here.

U-67 in Caribbean. Hans Burck is in the front row, center, on bridge. Note variety of headwear for tropics. December 1941.

16 FEBRUARY. It is 1:00 A.M., and we are slowly proceeding toward the outer harbor of Willemstad. The shore is lit up like daylight, and we are very excited and nervous. The clock moves slowly, and we can hardly wait, but finally it is time. With a calm voice, the commander announces throughout the boat: 'Make torpedo weapons ready.' I am sitting at my station between the bow torpedo tubes, and I have my earphones and microphone on. We are steering toward our position. The first order comes to me: 'Make tubes one through four ready for a surface shot.' Everything is all set. Exactly to the minute at 5:00 A.M. the first torpedo leaves the tube. It is running, and the seconds turn into hours. Finally a little jolt hits our boat, and hooray! a hit. A four-thousand-ton tanker is going down.

Suddenly, all hell breaks loose. Searchlights are lit up on shore, and we have to dive. After a little while we go back to periscope depth. Our commander explains what is happening on the surface as he watches. The water is burning, and the tanker has disappeared from sight. There are only lifeboats and fishing boats trying to save the survivors.

17 FEBRUARY. This morning we surface for a short while, and the

water is covered with oil and pieces of wood from the wreck. Debris is strewn everywhere. According to what we can learn, the tanker was Dutch, the *Rafaela*, four thousand tons. We are suddenly forced underwater by airplanes, and they drop two bombs.

At noon we surface again but have to immediately crash-dive because of an airplane that drops three bombs, and they are fairly close. We submerge again, because now the Tommies have our number, and their airplanes are hanging around all the time. Three bombs explode near us. We stay submerged until dark.

18 FEBRUARY. Today was another very exciting day. As usual, we stayed underwater all day long, and now at dark we are heading toward the Bay of Willemstad on the surface. It is a great joy, because we can go on deck and feel the cool air.

Then we get the order to man the cannons. This is our most beautiful moment, the one for which we all have been waiting. The coast is so close we can almost touch it, and we can see big beautiful white tanks, one after the other [lit up]. We get our cannons positioned and loaded with a certain type ammunition, ready to shoot at the oil tanks. Our first shot falls into the water, but the second and following shots reach their targets. Then we change from high-explosive shells to incendiary shells. Oh, what beautiful fireworks! On shore it starts burning in every nook and cranny. [U-boats rarely attacked shore targets.] Suddenly we notice a shadow off our stern, a Dutch torpedo boat, and we beat a retreat with course south.

19 FEBRUARY. In the morning we sight Venezuela. We want to take a day off and rest a little, but airplanes keep causing alarms, and we are rocked by three bombs. We stay submerged all day and it is red hot in the boat—68° [154°F].

20 FEBRUARY. We return to take a second look at Curaçao and see the oil tanks still burning. Even though we are submerged, two more bombs detonate near us. Then we detect propeller noises and go to periscope depth. The commander sees a beautiful tanker [*J. N. Pew*, American], and it is a big one of 9,608 tons. We make a well-executed underwater attack and sink him with five torpedoes. The water is on fire, and ashore the tanks are still burning. We withdraw toward the west for a new maneuver.

Now an American warship is on our tail, and they bombard us with eight depth charges, but no damage is done.

21 FEBRUARY. We stay under the water all day, and finally things are quiet. If only it weren't so hot.

22 FEBRUARY. Still submerged and traveling out of the danger zone. Otherwise, nothing special.

23 FEBRUARY. Now we are surfacing at noon and finally we can see the sun again. We move along on a southwesterly course.

24 FEBRUARY. We are traveling toward Venezuela, to a quiet place where we can transfer torpedoes from the deck into the tubes."

■ ■

The diary ends here, and U-67's patrol continues back to France.

Hans Burck's successful mission produced sensational headlines in the *New York Times:* "U-boats raid Dutch West Indies, Sink Tankers; U. S. Planes Attack. . . ." The story, with several large file photographs of hundreds of oil storage tanks and a map, revealed that more than one German submarine was in on the act, but no one knew how many. Actually, Werner Hartenstein in U-156 and Jürgen von Rosenstiel in U-502 made attacks at nearby Aruba at the same moment that U-67 surprised Curaçao.[1]

Lieutenant General Frank Andrews, commander of U.S. Caribbean defenses, happened to be on an inspection mission and was spending the night in the guest house of Standard Oil of New Jersey at Aruba. He was awakened by explosions at 1:30 A.M. when two tankers near the island were torpedoed. This was U-156 attacking the *Pedernales* and the *Oranjestad.* "There was a great flash after the first explosion, which almost split the tanker in two," reported the general. The oily waters of Nicholas Bay were ignited, and soon the entire harbor was ablaze. The second tanker was struck and later sank, but the general said it was impossible to tell how many U-boats had attacked. However, they did see that the submarine that sank the second ship surfaced afterward and began firing shells at the refinery, a short distance onshore.

The general's guest house lay between the shore and the refinery, directly in the path of the submarine's shells, but none hit the house. "One shell struck a diesel oil tank, glancing off and leaving a small dent," Andrews went on.

"At 1:30 A.M. an explosion knocked me out of bed," said Captain Robert Bruskin, who had come with General Andrews on the inspection tour. "I looked out the windows. Flames were shooting straight up and seemed mountainous. The ship just seemed to break apart." Bruskin said they all dashed out of the guest house and saw that the flaming oil was spreading over a wide area, under a steady wind. He then noticed that a second ship about a hundred yards away was on fire, and watched as tracer bullets streamed through the darkness— ten or fifteen shots, "apparently aimed at the refinery." No fires were started there, but at that point two hours had passed, and the bay waters were still flaming. They heard a second explosion and learned that this was the torpedoing of a tanker at her pier.[2]

No one realized that U-156, which had actually damaged two ships and sunk another, was accompanied by U-502, which sank the *Tia Juana* and the *Monagas* between Aruba and Lake Maracaibo on 16 February. Although the *New York Times* carried a photo of the oil tanks at Curaçao (at the Royal Dutch Shell Company), there was no mention of U-67's attack on the *Rafaela* nor of the fires started in the storage tanks. U-67, U-156, and U-502 managed to sink four ships and damage two on 16 February, and on the twenty-first U-67 sank one more.[3]

The German navy was fully aware of the importance of both islands, fifteen miles from the Venezuelan coast, where no harbors existed. Two enormous refineries on Aruba and Curaçao were producing great quantities of fuel for the war effort, and their deepwater ports serviced oceangoing tankers. "I decided to use this . . . [U-boat] group for a surprise blow in . . . part of the western Atlantic in which shipping was plentiful—the Aruba-Curaçao-Trinidad area," wrote Admiral Karl Dönitz in his memoirs. "Aruba and Curaçao were important oil centres in the vicinity of which a large number of tankers could be found." The admiral had instructed his commanders to bombard their coastal targets after they had accomplished the sinking of some ships.[4]

Japanese submarine I-30 arriving at Lorient, 21 August 1942. The boat picked up technical material and stayed for four-day visit. *Bundesarchiv, Koblenz*

The U-boats' surprise attack shocked the British, Dutch and American military men based on the islands and caught the Shell and Standard Oil Company executives off guard. Ships leaving Lake Maracaibo received orders to return, and war fuel supplies stopped flowing.

Since Aruba and Curaçao lay a short seven hundred miles from the Panama Canal, Allied military leaders now feared that German wolf packs in the Caribbean would raise new and urgent war problems. Mexico started to fortify her biggest oil refinery at Tampico and initiated searches along the Yucatán Peninsula coastline for possible secret U-boat refueling locations. In the United States, Secretary of War Stimson warned the country that major coastal cities could be attacked and told everyone to get prepared. The German navy's plan to "create chaos" had worked exactly as they had hoped.

U-67 continued to wreak havoc in the petroleum industry with her next mission into the Gulf of Mexico and the sinking of six tankers and two freighters. Arriving at her home base, Lorient, a huge welcoming crowd greeted the crew at the docks on 8 August 1942. There, U-67 had the honor of greeting a large, sleek Japanese submarine, the

Grand banquet at Lorient naval base in honor of I-30 visit. *Bundesarchiv, Koblenz*

I-30, when she came into France on 21 August to take on German technical material. After tying up to a buoy, the Japanese sailors were picked up by a French tender and brought to shore, where Burck's crew members awaited them on the deck of U-67 and cameramen hustled about filming the event.[5]

"The day after I-30 arrived we were involved in the official greeting of the guests, and that included a joint [Japanese-German] dinner in the grand hall of the arsenal." Burck remembers that "many speeches were made, and the next day some of us met our Japanese table neighbors and exchanged small presents." Hans developed a close friendship with two of them while I-30 spent several days at Lorient, and the sailors, following an old custom, exchanged hat bands. "But communications between us were very, very difficult."

"U-67 and I-30 were moved on the same day into the Keroman Bunker for overhauls, but we were not allowed to board the Japanese boat: we could only look at it from the outside. However, we were permitted to have the Japanese on our boat for one day, and I remember that they took many pictures inside U-67."

Hans Burck, who lived through all of U-67's eight patrols, first joined the German navy in 1939. Born in Frankfurt, he came from an honored fishing family that had plied the trade since the sixteenth century. When Hans returned to the ruins of Germany, he once more practiced the profession of river fisherman, "because it was important to get food to the hungry population." At the same time he worked as a ferryman, taking people across the Main River, where all bridges had been blown up. "Now I only practice my fishing trade as a hobby," he says, "and I like to teach young people about boats and the art of making fishing nets."[6]

6   Ernst Göthling, U-26

■■

A border of red, gold, and purple flowers brightens the walkway of the German U-boat memorial at Möltenort, giving a lively touch to the solemn surroundings. A curving wall, set below a grassy hill overlooking the Kiel Fjord, bears 30,003 submariners' names in raised lettering on bronze panels. Each of the 739 lost U-boats is listed, with every crew member and commander who went to a watery grave in World War II. Visiting this impressive setting, one gets a feeling for the devastating losses of good men at sea. Ernst Göthling, one of the fortunate survivors, comes here regularly, dedicated to helping maintain the beautiful monument to his fallen friends.

■■

"I am a blacksmith by profession, and I was born in 1920. My father, a tailor, died when I was two years old, so I grew up without a father." Although his grandfather had been a tailor as well, and German tradition held that sons of craftsmen should follow a craft, Ernst dreamed of joining the navy, even as a small boy.

"In 1933, when Hitler took over, he rebuilt the *Wehrmacht* [armed forces], and ads came out in the paper saying 'Join the navy,' with a list of preferred trades." One day Ernst noticed blacksmiths on the list and had an idea. "At that time I was thirteen years old, and agriculture was the main thing in our village, so there were only a few real professions to pick from, including the blacksmith." To get into the

Ernst Göthling

navy, Ernst chose to be a blacksmith and served the usual three-and-a-half years of apprenticeship in a local shop.

"I put in my application for the navy when I was seventeen and joined in April 1939, half a year before the war started, volunteering for U-boat service. After basic training I was sent to the main center for submarines at Neustadt, where there were many barracks and this diving tower." For six months the sub crews learned about the boats and practiced emergency escapes with their *Tauchretters* (breathing devices) in the five-meter-high tower.

In April 1940 Göthling went to Wilhelmshaven to take a course in submarine welding. Survival at sea often depended upon the art of metalworking, and a great many U-boat crewmen were trained in this skill. After completion of the course, Ernst was assigned to an old U-boat, U-26, built in 1935. "It was an IA, very old-fashioned, with no distilling facilities for fresh water and lacking many things. We had to go to sea like they did in the First World War."

"But I was just a young boy, the youngest one on the boat—nineteen years old. We went out on 20 June 1940 to our patrol area, the Bay of Biscay, and about two weeks later we received a message that a big convoy was leaving Gibraltar, bound for England." Successful in finding the mass of ships, U-26 made a night attack. "We had compressed air-driven torpedoes, which we could only use at night, because they made a streak of bubbles on the surface. I was unaware of this at the time, but the rest of the crew told me about it." Not only did the torpedoes leave a telltale wake—they were often unreliable, going too deep and passing under the ships or rising to the surface. "The two props on the torpedoes turned in opposite directions, making a noise, and we thought that the destroyers must have heard it."

Whatever the reason, two destroyers turned and charged U-26. Commander Scheringer gave orders to fire one "eel," and another a few seconds later. "Then we crash-dived in a hurry, but only to thirty meters. Both destroyers crossed over our position, dropping depth charges on us." As blasts shook the boat, water rushed into several compartments, and "we started sinking deeper and deeper, but the chief engineer, a very skilled man, got the boat under control. Those of us who were not needed at a station ran to the bow room and piled ourselves in between the torpedo tubes, and they put some air in the aft pressure tanks so that the boat became level again."

The battle continued for six hours, with depth charges roaring and booming, destroyer propellers thrashing, and eerie asdic pings. "After the third series of depth charges, all the lights went out, and it was a terrible feeling. But the crew had been trained in 1936 as a peacetime crew and was extremely capable. They were doing things by intuition, without thinking, and they managed to get the lights back on." Göthling said he owned them his life, for he was a complete newcomer.

The depth gauge indicated that they had gone down to 230 meters, more than twice the distance guaranteed by the boat builders, and the men were gasping for breath. Scheringer decided to bring U-26 to the surface just before dawn, hoping to escape. They had lost some oil from damaged fuel tanks, and pieces of wooden decking had floated to the top, creating the possibility that the destroyers would notice the debris and consider the boat sunk.

After spotting a Sunderland airboat circling the attack area, U-26 attempted to get away from the site of the attack, farther into the Atlantic, where they could assess her damage, "but we didn't have a chance to. We met another destroyer, the *Rochester,* headed for England." A British sailor in the crow's nest spied what he thought was floating debris, contacted the Sunderland, and the plane headed toward the traveling U-boat. As soon as it located the sub, the plane dropped six bombs, but by that time U-26 had nosed downward.

"But then the boat went out of control. It was like a seesaw, going up and down, deeper and deeper." Then the chief engineer told the commander, "We *have* to surface now; it will be our last chance." Air hissed into the tanks and the boat rose to about forty meters but could go no higher with so much water inside. Finally, one of the sailors, after great effort, managed to get some of the water pumped out, and the boat again rose gradually. "But we thought the Sunderland considered us done for, and instead, when we made it to the top, he let us have another six bombs, three on one side and three on the other, but we didn't get hit."

Their old foe, the *Rochester,* had by now come on the scene and was blasting with her guns. Recognizing defeat, Scheringer ordered everyone overboard. The men put on life belts and *Tauchretters* (breathing devices) and climbed up the tower and down to the deck, where they stood ready. When the chief engineer, charged with scuttling the boat, appeared and told the commander it was time to go, everyone yelled the customary "Hurrah, hurrah, hurrah!" and jumped overboard.

"Scheringer had given us orders about what to do in the water: no big swimming motions, just treading water and staying together, keeping all clothes on for warmth, and taking any notes out of our pockets. We were also supposed to say nothing at the interrogations or tell the number of the U-boat." Fortunately, in mid-July the Atlantic was not as cold or rough as it could be, giving a better chance for survival. The floating submariners watched the Sunderland flying around above them and feared they might be shot. "It was an awful feeling. We had heard rumors that the British airmen were shooting survivors."

After waiting a while, the men spotted the destroyer, which had gone off at a distance. Then they saw the plane fly over to the ship and exchange flashing signals; as they later found out, the pilot had lost the position of the survivors. "We were only small heads sticking out of the water, so they couldn't see us. Then the plane came down very low, and a man in the upper part opened the window and waved. We were very relieved." After two hours in the water, every crew member was picked up by the *Rochester*. "We were too weak and cold to climb the ladders, so they put ropes around us and pulled us up."

"The treatment on the British destroyer was excellent, and one of our men, who had been a merchant marine captain, helped everyone with translations." *Rochester*'s captain explained to the Germans that he did not have much food left on the ship and told them, "Don't blame us if you don't get enough to eat." However, the British sailors shared their meals with the submariners, and no one suffered. "It was very, very nice," remembered Ernst.

After Göthling's voyage to England, a lengthy period of imprisonment began. At an interrogation camp near London the crew members were questioned, then transferred to a POW camp at Banff, Scotland. If they felt safe in Scotland, they were mistaken, for a Heinkel-111, in an air raid, dropped four bombs on Ernst's prisoner of war camp by error. "Six crew members of U-26 and two British guards were killed. I was pretty badly hurt by having several splinters go into my right lung."

After treatment at a local hospital in Banff, Göthling was sent to a new camp near Manchester, England, where he and fellow prisoners experienced the Blitz. For eight shattering months the Luftwaffe blasted British industrial areas, airfields, and harbors every night. "We spent our nights in the bomb shelters."

Traveling in a large convoy, the crew of U-26 was shipped in January 1941 to Canada: the British, lacking sufficient housing and food for prisoners, were sending thousands of captured Germans to Canadian prison camps. "Our first camp was at Angler, really just a railway station on the beach of Lake Superior. It consisted of wooden barracks surrounded by strong barbed wire fences and watchtowers. But in spite of being heavily guarded, the men managed, with teamwork, to dig a seventy-meter-long tunnel."

"I was still suffering with lung problems from the air raid, and so I did not dig, but I helped prepare food for the escapees and make candles," Göthling continued. "The tunnel was under a barracks, and there was no light down there, so we made candles out of string and grease from the kitchen. One of our men took meat scraps, and we boiled the pieces to make meatballs, then packed them with fat inside tin cans. We made toast, too, since toast keeps better than bread." Some of the prisoners had constructed air vents for the long tunnel, as well.

"We had a warning system. When our lookout saw a guard coming through the gate, he said, 'Fifteen.' That was our code word, and everyone stopped all tunnel work."

On 18 April 1941 twenty-eight Germans fled through their underground passageway to the forest. A small group of them found an abandoned shack and were sleeping there when Canadian guards found them. Before two of the escapees could get out of their blankets, the guards, in a frenzy of gunfire, shot them dead and wounded three others. Ernst learned about the incident from one of the prisoners who escaped from the hut unharmed. In two weeks all the escapees were rounded up and brought back to the camp, where they were placed in a detention area for twenty-eight days, with short rations.

From Angler, Ernst Göthling and crew were sent to Ozada, in the Rocky Mountains west of Calgary. "It was intended to be a summer camp for approximately ten thousand prisoners from Rommel's Afrika Korps. They set up this tent camp to house the men while they constructed permanent barracks, but there was a delay, and we had to stay there until 1 December."

On 1 September came the first blizzard, and the tents had no heat. "We took pails and filled them with roots and things and burned them to try to stay warm. Every night we stayed up until two o'clock, then lay down on our sacks stuffed with straw. It was hard to sleep." In the six-man circular tent, each person had to lie with his head next to the side of the tent, where freezing air seeped in. They piled on many blankets, but it was difficult to keep arms, legs, and shoulders warm.

"We were there for three months, and we had no water, among other things, so we melted ice shavings. But in spite of everything, we did not blame the Canadian government, because they had tried to build a camp at Lethbridge and the main dining hall burned down during construction. That is why we could not be sent there."

Göthling became ill with pleurisy and went to a hospital in Calgary, where he stayed for four weeks. That December of 1942 Ernst and friends spent a dismal Christmas in Lethbridge camp. "In spite of our fervent hopes [of getting home], we still had to spend several Christmases behind barbed wire. Holiday times were always very hard on us."

At Lethbridge the camp leaders organized classes, cultural exhibits, and various events for the prisoners. "We were able to further our education during that interminable time, and after so many years of idleness, it took an enormous amount of energy to do it." Ernst studied English, mathematics, physics, chemistry, and other subjects, trying to prepare for his future.

"So the time passed. Our greatest handicap, besides not knowing when the end of the war would be, was not being able to work. The Canadian government kept all prisoners from doing labor until the end of 1943. At that time I was able to work in a sawmill in the north of Alberta, and those were good days."

In May 1945, "The war was now lost for us, and the Canadians, acting very much like victors, let us go hungry and interrogated us several times. They installed camp radios in our barracks and broadcast propaganda, telling us that everything we had done was wrong, and so on. But things were really not too bad there."

"Finally, at the beginning of April 1946 they shipped us back to the United Kingdom and started interrogations again, trying to make us say, 'We are guilty in every way.' Each man was quizzed at great length as to his political beliefs, and they put everyone into categories: 'A' for Democrat, or believer in democracy; 'B,' a neutral person; 'C,' a Nazi; and 'C+' for Supernazi." Those in category "C" were kept in England and forced to work; those who were "C+" went back to prison camps and were given minimal food rations. "If we reminded the British that we were not criminals, but prisoners of war with a right to go home one year after the war (under the Geneva Convention), they classified us as Supernazis."

Ernst made the mistake of protesting and had to serve ten months in a punishment camp in Northern Scotland. At the beginning of July 1947, after seven years of incarceration, Ernst Göthling was discharged and went home.

"In retrospect, after writing this report, I have come to this conclusion: in spite of the long imprisonment and occasional problems, it was not a lost time for me. The Canadians treated us correctly during the war, even though the impossibility of working created a hardship for us psychologically. I improved my education immensely and my ability to get along with people, both of which helped me a great deal in later life."[1]

7   Hermann Frubrich, U-845

■ ■

Matrosengefreiter (Ordinary Seaman) Frubrich, battle station helmsman, manned alternate positions on the boat—the central control room or the tower—and in both areas he operated the rudders by means of an electrical box with two buttons, one left and one right. If the controls were damaged, he could go into the stern torpedo room and use a manual one at the emergency station. Hermann, who left home at age fourteen, went to work as a sailor's apprentice for the Neptune Line of Basel, Switzerland, and in 1942 joined the navy. Assigned to submarine duty, Hermann was chosen by Commander Udo Behrens to be his personal helper, or valet, a special honor for a young sailor, and a sought-after position.

■ ■

Before a submarine could go out on war patrol, the commander took the boat out into the Baltic for tactical maneuvers. Engineers from the navy base, nicknamed "Silberlings," accompanied the crew, and once at sea, they created emergency situations for the boat, to find out whether the crew could cope with system failures. "In one case [June 1943]," Frubrich pointed out, "an engineer blocked a diving cell with a piece of metal. Normally, such a thing would never happen, and a boat could not survive it. Right away, the chief engineer (diving officer) lost control of the boat, and we rushed toward the bottom at a sixty-degree angle."

Hermann Frubrich

U-845 plunged into the floor of the Baltic, but, by a stroke of fortune, the area was soft, not rocky. "When we hit, everything in the boat flew all over the place, and I was thrown against the iron wall of the tower, facing it. Then the navigator flew into me, hitting me in the back. I felt like my back was broken." U-845 was now trapped in the mud.

When the sub smacked into the seafloor, bags of potatoes in the aft torpedo room flew into the air, and a barrel of pickled herrings burst, spewing fish juice into the bilge. "The batteries were running over, as well, and that released poisonous acid fumes, so we had to put on our breathing devices."

Skipper Behrens and the chief held a brief discussion, then Behrens announced: "We will put the electric motors at slow and move the rudder from side to side until I rescind the order." Frubrich followed instructions, and as the boat strained one way and then another, nothing happened. Then, slowly, there was a slight movement and a scraping noise was heard in the bow. "Both engines stop," barked the captain, and he said to the chief, "Now both engines back, and if the boat moves, blow the bow tank slowly. You must catch it just right so the stern does not sink into the mud."

"That's exactly what we did. Slowly the boat righted itself, but we were struggling in there, trying to work at a steep, sixty-degree angle and breathing through tubes." When the boat again surfaced, the chief quickly opened the hatch and turned on the ventilator system. "I had never seen the commander so mad. He told the Silberlings, 'The likes of you will never again set foot on my ship.'"

Udo Behrens, suffering with eye problems, was taken off U-845 and replaced by Rudolf Hoffmann in July 1943. As the war progressed against Germany, the U-boat force was disappearing in ever greater numbers, hunted down and bombed by planes from aircraft carriers. "In August," explained Frubrich, "we went to Kiel, where our 10.5-centimeter gun was taken off, and we were given a 'Quad,' or antiaircraft gun." U-845's assignment on 20 September 1943 was to head out into the Baltic, where training exercises were held, and to listen for noises from U-346, which had made an error in submerging exercises and was sitting on the bottom. "We were directed to go to eighty meters and stay near the boat till we could not hear any more knocking [by the sailors] on the hull. Only one man survived—the first watch officer; forty-two other crew members died." In emergency situations the crew sometimes was able to make it to the surface using their breathing devices and could be picked up.

A week later, back in Kiel, a group of Japanese naval officers came aboard U-845, as Hoffmann had been assigned to sail into Japanese waters. However, the mission was abruptly canceled when *BdU* relieved Hoffmann of command. Admiral Dönitz had issued orders that no longer could the navy men use a standard military salute but must give the "Heil Hitler" gesture. When Hoffmann heard this he made a remark to a propaganda man who was on board, that if his men had to use that Hitler salute, he would not return to Germany after his next mission. "We felt sure that must have been the reason he was relieved. To us, he was always friendly, and he liked to be part of any mischievous goings-on. Whenever we were doing torpedo practice underwater, he sat on the periscope seat, swiveled around, and sang a song called 'Jumbo the Elephant.'"

In October 1943 Werner Weber took command of U-845 in Stettin. "He had been on the *BdU* staff in France and was one of Dönitz's relatives," said Hermann. In preparation for their next patrol, the crew had to endure Baltic maneuvers for a third time. With every new commander came another training session for his men, to be sure that crew and skipper worked well together.

After all supplies were laid in, U-845 pulled away from the Kiel pier bright and early on the morning of 1 January 1944. "The band was playing a march, and women and officers from the base were waving good-bye to us." The weather grew steadily worse, with tremendous winds, huge waves, and a mixture of rain and snow. As they went into the Skagerrak, between Norway and Denmark, the sea grew calmer.

"One day about midday we had an air raid alarm and manned the antiaircraft weapons. We put a short burst of fire in front of an airplane, and all at once it turned and shot a recognition flare. The first watch officer shouted, 'Hey, it's German!'" So the guns were secured, and U-845 went into Stavanger, Norway, to pick up a spare part for a damaged detection device.

The next day they departed once again in quiet seas, and after a second stop in Bergen, U-845 headed into the north Atlantic. "We had rains and storms to almost hurricane force, and there were snowstorms, fog, and waves as big as a house. Part of the deck got torn away, and some sheet metal on the conning tower was bent." One of the sailors, Rudolf Voigt, injured his right arm working as lookout, so the captain told Frubrich to man the watch and let Voigt handle the helm.

"I put on my gear and went up to be the new lookout. As I was passing through the tower, I saw Voigt and said, 'Watch the rudder, or we may sink.'" Then Frubrich climbed up onto the bridge, snapped on his harness hooks and was surprised to feel himself being slowly lifted. "I hollered to First Watch Officer Theimann, 'Sea coming from astern. Close the lid!'" A few seconds later Frubrich was standing in Atlantic water, clinging to his safety harness. "Frubrich," yelled Theimann, "get the heck back down in the tower and take over the rudder!" Hermann heard the words with satisfaction. "I would have liked to kick Rudolf in the ass, because I got completely soaked."

Frubrich drained the water out of the tower bilge and checked everything carefully. "We had seawater in the two front cylinders of the diesel, so we submerged, and Chief Engineer Otto Strunk rolled up his sleeves and worked, up to his belly button, in one of the diesels." After ten hours the job was done.

In the meantime, Hermann lay down on the floor of the engine room to catch a nap. "It was nice and warm in there, and my clothes dried on my body. Suddenly Adolf Helfers was shaking me, yelling, 'Hermann, to battle stations!' I got myself together and reported to the tower." Weber gave orders to surface, to check the diesels. Both engines started promptly, except that the port side ran a bit slower, then faster. When the two engines were performing well, Engineer Strunk told the captain that the boat was "completely able to do battle."

North of Scotland, between the Shetland and Faroe Islands, U-845 ran into a dense wall of fog. "It was the middle of January, and I was on watch, and the fog was so thick we could hardly see the bow of the boat, so we stayed surfaced, cutting through the calm sea at a speed of eighteen to twenty knots. It was the perfect time to charge our batteries."

"All of a sudden we broke through the fog bank and encountered a blue sky, sunshine, and a calm sea. The starboard lookout shouted, 'Big steamer at thirty degrees. Three smokestacks.'" Theimann ordered the rudder ten degrees to port and yelled a message to the commander: "Passenger ship on starboard at thirty degrees!" He told Frubrich to stay on course, and the commander climbed up to the bridge.

"At the same second, the passenger ship had sighted us as well," Frubrich went on. "Great clouds of black smoke were discharging from the funnels, and, as the liner went into full speed, the bow of the ship lifted somewhat. She was zigzagging."

Weber turned to Theimann. "Why didn't you turn, too?" he asked.

"Then we could have had her." Theimann replied, "But commander, we have orders to stay invisible until we get to Newfoundland."

"That's a different story, Mister Theimann," shot back Weber.

Frubrich said that the skipper only called Theimann "Mister" when he was angry. Weber then asked the navigator to look in the ship description book and find out what type and class of vessel it was. Soon Mai reported that it was the *Queen Mary.* "Shit," said Weber. "That would have made a nice catch." The 81,235-ton British Cunard liner *Mary* sailed alone, too fast (31.7 knots) to be in a convoy, and there were no warships protecting her.

"So we went down to the basement, because sure as heck she was going to send airplanes or destroyers our way." Captain Weber learned from Mai that the *Mary* was being used as a troop transport and that some of the troops could be German prisoners of war being taken to America. "That meant that if we had sunk the ship, we might have killed our own comrades," commented Hermann, not realizing that he would be one of the German prisoner-passengers in the near future.

At the beginning of January 1944 Weber notified headquarters that he had arrived at his destination off Newfoundland and asked for further instructions. "It's free hunting," came the reply. With that, Weber called his officers into the tower and asked Chief Engineer Strunk how Prien had prepared his boat before he entered Scapa Flow. Günther Prien's mettlesome exploit on 14 October 1939—sinking the British battleship HMS *Royal Oak* in the harbor at Scapa Flow, Scotland— had fired all submariners' imaginations, and Otto Strunk had been first machinist on Prien's boat.

From the beginning of the war Newfoundland was the point of departure for aircraft and large convoys headed for Great Britain and Russia. At St. John's (nicknamed "Newfyjohn's" by British sailors) the Canadian navy operated a large base, and it is probable that Weber had hopes of finding a warship and accomplishing a coup similar to Prien's. Getting into and out of the harbor, however, presented a major problem, in that the entry from the sea was short, curved, and flanked by hills. James B. Lamb described it neatly: "In Newfyjohn. . . you are either in the harbor or out of it; there is no long estuary leading to the sea."[1]

During the next few days, the commander questioned Strunk to find out the exact horsepower and other requirements needed to get the boat into top battle condition. "We put the torpedoes into the tubes, and the reserve torpedoes were worked into perfect shape. A report came from the bow and aft torpedo rooms that everything was in order, and the navigator and Able Seaman Ferdinand Heger worked out the course needed to enter the harbor of St. John's."

At 10:00 P.M. on 4 January the bow of U-845 was headed toward the entrance of the harbor, and creeping through the water with little vibration, the boat submerged carefully, avoiding telltale eddies on the surface. Weber remarked that "conditions could not be better." Everything appeared routine.

Through the periscope, the skipper observed a small port but, strangely enough, saw no ships of any kind. One small escort appeared, coming toward U-845, so the boat submerged five or ten more meters. "The escort ran over us three times," said Hermann. "But the captain told us, 'He doesn't have any depth charges on board.'" Then, "What are those barrels on the surface, Mai?"

After taking a look, the navigator replied, "Mines, sir. There is a mine barrier and no way to get through." So they turned around and steered 180 degrees from their former course. As they crept toward the outlet of the port, watching their surroundings, Weber noticed a big pipe on the shore with a large volume of water gushing out.

"We should put a torpedo in it, because I don't want to carry the Atos [torpedoes] home," muttered the highly frustrated commander. "He shot one off, and the explosion would have waked the dead, but nothing more happened. We heard no sounds whatsoever. After a while we were dismissed from battle stations."

"I asked the second watch officer where I could sleep, since my bunk in the rear torpedo room was folded up. He said I could sleep in his, and I did what he told me: I removed my boots, put them next to his, and climbed to the top bunk. I went to sleep at once." Loud scraping noises woke Frubrich, and a voice on the loudspeaker system announced: "To battle stations."

"I zipped out of my bunk and into my boots, but oh, my God, they were much too big. But it didn't make any difference. As I arrived in the tower, orders were flying thick and fast." U-845 surfaced and the engines were stopped. "We had run into something." As Weber ordered both diesels slow speed ahead, Frubrich manned the rudder and tried to follow the captain's orders, but there was no response. "I can't move it," he said. "Do it by hand," ordered Weber. So Frubrich called on the speaking tube to the aft torpedo room to move the rudder by hand. This failed, as well.

"You'll have to steer with the engines," said the commander. With constantly changing engine speeds on both sides, Frubrich directed U-845 away from Newfoundland, while engineer Strunk checked to see if there was any interior damage. "The boat was still able to submerge, and that was very calming to us."

From the hydrophone operator came word that he was hearing ship propeller noises, so the "Old Man" took the sub to the bottom. "Extreme quiet in the boat," he instructed them. After a tense silence, the noises disappeared.

Next morning, steering with its engines, U-845 traveled to a point about two hundred miles from St. John's and made ready to repair her damaged rudder.

"At nine o'clock Canadian time the boat was lying quietly in the Atlantic, with a light sea. Items needed for repairs were transferred to the deck and we strapped on our diving apparatus, flooded some tanks in the bow so the boat would be lower there, and released the aft end so that it was high out of the water."

Chief engineer Strunk sent Erhard Hennig and Erich Torunski into the water, and with power from a diesel engine they used a blowtorch to do the job. "Each time a wave freed the rudder blade, Hennig applied the torch to one of the blades, but the water, being highly conductive, occasionally gave him a good shock. It affected his eyesight somewhat, but in spite of that, he managed to finish the work."

While the welding was going on, another mate in a diving suit swam around the boat to see whether there was further damage, but he found no more problems.

On deck, the watch scanned the skies for aircraft and kept the guns manned until late afternoon, when the work was finished. Then the lookout reported masts on the horizon, and all equipment was quickly brought back into the boat. The doctor, Wilhelm Heinrich, treated Hennig for electric shock and the others for minor injuries. Hennig lay on his bunk, completely stiff, but finally limbered up again two days later.

"During all that time we were charging our battery with the other diesel and the boat was now fully operational." U-845, with all stations crewed, made ready to submerge, then dived. "The Old Man raised the periscope and reported the mast as a frigate." After the navigator took a look, he told the captain, "You should let him go, because sure as hell, there are others coming afterwards." And as predicted, a freighter with four escorts came into sight. "The hunting dogs are circling the freighter like it's a jewel," remarked Weber, who prepared for attack and headed in the direction of the target.

"Fire!" came the order, and two shots zipped out. The navigator activated his stopwatch, and they waited—one hit, one miss. "The Old Man sent a third, and that was the hit that sank the ship. A lot of breaking up noises were audible, sounding like a thunderstorm over our heads." The navigator told the captain he thought it must have been an ammunition ship.

Four days later they spotted another target, the British freighter *Kelmscott.* After attacking her, Weber thought he had sunk the steamer and rewarded the crew with a sip of brandy, but later records showed that the freighter only had been damaged.[2]

Although the chief engineer kept warning the captain that they were running low on fuel, Weber "wasn't thinking of going home yet," said Frubrich. "On 14 February we were cruising along on the surface, with blue sky and sun overhead. The Old Man was getting kind of careless, because no one was paying any attention to us. He thought the Canadians must have been asleep."

But then a plane dived out of the sun and attacked. "The alarm sounded, and we crewed our weapons while the plane was shooting. I had been off duty and was climbing into the tower just as the aircraft crossed our boat. Bullets were hitting the sides of the conning tower like peas rattling in a pod."

Frubrich took over the rudder as instructions came: "Hard star-

board. Both engines two times full speed ahead." Hermann moved
the engine telegraph, and the diesels roared deafeningly, swerving the
boat hard in one direction, then another, as the attack went on. "As
the plane flew for the second time over us, it released many bombs, so
close that the pressure from the explosions made our boat lean to port."

From the bridge came a message that the 3.7 gun had failed. In the
tower, Franz Vorstheim rushed past Frubrich and climbed the ladder
to the bridge as the plane made its third pass, with bombs exploding
and machine-gun bullets rattling the superstructure. "A salvo tore into
Franz's throat, and it looked like his head was hanging on some strands
of flesh. I guided his body down into the control room and hollered,
'Attention, wounded man coming down!'"

Spots of blood splattered onto the tower instruments and floor. "I
handled things by instinct, because in my head, I was concentrating
on the maneuvers we were supposed to be executing." From the bridge
the captain yelled, "When the plane passes next time, we are going
down to the basement!" As soon as the plane reappeared, Weber gave
orders for alarm dive. "That meant it didn't make any difference what
came, we were going deep." The men, ammunition, and machine guns
came tumbling through the tower hatch. "I was busy with my feet,
trying to clear the hatch into the control room. Many of the men were
yelling with pain."

As the boat careened downward, the skipper dropped through the
hatch, along with a gush of water. "I tried to close the hatch into the
control room, and he managed to close the tower hatch, so I opened
the control room hatch again." At a sixty-degree angle U-845 roared
headfirst toward safety.

"In about thirty seconds we were at thirty meters, then the depth
gauge needle went to one hundred meters." The chief engineer tried
to keep the boat from going any farther, and Frubrich sensed that the
sub was not obeying. "I put the rudder hard over to port, and that
acted something like a brake." Weber then ordered both engines to
stop and slow back. The chief blew one tank on the bow slightly, so
the boat would sink at the stern, and U-845 lay with the bow at 210
meters and the stern at 250 meters, under control again. "We survived

that great depth quite well. We could hear some popping and groan-
ing noises from the steel plates and pressurized hull, but otherwise,
everything was in good shape."

Weber ordered the boat to fifty meters, and U-845 slowly climbed
until he said, "Discharge old uniforms and other useless things from
a torpedo tube." With this desperate measure, they were going to
attempt to convince the enemy that they had been sunk, and it worked.
"So we did it. We had been trailing an oil slick, as well, because one of
our empty fuel tanks was damaged."

In preparation for the burial at sea, Herbert Kling had sewed the
body of Franz Vorstheim into a canvas sack with a heavy weight at the
feet. The commander announced that when dark came they would
surface, rinse the oil tank, and commit their fallen comrade to the
ocean.

"All this had happened in a little under an hour, but to me it was an
eternity." He noted that after the captain had jumped into the tower,
the water that rushed in with him rinsed away all Vorstheim's blood.
Later the skipper said to Hermann, "Sometimes things rectify themselves."

"At about nine at night we started upward. When the bow
breached the surface, the skipper opened the tower hatch, and fresh,
cool Atlantic air streamed into the boat. After he took a look from the
bridge, he ordered the men to watch stations." Hermann heard the
commander yell down to him in the tower, "Give me a cigarette."
Frubrich kept the captain's cigarettes in his pocket, ready to hand him
one at any time. "I got one out, lit it, took a deep drag, and sent it up
to the bridge."

"It was a clear night with a full moon. The water and mist coming
over the boat adhered to our beards and eyebrows in a phosphores-
cent light. It was a remarkable sight." Behind the boat a streak of glow-
ing foam ribboned through the dark. Following the rinsing of the
damaged tank, orders went out to make ready for funeral services.

The men laid a platform on the starboard railing, two sailors supported it, and a third sailor laid the body on the platform. Petty
Officers Böhme, Heger, and Behnert stood at the second gun station,
next to the war flag. "Attention, face our dead comrade," ordered the

petty officer. They lowered the flag to half-mast, and Weber said the Lord's Prayer. "Commit the dead comrade to the sea," he continued. As the commander spoke, the petty officer whistled, "Attention on deck." The two sailors lifted the platform, and Franz Vorstheim's body slid into the dark Atlantic.

"Raise the flag," ordered the skipper. Then, "Dismissed from deck. Man your diving stations." U-845 glided once more into the depths. "Give me the microphone," said Weber to Hermann, and then announced to the men: "We lost a comrade, and he is not going to be the last one. . . . I was very close to getting killed myself, because several bullets went through my jacket and my cap. . . . Our mission is to inflict as much damage as possible to Germany's enemy. The battle is going to continue, so forget what happened, and think about tomorrow."

"He handed me the microphone and disappeared into the control room," said Hermann. "I believe the whole thing was very hard for him to take."

Cruising on rough seas a couple of days later, U-845's radio room sent a message to the bridge that there were noises at forty degrees on the starboard side, fading away toward the stern. Weber, standing next to Theimann on the bridge, looked in the direction of the noises but couldn't see anything. He climbed down into the tower, sat on the periscope seat, raised it, looked around at the sea, and found nothing.

"Who knows what it is—let's get under," said Theimann. "Maybe we can identify the noises then." The order came for diving, and those on the bridge came scrambling down into the tower and thudded into the control room. "That time it was much better and easier than a couple of days before, when we were being attacked by the plane."

At periscope depth the radio room reported propeller noises aft. Weber turned the boat and again raised the periscope, as another message came that the noises were dwindling. The skipper thought it might have been a submarine that surfaced. So U-845 headed upward, as gun crews and the bridge watch were getting ready. In the tower Weber ordered, "Heger, come up to the bridge with your signal box and flags." Heger, once on the bridge and ready to signal, saw nothing, and U-845 went to periscope depth again.

"Sir," said the chief, "isn't it better that we dive to fifty meters, because if that is another submarine and he lets loose a torpedo at us, he could hit us if we stay here." Weber agreed and took the boat down to fifty meters.

From the radio room came word that they could hear a fast-running propeller noise from the starboard side amidships, headed toward U-845. Weber asked the chief, "Do you think we should go deeper?" Strunk replied: "No, this is deep enough." All of a sudden the crew could hear a kind of whirring noise, coming quickly from starboard, running over the boat and disappearing on the port side. "That was a torpedo," said the commander. "Is there another boat near our location?" he asked the navigator, who replied, "Not that I know of." Weber, looking mystified, commented, "What kind of damned situation is this?" No one could explain the incident.

U-845 remained submerged until nightfall, then proceeded on a northerly course, until a message came from the forward torpedo room that they were bumping into ice blocks. "Make a 180-degree course change," instructed Weber. "We are not going to freeze our asses off here."

Days passed, and by radio the commander received a promotion from the *BdU* staff to the rank of *Korvettenkapitän*. With a feeling of pride, the engine crew changed the insignias on their commander's jacket and cap and added gold stripes. From that time on, Strunk "was on the captain's case to go home," said Frubrich, "because the fuel was going to be gone soon." But Weber told him with a grin, "Then we'll do like the Vikings, and sail into the harbor or row the boat. Won't everyone be surprised to see us sailing in." But Strunk had a worried look on his face. "He was dead serious, and knew what he was talking about."

A week or so later Weber relented and gave instructions to the navigator to set course for France. "If we make it back all right, I'm going to invite the whole crew to my home in Sauerland, and they can all learn to ski. That's going to be some sight—sailors on skis."

U-845's bow pointed eastward toward home base, both engines at half speed. "We settled into a daily routine, traveling submerged by day and surfaced at night." Then came a message from *BdU:* "Enemy has new aircraft equipment. Can bomb accurately at night. Looks like a full moon, or red circle in sky. After it appears, bombs fall immediately, and boat has no chance to escape." Weber increased the lookout to three men, who scanned the sky incessantly, but once again, the Allies had come up with a new weapon against the U-boats: this time, a "Leigh Light" system, combining a powerful searchlight with radar that enabled aircraft to attack the subs in the dark.[3]

On a misty March day, the boat was humming along on the surface, when the lookout spotted tops of masts on the horizon. Weber sent a message to headquarters that they had a convoy on the starboard side, then received the reply that U-845 should stay in touch with it. "We could forget all about running for home," said Hermann, and Weber told Strunk: "We'll stick with the convoy even if we have to be towed into the harbor."

"From then on, nobody even mentioned going home. All our thoughts were directed toward chasing the convoy, and our nerves were very taut, because every minute there was a chance that they could sight us, either from an escort or a plane."

That same day, 10 March, an escort destroyer spotted U-845 and churned toward them. "We had no choice but to submerge." Even though he kept his distance, Weber gave the order to dive, and U-845 went down to periscope depth.

"Load tubes one and two with T.5s, [the type that responds to propeller sounds] and let me know when ready," barked Weber. Thirty minutes later the tubes were ready to fire. "The Old Man turned his cap backward and looked through the periscope at the destroyer. The electric motors were humming at slow speed, and the tension increased as the commander lined up to shoot. I was thinking that if the torpedoes hit, we would have to dive really fast to keep depth charges from exploding under us and blowing us to the surface."

Suddenly Weber interrupted Hermann's thoughts, saying: "Tube one, clear for shot. Open outer doors." Then a return message: "Tube one ready." Weber: "Tube one, Fire!" As a light shudder was felt in the boat, Weber withdrew the periscope, ordering U-845 down to forty meters so their own torpedo would not hit them. "As the navigator's stopwatch was running we took her down to forty meters. All of a sudden, depth charges hit," said Hermann. "It's a ground-runner," yelled the navigator. Weber quickly brought the boat back to periscope depth, took a look, then shouted, "Alarm! Dive!" A destroyer was speeding toward U-845.

"We rushed downward and were at 150 meters when the first depth charges rocked the boat. But they were not well-aimed, and we didn't get any damage." Everyone in the tower except Frubrich had climbed down into the control room for more safety. "I was the only one up there, steering our course with the magnetic compass, since the gyro-compass had stopped working when we were first bombed."

Another spread of detonations shook U-845. "There was an awful lot of noise, and all of a sudden a stream of water hit me in the back." Frubrich turned, saw the gasket rings on the periscope were spewing water, and reported it to the captain. Weber stuck his head into the tower hatch and shouted, "Clear the tower!" As powerful explosions boomed above them, Frubrich switched the rudder controls to the control room and climbed down.

Frubrich remembered that after taking his place to steer the boat, he noticed the ham hanging over his seat, left there to see how long it would last. "From then on, it was hit after hit. The attacks were short, so the skipper figured that there were at least four ships up there." By now U-845 had reached almost two hundred meters. The explosions were getting closer, causing the lights to burst, and gaskets started leaking. "But the crew could cope with it, and there was no danger to our lives."

As the electric motors ran on slow speed, each charge that hit nearby caused the magnetic compass needle to swing back and forth. "I had just enough time between attacks to find the course I was supposed to steer. We had practiced that in training."

Weber started evasive maneuvers by turning the boat toward the departure course of the enemy when the bombs were on the starboard side. If the attack came from port side, he headed toward starboard, and U-845's propeller noise and that of the destroyer overlapped for a while. "After about an hour they either lost us or withdrew to rest."

"Can you hold the boat with no engine speed?" Weber asked Strunk. "Yeah, sure," replied the engineer. "If they don't throw any more charges, I can hold it at a certain depth for a while without moving through the water." With that, Weber ordered: "Both engines stop."

When all was totally silent in U-845, Weber told the crew to lie down and rest or sleep, if possible. "I couldn't do that, because the battle station helmsman can't get tired or fall asleep, so I got some strong coffee, chocolate, and Dextroenergie from the cook."

"Another hour went by, then the hunting dogs found us again. The regular *ping-ping-ping* in a shrill tone was getting on our nerves. They started throwing again, and I could hear the cans hitting the water." After a short hissing noise, came the boom. "The game had started all over again." A rain of hellish explosions descended, coming closer and closer to U-845.

Weber asked the chief engineer if the boat could withstand a deeper level, and Strunk replied, "Yes, we could make it to three hundred meters without too much trouble. I'll take responsibility for that." Weber: "Let's go, then, before they know exactly where we are." Sinking lower and lower, the depth gauge now read three hundred meters.

With both engines slow speed ahead, they were now safe from the deathly booms. "They didn't have any effect on us. It sounded like rolling thunder in the distance, and we could not feel the pressure waves." The boat was again quiet.

"Skipper, I can't keep my eyes open any longer," mumbled Frubrich, and with that, Weber assigned Navigator Leucht to take Hermann's place. Completely exhausted, Hermann collapsed on the floor of the control room and fell soundly asleep.

At about 10:00 P.M. the skipper woke Frubrich, told him to get to the tower, then made the announcement, speaking softly: "Comrades, we must go to the surface. Our air and electricity are almost gone, as well as our high-pressure air. If we wait too long, we won't be able to make it. Do everything as you have been taught and go to your stations. I know I can depend on you."

"Let's do it," Weber said to Strunk. The chief gave orders to drain the tower, slowly. Machinist Mates Schneider and Uberschär had their hands on the handles of the air valves, and Strunk instructed them: "Gentlemen, the high pressure air has to hit the tanks in unison. You must open the valves in synchronization. If that doesn't work, we'll never get to the surface. Do you understand?" Both answered, "Yes, sir."

"Wait for my order," said Strunk. Then, "Blow." Hissing air could be heard going into the chambers, "and it sounded good," said Frubrich, "like it was a unit." The electric engines were barely humming, and then the lights grew dimmer and dimmer.

"Fascinated, I was watching the depth gauges on the wall." Nothing happened. "Come on, baby, come on, baby, come on," urged the navigator. "We thought it was all over," Frubrich admitted.

"The depth gauge had been stuck on three hundred meters, but now it was rising slowly, so that was a sign it was functioning properly." Then a light cracking noise could be heard, and another and another. "The boat is rising gradually," announced Strunk. Weber ordered that the tower draining be accelerated and told the bridge watch and gun crew to get ready and put on their diving apparatus and life belts.

U-845 began to shoot upward, indicated by the hand on the depth gauge. Strunk reported that the boat was breaking the surface. Weber opened the hatch into the tower and climbed up, then opened the top hatch, holding on to the ladder so as not to be sucked outside. He ordered the gun crew to man their weapons, and they scrambled onto the deck.

"We then started the diesels, and they howled like whipped dogs, going at full rpm's. The chief gave the order to start the compressors, to replenish the high pressure air. I quickly climbed into the tower to open the speaking tube to the bridge, then went back to the control room to steer." As U-845's diesels went roaring into high gear, the boat bucked forward like a wild horse.

"I could hear our weapons firing through the speaking tube, and also the enemy's shells. We could hear them hitting in the area of the diesel engines, as well as the port side of the tower. Where my station was, an explosion went off, making a hole as big as a door."

U-845 was wounded, but "the Old Man was fighting bravely." Weber ordered tubes one and two to be made ready, and as soon as they were prepared, the outer doors were opened. "Judging by the course I was steering, the skipper was trying to shoot a hole through the enemy surrounding us, but our boat was headed straight for a destroyer."

"Torpedoes, Fire!" shouted the captain. Nothing happened. Then came a message from the torpedo room that the "eels" were stuck in the tubes with their motors running. Frubrich relayed the message to the bridge, then heard Weber yell, "*Rohrläufer,* shit!"

"We stayed on course," Hermann said, "and I had the funny feeling that he was going to ram the destroyer, and if he did, we would all be blown up—the enemy as well as us." With four armed torpedoes in her bow, U-845's explosive power could have demolished three ships, at least. "I heard heavy firing from the bridge, and the bullets were pummeling our boat like rattling peas. The ship we were shooting at must have done some fancy maneuvering, because we ran by it doing twenty-three knots."

No orders were heard from the bridge. "I hollered through the speaking tube, 'Bridge, bridge, report in!' But there was no answer." Chief Strunk sent a man up to check the bridge who quickly returned, saying, "Everything is shot to hell. The first watch officer and the skipper are dead—they're draped over the railing of the bridge. There's no sign of life anywhere up there."

With Strunk now the highest-ranking officer on board, he took command of U-845. "Both engines half speed. Make ready to abandon ship," he ordered. Then after a few minutes, "All personnel overboard. Use the galley hatch to get out."

As the men disappeared one by one, the engines were set at slow speed ahead so as not to pull any swimming survivors into the props. "I steered U-845 straight, and the chief said to me, 'Run up to the bow and see whether anybody's left aboard, and I'll do the same astern.'"

Frubrich and Strunk met again in the control room, and the chief said, "Get out of the boat now. I'm going to pull the vents [sink the boat]." Frubrich wished him good luck, went into the tiny galley, climbed the ladder, looked right and left, and jumped into the sea. "Right away, I sank. I had the mouthpiece of my diving apparatus in my mouth and the clamp on my nose. I could breathe, so I closed the pressure valve and balanced myself so that I submerged two or three meters below the surface, to escape the hail of bullets." After a few moments Hermann surfaced, tilted his head back, and looked at the night scene. "Orange rockets were illuminating the sky, and U-845 was still making a little headway through the waves. Then suddenly the stern part of the boat started to sag, then went down faster and faster, and the bow reared and disappeared into the sea." Just at the dramatic final moments of the boat's disappearance, the sounds of "Hooray, hooray!" came from the enemy ships.

"I was lying with my ass in the cold Atlantic," remembered Hermann. "I turned around slowly and looked for some of my comrades, but the waves took me down into a valley, and I couldn't see anything. Then up again, and I saw a warship, moving like a shadow through the moonlight." Hermann attempted to swim toward it, but it was farther than he had realized. "I was not anywhere as near as I thought, and so I gave up and let myself drift."

Afraid that his wet clothing might drag him under, Hermann pulled off his right boot, and "Oh, my God, my foot was extremely cold, so I left the left one on." He decided that it was better to stay warm and drown than to freeze to death. "We had learned in training that we should keep moving, breathe very deeply, and exercise all parts of the body—then maybe we had a chance to live until they found us, if they were willing."

"I had to pee. Lukewarm urine ran down my leg. Oh, it was wonderful, and I wished I could pee all night." Hermann did not remember how long he drifted in the icy water. He lost all sense of time, thinking about what he had learned in the diving tank in Plön and remembering that if he turned off the oxygen on his breathing apparatus, he would "wander slowly but surely into the afterlife."

Occupied with these musings, Frubrich hardly noticed that someone was pulling him by his jacket collar, urging, "Come on, boy." Then he felt himself being hauled out of the water into a rowboat. "A British sailor pushed me into one of the seats beside him, bent my stiff fingers straight, then forced them around an oar so that I had to do the same movements he did. The boat crew rowed toward one of the warships, and as we came alongside, we were pushed up by a large wave, and a big guy grabbed me by the collar and stood me up on deck. There I was, standing, with water running in puddles all around me."

Noticing a sailor walking toward him with a knife, Hermann thought, "Why would they fish me out of the water and then knife me?" For a second he considered jumping over the side, rather than be "stuck like a pig." But the sailor poked a cigarette in Hermann's mouth, cut off his life preserver belt, removed his wet clothing, and pushed him through a door. There, another sailor stripped off his underwear and put him under a shower. "It was nice and warm, and the ghost of life slowly came back to me. My comrades from U-845 were there in the showers, too."

Seabags were distributed to all the survivors, who found every-thing they needed "to become a human being again." When Hermann started to shave off his bushy beard, a sailor stood next to him to see that he did not commit suicide. "After that I drank half a glass of hot rum, and they escorted me to the quarters, where I found some of my friends from U-845." They remained on the ship for two days, enjoy-ing good food and excellent treatment.

"Two or three times we had a submarine alarm, and they gave us life preservers, but they were different from ours. They were black with a hood and a little light on top which would start blinking when wet. The vests were filled with cork, whereas ours were filled with air."

A few days later the *Swansea* landed in Londonderry, Northern Ireland, and U-845 crew members were escorted off the ship. Later, at an inquiry in London, Canadian officers asked the men if U-845 had been on a mission to blow up the power plant at St. John's, because they had torpedoed the discharge pipe. "They said if they found out we were, we would be sent to Canada to rebuild it." (Hermann was never able to ascertain the outcome of the inquiry.) From London he was sent to Scotland, and from there to New York, and by a great twist of fate, Hermann traveled on the *Queen Mary,* the troop-carrying liner Captain Weber had wanted to sink.

In 1993 Frubrich's friend Ferdinand Heger corresponded with one of the Canadian seamen, Norris Jones, who helped rescue U-845's crew in a whaler. "It was the HMS *Forester* and the *St. Laurent* that left the convoy to track the U-845; we on the *Swansea* left some time later to join them. We had just arrived at their position when U-845 broke the surface. I saw her with my night glasses from the bridge. . . . The *St. Laurent* then made her attack on the U-boat; it was very fierce while it lasted. U-845 put up a tough fight, but the odds were against her."

Jones said that after the destroyer raked the submarine with heavy fire, U-845 attempted to ram her. He saw dead German crewmen hanging over the side of the sub and watched as the others jumped overboard. As soon as possible, the *Swansea* lowered a whaler with six armed sailors, including Norris Jones and one officer. As Jones wrote to Heger: "Our job was to get on board U-845 and take your code books. We got as close as 10 feet when her bow went straight up and she slid under. The conning tower was a mass of holes, a good 1,000 of them."

"Anyone on the whaler could not forget . . . the bow of a sub nearly three stories high over your head sliding into the sea, wondering if it's going to slide on top of you . . . only fifteen feet away. It exploded under us with a small rumble." After the boat disappeared, Jones and crew began to pull German sailors from the icy waters, using a lantern to locate them. In a short time they had rescued twenty-three survivors, filling the whaler completely, with several others hanging on to the sides. Exhausted, two of the submariners gave up and let go, and two others were sucked into the *Swansea*'s propeller. All the rest of U-845's crew had been killed by gunfire.

Just after the destroyer reached Londonderry, "we felt sad to see you all in blindfolds," wrote Jones, "marching out onto the wharf." When the Canadians noticed the Irish guards roughing up some of the submariners, they yelled, "Stop! Those German sailors are real fighting men!"[4]

In the end, Hermann was shipped with other submariners to prisoner of war Camp McCain, Mississippi, where he picked cotton and acted as a translator. In 1948 Frubrich returned to his hometown, Hamm, Germany, and became harbormaster for the city of Hamm, as well as organizing and supporting U-boat veterans' groups. After retirement Hermann created a private tour business with his excursion boat, the *Doris,* on the Weser River. He calls it his "dream job."

Looking back on his battles at sea, Hermann comments: "During the war, whenever we met the so-called enemy, I never had feelings of animosity, because every sailor wore the blue uniform with three stripes around the collar—a tie that bound us all."[5]

8   Hermann Wien, U-180

■ ■

Born in 1916 in Munich, Hermann joined the then-called "Reichsmarine," or Navy of the Reich, at age eighteen, serving in the engineering division on two torpedo boats. In 1937, after Germany had been allowed again to have submarines, Wien took training on U-2 and U-7, both constructed and used in World War I. The old boats, stripped of all deck guns, still had two torpedo tubes in the bow and two in the stern and could muster up just thirteen knots per hour on the surface.

■ ■

In early 1943 Wien was assigned to a "completely new boat type with nine thousand horsepower." U-180, a 270-feet-long vessel, was one of the two fastest U-boats in the German navy and could make twenty-one-and-a-half sea miles per hour. "The high speed had a great advantage in that it helped us escape from planes with the new radar, but at the same time, the diesel engines, when we went from low to high, gave out dense black smoke. This was dangerous—one could say almost intolerable." (The enemy could spot the smoke from a distance.)

U-180, ready to go on war patrol in January, had been selected to carry out a distant secret mission. When the sailing date was set, crew members started speculating about where they would be going, but then the date of departure was changed. "Finally they told us, 'Tomorrow you are definitely sailing,' but the date kept getting put off. We thought there was something funny going on." They guessed that the

Hermann Wien

mission would probably take them to Japan or Singapore—somewhere in the Far East.

The ninth of February became the final sailing date, with a destination known only to *Korvettenkapitän* Werner Musenberg when he opened a sealed envelope at sea.

"I was the *Obermaschinist*—head of the diesel engine systems, and on the evening before we departed from Kiel, I had watch duty, and I was spending the night on board." [The rest of the crew were not allowed on the boat, as this was to be a secret mission, and the enemy could have observed them and calculated when they were leaving.]

"So at 2100 the post guard who was watching the boat announced that a private car had arrived on the dock. An officer of the flotilla came up carrying some suitcases, identified himself, and told us to keep quiet and stow away his baggage."

Early the next morning, with the crew on board, Wien went into the engine room to get the diesels ready for sea by starting and warming them up. The flotilla chief gave a short farewell speech for families and friends on the dock, everyone waved and cheered, and U-180 cast off. "Nothing special happened—it was like every other departure," recalled Hermann. "As we passed through the middle of the inlet, on the right we could see Laboe [a village near Kiel]. We stopped there in the inlet, a motorboat came alongside, and two gentlemen got off and climbed aboard the submarine."

A few minutes later U-180 picked up speed and headed out. "We were all saying, 'What's going on? Who are these two men?'" Hermann and his friends had the impression they were foreign, not German, as their complexions were slightly yellow brown, and they were dressed in dark clothes and hats. "Also, they were wearing dark horn-rimmed glasses and looked mysterious."

Wien finished watch duty at twelve-thirty, and by that time rumors were circulating throughout the boat that the two strangers were submarine experts. The two were now wearing "the same clothes we had on": gray-green leather pants, jackets, and officers' caps. One, about five-feet-seven, was strong looking and stocky, and the other was short in stature and small-boned.

As U-180 traveled along, German escort boats arrived and accompanied them past the Danish islands up to Kristiansand, on the southern tip of Norway. At the dock, the commander told them that none of the crew would be allowed to go ashore. "Then we really started circulating wild rumors. One of my friends said, 'I am sure I saw one of those men not long ago in a magazine picture, and he was visiting Hitler. He is the Adolf of India.' Commander Musenberg told us that it was just two special engineers coming along with us to build some submarine bunkers, and they would be going ashore in Norway."

The next day they traveled on to Bergen, and again, no one was allowed to leave the sub. "The guests made no signs of getting off the boat, either. The next morning, we made our way for a long time without any escorts, and after we had Norway behind our backs, Musenberg told us about the identity of our two guests and the purpose of our trip, which was so secret."

The commander explained that the mysterious men were Indian

Subhas Chandra Bose, leader of a revolt faction in India, traveled secretly on U-180 to the Indian Ocean.

freedom fighters Subhas Chandra Bose and his adjutant, Abid Hassan, an Arab nationalist leader. "Our job was to take them both, without harm, to the sea area of Madagascar. There we were to meet the Japanese submarine, I-29, and exchange them, then they were to go on to India or the Burma front."

In 1941 Subhas Bose, leader of the Forward Bloc Party and advocate of the overthrow by force of the British government, had escaped house arrest and fled in disguise through Afghanistan, thence to Moscow. From there he flew to Berlin and was welcomed by Hitler, who helped him beam radio broadcasts to India, urging violence. His pleas for help in Europe succeeded in arousing the sympathy of numerous Indians living in Germany and other countries as well. "He got the support of many of the British Indian army prisoners of war who had been captured in Africa by Rommel and sent to Germany. And with the help of Hitler's army, he was creating an elite corps, trained by the Germans." Bose called his outfit "The Legion of Free India," and he hoped to return with his trainees to India and wage war against the British colonial government.[1]

Hitler went along with Bose's schemes, hoping that with a military uprising in India he could force great numbers of European troops to go to the aid of the British there.

Bose had plans to get to Burma, where he expected to raise an army of Southeast Asians, and the safest way to get to his destination surreptitiously was underwater. The men of U-180 carried out their mission to transport Bose and Hassan, but the journey brought their passengers a variety of difficulties.

After leaving the coast of Norway, U-180's bow pointed northward, and, without escorts, the boat started on her long voyage. The seas grew increasingly higher and the squalls more frequent as the U-boat traveled parallel to the Norwegian coast. "This was the kind of weather we wanted, because the British couldn't see us very well, and we could get past the point where they had their ships watching to see who was leaving Germany. Every day we had to dive for alarms, so we started getting used to this kind of activity."

As the trip progressed, the Indian guests became more and more taciturn and started keeping to themselves. "They didn't know that the conditions were normal for U-boat sailors, and it was putting a strain on them." Packed to the brim with torpedoes and foodstuffs, plus boxes of supplies to be exchanged with the Japanese, the boat's living space was cramped to the utmost and they traveled underwater most of the time. "We never were able to see daylight because we knew we couldn't dive fast enough in an emergency." The vicissitudes of traveling submerged—breathing stale air, living in horribly crowded conditions, and listening to the deafening noises of the engines—were making the foreigners uncomfortable and depressed. The "noble" anarchists had little spunk left in them.

"All this grew worse when we came to the tip of England. From here we turned from north to west." A dangerous passageway between England and the Faroe Islands allowed their only route into the Atlantic, but it was heavily patrolled by Allied boats and planes, "because the enemy knew that all submarines had to go through there."

Increasingly vicious weather and terrible visibility brought good luck for U-180, in that "the enemy watchdogs also had trouble seeing." As the seas billowed straight toward the submarine, the winds grew incessantly stronger, up to a force of twelve. Dressed in oilskin suits and hats, the four men on watch were securely attached to the bridge with wide steel belts to keep them from being washed overboard, as mountainous waves smashed over the boat.

"Our commander said that we would travel only at night [on the surface] and that during the day we would go slowly, staying submerged. We thought we had gone 240 nautical miles by counting the engine turns, but we really had made only one to two hundred miles because of all the waves, wind, and so forth. That's how strongly the sea was running against us."

The executive officer, an older man who had served in the merchant marine, could not remember worse weather in all his years at sea. Happily for all, one day U-180 dived to about sixty meters, where the waters were quiet, and traveling became far more bearable.

"After ten days we reached the free Atlantic, and the main dangerous sea area lay behind us. The weather was getting better and better as we went on course south." The two guests, who had been lying in their bunks and eating hardly anything until now, came to life. "They seemed very happy and had hearty appetites, and they started to mingle with the crew. They became good comrades on the trip."

The sailors soon noticed that Subhas Bose's command of the German language was rudimentary, and they tried to make him understand by speaking slowly to him, but conversation was frustrating. Bose spent a great deal of time writing, and Abid Hassan told Hermann that Bose was working on a book, entitled *My Fight for Indians' Freedom.*

Hassan spoke somewhat better German, with a Berlin dialect. Educated at Oxford University and now twenty-eight years old, he had studied street construction in Germany. "I talked with him often, because he had the upper bunk over me. You could say he was a joke teller, and he had many about the Third Reich. He knew a lot of them and didn't hold back." Abid told Hermann that the British government had offered rewards for him and Bose of a thousand pounds apiece. He explained that in India Bose had as high a status as Mohandas Gandhi, but that they had different ideas. Gandhi believed in peaceful means to evict the British, and Bose advocated military force.

As U-180 traveled south, bad weather again set in, and with it the boat consumed higher than normal amounts of diesel, forcing them to stop for resupplying. They met U-462 and transferred diesel oil and more food supplies. Every day the weather grew warmer and the temperature inside the boat rose as they neared the equator. "We in the engine room felt most of the heat, especially when we dove and surfaced frequently. The temperature where we were was 60°C [140°F], while in the control room it was around 40°C [104°F]. But good old Saint Peter, our weather god, felt sorry for us sometimes, and we had a good shower."

Captain Musenberg decided to celebrate the equator crossing in spite of the enemy plane hazard. "We all had to take part in this ritual, and afterward we were clean from top to bottom." Baths were not part of U-boat life, but on this occasion every man went through a rigorous baptism where he had water sloshed on him and was scrubbed with brushes. "Even our guests had to submit to this torture, and they endured it like men."

Because Musenberg had been instructed to keep the two special passengers safe, the boat could not make any attacks on single ships or convoys. As they passed by Ascension and St. Helena islands, where enemy bases and air strips were located, they had to "watch like hawks."

Then, bad luck struck. The freshwater-maker broke, and there were no spare parts, but one of the engine men managed to weld a small piece into it by hand and got it going again, much to everyone's relief. The boat needed freshwater for drinking, as well as replenishing the water in the batteries.

Days passed, and things were uneventful until one of the crew caught a shark. "We put the shark's tail on our tower, and that was our good luck symbol," said Hermann. The boat traveled on around the Cape of Good Hope and headed northeast toward the Indian Ocean.

There, in the vast sea, a British ship crossed their path. "It was the tanker *Corbis,* loaded with heating oil and headed for Capetown. It was 18 May 1943, and we sank her in a surface attack at night." Wien said that after the second torpedo struck they could see the fire billowing up and some of the crew members getting away in dinghies. The men in the dinghies rowed toward the U-boat and came alongside. "We gave them whatever we could, which wasn't much, so that they could survive." U-180 had been able safely to make the attack, as the Indian Ocean at that time was almost free of Allied planes.

"All our lookouts started to focus on our meeting with the Japanese sub, and on the evening of Hitler's birthday, 20 April, the wireless operator heard noises and recognized them as diesel engines of a ship. We surfaced, looked toward the black horizon, and saw something moving from left to right with the waves and traveled toward it, keeping out of their sight." They checked the chart and saw that their position was correct, east of Madagascar. Judging by the size and shape of the vessel, it had to be the Japanese submarine cruiser I-29.

"He still didn't see us, and he could not hear us because his tower was much too high out of the water. What luck for the sons of Nippon that we were partners of the Axis."

To play it safe, they dived again and waited until daylight, then surfaced and saw I-29 standing three miles away. "We started exchanging signals with flags to see if it was the right one, but this was only a matter of form, because we were sure it was them."

The two submarines attempted to get as close together as possible on a parallel course, but choppy seas prevented their maneuvering, and the transfer of men and bulky boxes had to be delayed. For two days U-180 trailed behind the larger boat on a northward course, until the seas and winds had quieted sufficiently.

Finally, conditions were right. "The weather god was on our side, and everything went fine, with no trouble." First, the exchange of the valuable cargo, packed in oddly shaped crates, was started. All the transferring was done by dinghy, and some of the larger boxes had to be loaded through the torpedo tubes. "We exchanged new weapons, new designs, and technical data."

Some of the German U-boatmen went over to visit the Japanese, and the Japanese came to see U-180. "Lots of discussion went on among ourselves that their boat was as good as ours, but that they had more space for their people." When all the equipment had been exchanged, it was time for the two mysterious guests to make their departure. "Wearing life jackets, Bose and Hassan expressed their farewells. They climbed down into the dinghy and went over to the Japanese boat, waving at us."

In return, U-180 received two Japanese shipbuilding engineers—Commander Emi and Commander Tomonaga, who had orders to go to Germany to be trained in submarine construction and to acquire technical data.

When the operation ended, all the men on U-180 gave three hurrahs, then departed. "We were full to the top with everything imaginable. Besides the huge boxes and odd-shaped crates, we also had fifty gold bars. Every bar weighed forty kilos [eighty pounds], and it was pure gold—every bar clean and fine, sealed and packed in hardwood boxes." Each box weighed two tons, an extremely dangerous load for a submarine, as there would be problems keeping the boat balanced, but after a bit of intense studying, the chief engineer came up with a practical way to manage everything. With instructions to spread the gold throughout the boat, the crew placed most of the boxes in the living quarters and bilges, so that they now had even less space for their own needs.

U-180 now ran along on the surface in the latitude of Durban, South Africa, when suddenly, out of the sun, an enemy plane came right at them. "We had no chance to dive, so immediately one of our sailors manned the two-centimeter gun and hit the airplane. It went down, trailing black smoke, into the sea. Then we made a crash dive and got away as fast as possible."

The two Japanese officers observed everything in the U-boat with evident interest, especially the new engines and other equipment in the engine room. "Their thirst for knowledge couldn't be quenched," observed Wien. During their conversations with the crew, the Japanese politely described the time they had spent on ships during the war and their experiences at Pearl Harbor.

Orders from U-boat headquarters instructed U-180 to meet supply boat U-463, but the larger sub never made it to the rendezvous. The crew learned several weeks later that U-463 had been sunk by a British bomber, with no survivors. "My brother Eberhard was on this boat as *Obermaschinist*," said Wien.

Still in need of fuel, U-180 met slightly crippled U-530 on her way back to France. "They could travel only at a slow speed, requiring less fuel, and were able to transfer a small amount to U-180. We barely made it back." U-180 traveled submerged for safety and surfaced only at night to recharge the batteries. The farther they went eastward, the more planes they saw, day and night. "Sometimes we almost went nuts because it was hard to get enough juice into the batteries."

One afternoon they were almost caught while charging the batteries, traveling on the surface. With no warning and from the direction of the sun roared a two-engine bomber. There was no way for U-180 to dive, and her deck guns were not functioning properly after the long sea trip. "Right toward us the bomber came, and the commander yelled three times through the speaker: 'Highest engine power!' I was on duty in the engine room, and I pushed all six diesel engines to full speed and started up the two electric engines. The boat started tearing along at twenty knots per hour, and the British bomber didn't expect such speed."

The plane rushed past the U-boat, dropping his bombs in the open water. "I thought, boy, how nice it would be if they had the same trouble with their guns as we are having with ours." U-180 then turned with hard rudder to starboard, and the crew could hear the sound of a machine gun. "He just missed the boat by about one meter, and the bullets splashed into the sea." But before the "big bird" could turn, the submarine plummeted down to three hundred feet, and the chief engineer told them to go deeper. No more bombs could be heard, and the men figured that the plane was having trouble. "The dear Lord was holding His thumb between that bird and our boat."

In July 1943 U-180 started across the Bay of Biscay, the last leg of her trip home. The boat crawled along, watching for enemy planes, but "Göring's air force let us submarines down. We had no air escorts, and mines were everywhere." After a day's travel, the crew was relieved to see a German destroyer coming out to meet them. "We figured that this was mainly because of our valuable cargo and two Japanese guests, because help was usually impossible to get. We were all glad when on 9 July 1943 we arrived in the mouth of the Gironde River [at Bordeaux]."

U-180 had traveled fifteen thousand miles, spending five months at sea on her secret mission. "I think many of us quietly gave thanks for being back." As the boat motored through the river toward her base, most of the crew were allowed to go up on the deck and enjoy their first sight of land. The cook, using all remaining food supplies, prepared an excellent feast that included schnitzel and cutlets, and as Hermann put it, "The happiness of life took over our bodies again."

Upon arrival at the bunker, the band played and a rousing speech was given. To protect the vital cargo, a band of Gestapo and military police watched the area closely, and special railroad cars stood ready to be loaded. "Everybody was running around, and then all hell broke loose. A bar of gold had been discovered missing. After they looked and looked, they found it hidden under the mud of the bilge in the engine room."

Forty-seven years later several of the crew of U-180 contacted each other, and out of the original sixty-one men, fifteen were still alive. "It took a long time to find out who was left," wrote Hermann, "and every year about ten or more of us get together at different places— sometimes in the north, near the sea, and sometimes in the mountains of the south. The camaraderie of our war experiences holds us old submarine sailors together."[2]

9   Otto Dietz, U-180, U-505

■ ■

One cool October afternoon in 1990, Otto and I strolled along the shore of a lovely little lake near Klagenfurt, Austria. Engrossed in the beauty of the scene, with the Alps in the distance and sailboats skimming along the blue surface, I hardly could take in what Otto was saying. His submarine adventures and his prisoner of war days sounded like a best-selling book of fiction, but every word was true. I visited with him on several other occasions to record as many details as possible of his war experiences. Four years later I heard of Otto's death on 6 May 1994.

■ ■

In 1939, at the age of seventeen, Dietz joined the German navy and went into training at the Naval Medical School in Wilhelmshaven. With the outbreak of World War II, he started to work as pharmacist's mate in the navy base hospital, and "a few days later we had the first air raid over Wilhelmshaven." The light cruiser *Emden* had been heavily damaged by bombs, and many wounded sailors were brought into the hospital.

Otto worked in the hospital until 1940 and was then put on a floating submarine repair boat, the former motorship *Cameroon*. "It was a floating dockyard, and the crew were dockworkers who just put on a uniform and learned to salute, that's all." When Germany occupied Norway in the spring of 1940, the repair ship went to Bergen and

Otto Dietz

remained as a small submarine base. "I spent a happy time there with some Norwegian friends. It was wonderful."

This kind of life, however, grew monotonous, and the young sailor longed for action and adventure. "So I volunteered for the submarine forces in September 1941." Dietz was assigned to the crew of U-180 under the command of *Korvettenkapitän* Werner Musenberg, with Harald Lange as first officer.

"We were testing and exercising a new kind of Mercedes high-speed engine. From Kiel we went out on patrol in February 1943, and it was a top secret mission." Otto said that two "very important personages" traveled with them—Subhas Chandra Bose and Dr. Abid Hassan.

"As we sailed around England in rough seas, the German radio stations broadcast interviews between Bose and Hassan and Hitler. These were supposedly live interviews, but they had been recorded and rebroadcast to make people think they were still in Germany." Otto talked to Bose and found out that after he had conferred with Hitler, Bose did not think the Germans would win the war.

"We reached our meeting point with the Japanese submarine cruiser, I-29, under the command of Commander Mokuri Yoichi, on 23 April 1943. Without any problem, we exchanged some secret war materials, designs of new weapons like the V-2 rocket and the latest jet engine, and they gave us three small Japanese one-man submarines called 'suicide subs.'" Along with the midget boats, the Japanese loaded U-180 with a large amount of gold for the Japanese embassy in Germany.

"We then followed orders to sail back home to our new base at Bordeaux, France. There was no way to sink anything on the way because the new diesels were smoking like an old coal steamer and needed repair."

Back at the base, Otto's career took a turn for the worse. "After the long patrol, we all tried to enjoy life as much as possible, and because I got drunk and missed the daily test dive, they punished me very hard." U-boat officials put Dietz in the stockade for a few days, then sent him off to the Russian front, the customary punishment for misbehavior. "There we were cannon fodder."

Otto was shot in the chest by a sniper and flown to the front hospital, where he spent the rest of 1943. In January he was allowed to go back to the submarine forces, but to a boring job. "I had to do easy work in the sick bay of the Ninth U-boat Flotilla at Brest, and what a change *that* was."

U-505, under the command of Harald Lange, former first officer of U-180, arrived at the Brest dockyards for repairs. One day Lange came into the sick bay "to chase one of the nurses," said Otto. The truth is that Lange's U-boat had picked up thirty-six survivors of a German torpedo boat in the Bay of Biscay, and some of them were being treated in the hospital. At any rate, the commander recognized Otto Dietz from U-180 and asked him how he was doing. When Otto expressed a desire to get on submarines again, Lange offered him the job of pharmacist's mate on U-505.

The ill-fated U-boat started her last voyage in February 1944, bound for West Africa. For four weeks they patrolled along the Gold Coast without sinking any ships. As they started their trip home, the *ping* of radar sounded, meaning a plane or ship had spotted them. With each occurrence they dived, descending for longer and longer periods. Back on the surface, the *ping* always repeated. There seemed to be no escape from the maddening detection, and Lange guessed that there was an aircraft carrier nearby with scouting planes. Things were getting desperate—the batteries were down to nothing, and very little air was left in the boat.

One day at noon the men heard the sound of approaching destroyer propellers, and Lange ordered them to the surface, where they made ready to fight. This proved disastrous, for the enemy spotted their periscope and immediately let loose a heavy barrage of depth charges, jolting the boat. "We survived 164 depth charges, and everything was broken—all the meters, everything, including the lights." U-505 fell into the ocean depths at a terrifying speed. Almost all the controls, including steering mechanisms, were nonfunctional.

"The only thing that was still okay was the air pressure. The captain ordered the air tanks pressurized and when we did it, the boat jumped up like a cork, out of control." When U-505 hit the surface, planes came in from all directions, firing machine guns. On the submarine, an antiaircraft gunner was killed and a bullet hit Lange in the knee. All of U-505's crew jumped off the slowly moving boat, and the commander, after ordering the sea strainer removed, leaped in as well. The attacking destroyer escorts *Chatelain* and *Jenks* sent out a twenty-man lifeboat, and Otto and the others assisted Lange aboard. The entire crew of U-505, except for the gunner, was rescued by the destroyers on 4 June 1944.

A party of nine U. S. Navy men from another destroyer escort, the *Pillsbury,* boarded U-505, stopped the engines, and shoved the sea strainer back into place as the vessel rapidly sank. After a mighty effort, another member of the killer group, the *Guadalcanal,* towed the German submarine, with a large American flag waving from her conning tower, back to Bermuda. The U.S. Navy had made one of their prize captures of the war.

Aboard the *Guadalcanal* Otto assisted the doctor in tending to the wounded. "The Jewish physician did not treat Lange's knee. It had

U.S. Navy personnel raise an American flag on U-505, captured 4 June 1944 and later placed at the Chicago Museum of Science and Industry.
Bundesarchiv, Koblenz

a bullet in it, and during our two-week trip to Bermuda, the joint became so badly infected that his leg had to be amputated." Otto remembered that the doctor really hated the U-boat officers but was quite friendly to him and that they became friends.

In Bermuda the German crew was housed in large tents. Their rations, short on salt, caused many to suffer from stomach problems. After four or five weeks a destroyer took U-505 survivors to Norfolk, Virginia, and from there they went by train to Ruston, Louisiana, a small town near Monroe. "The train trip took us two days, and even though it was hot, they had the windows nailed shut. They were afraid we would escape. And nobody knew we were still alive." The U.S. military was keeping quiet about their seizure of the U-boat, and families of U-505 crewmen were informed by the German navy that the boat had been sunk with the loss of all hands.

Ruston's large prisoner of war camp was divided into several sections for different types of military. Otto Dietz and his fifty-eight companions were the sole occupants of their section, built to house a thousand men. Commander Lange arrived after a four-month hospital stay, making the crew complete. "We could not get in touch with any other POWs, and we couldn't write to our parents. There was no work to do, but the food was excellent, and the canteen paid us eighty cents a day. That was enough to buy Coke for five cents and Falstaff beer for fifteen cents and cigarettes for ten cents."

On several occasions Red Cross commissions from Geneva toured the United States to inspect prison camps, and every time a commission was due at Ruston, the camp commanders moved Otto and friends to neighboring Camp Livingston. After three or four days, when the inspection was over, they were brought back. "We knew what they were doing," said Otto.

At war's end in 1945, the crew of U-505 was ordered to pick cotton—a hundred pounds each day. If it rained one day during the week, they had to make up for it on Sunday. "The French farmers in Louisiana hated the Germans. It was terrible. And there were guards all around the cotton fields, even though it was after the war."

Then the crew was split up, and Otto went by train to Camp Mexia near Dallas, Texas, another "cotton" camp. There the situation was far worse, for food was practically nonexistent. "They took away the corn we had hidden in our pockets, so we had to catch sparrows to eat. It's true." Otto said they caught the little birds between the barracks by making traps of bricks and string, with bits of bread as bait. "We cooked them in salt water and ate them. They tasted good." No cigarettes were available, and the three or four months they spent at Mexia seemed to drag on forever.

Every day the prisoners were forced to pick 150 pounds of cotton, no matter how long it took. "We had to stay in the field until the last man had his 150 pounds—maybe ten hours, it didn't matter."

One day Otto and one of his friends hatched an idea to avoid any more picking of the hated cotton. "We waited until dark and made our move. The whole place was fenced in, but near the watchtower there was a place with high grass, so we used a board to separate the fence wires and ran for our lives." The two men calculated it would take about two or three days to be caught, put in the brig, and then no more time in the cotton fields.

"They did catch us in three days. We had been walking at nighttime along a railroad track and were going across a bridge over a swamp, when a train came. We had to hang underneath the bridge." The next morning Otto told his friend he had had enough and that he wanted to just walk along the highway, and they did just that. As soon as dawn came, they noticed airplanes flying back and forth, and as expected, the law soon arrived: about fifty Texas Highway Patrol cars came roaring up with sirens wailing.

When they saw the police approaching, the two escapees, wearing striped prison suits, ran into a field. "Hands up!" they heard the lawmen yell. Ready to be captured, the two tired Germans dutifully raised their arms and walked back to the road. Inside the police car Otto and his friend were made to sit in front with the driver, while a policeman held a gun on them from the back. "You're a hero, catching two Nazis," Otto remarked.

The fifty police vehicles drove back to Mexia in a grand parade with their two prisoners. Back at the camp, Otto and his buddy gratefully ate some sandwiches before they were put in the stockade at nearby Camp Hearne with some Japanese internees. "The war was still going on with Japan in July 1945, and the guards treated them really badly. To us the guards were friendly because the war was over for Germany."

After two weeks in the stockade, Seaman Dietz went to work in the camp library. "No more cotton picking," he gloated.

Finally, in January 1946, the crew of U-505 shipped out by train to Long Beach, California, and boarded the *Ernie Pyle,* a troop transport. "It was a big one, and there were four or five thousand POWs on board. They told us we were going home, to Bremerhaven." Now, at last, *Oberleutnant zur See* (First Lieutenant) Lange was allowed to write to his wife and tell her that he was still alive, as was the rest of the crew, and that all would be coming home. Frau Lange then sent letters to the other families, giving them the wonderful news.

As Otto and crew were traveling through the Panama Canal, they heard a rumor that everyone was going to end up in French coal mines.

Otto, disturbed about the possibility, told a friend: "Ernest, we are going to escape in Colón." The black cook in the kitchen told them he thought they could crawl out a long window in his cabin when they reached port, but when they arrived, Otto saw that there were many guards on the dock, making the plan impossible.

After departing Colón, the *Ernie Pyle* was cruising slowly along toward the Atlantic when a hurricane struck. The devastating assault of the wind and waves caused the ship to lose all her lifeboats, and some of the POWs suffered broken bones. Forced to return to Colón, the *Pyle*, instead of landing, sent the wounded ashore in motorboats, and again Otto and friend were foiled.

"The *Ernie Pyle* continued slowly moving around in the bay, and one night when the moon was shining, we crawled down the side of the ship on a rope, without any life belts, just wearing our trousers. We had maybe two miles to swim to a boat at anchor, where we could rest, but we didn't realize there were sharks in the water."

As soon as they jumped into the sea, the two men dived under to keep from being seen by guards on the ship. Unaware that the tide was going out, Dietz and his friend made no progress at all, even swimming as desperately as they could. "Our lungs were full of sea-water, and after about an hour, we saw the ship coming back to where we were. I cried 'Help!' But by this time my buddy had disappeared, and I thought he might have been caught in the ship's propellers."

All at once Otto heard a yell from the *Ernie Pyle:* "Man overboard!" and bells ringing. Crewmen lowered a lifeboat into the rough seas, and Otto thankfully climbed into it. When he arrived on deck, everyone was shocked to see a German prisoner, because they had presumed the lost man was a member of the American crew. As Dietz explained: "I had yelled the English word 'help.' If I had called, *Hilfe,* they would have shot me with machine guns, because they had to kill escaping prisoners. I thought it was best to call in English, so that was lucky."

Otto was assigned to the stockade at the stern of the ship next to the propeller for the next two weeks. "What a noise it made—*rrrr, rrrr.* They gave me my seabag but took away my cigarettes." At the end of the two weeks, the ship landed at Liverpool, and "we were glad to see it wasn't France." The crew, under heavy guard, boarded a train and traveled to Camp Sheffield, an enormous camp for ten thousand prisoners, where at last they began to feel free. Rules permitted the men to walk into town for Cokes and movies, and they enjoyed working at a nearby women's camp, emptying ashtrays and sweeping. "We had a very good time," smiled Otto. "At the canteen we could buy yellow army cake and coffee in any amount, also all the cigarettes we wanted, because we worked."

From Camp Sheffield Dietz was sent to Camp Hartford Grange, where he lived in a Quonset hut and worked on a nearby farm. "The family liked me. But I remember one day the farmer's wife said, 'I can't understand how people like you could destroy Coventry.' 'And I can't understand how people like you could destroy Dresden,'" Otto replied.

In April 1948, Pharmacist's Mate Dietz returned to his home in Germany, three years after the end of World War II. Twenty-nine years later, he retraced his steps to England to try to find the family who had befriended him. After a ferry trip down the Elbe River from Hamburg, Dietz traveled to London, and from there rode a train to Yorkshire. "I saw the old prison camp, but the Quonset huts had collapsed, and I found the farm, but the old farmer had died from smoking too much. His wife and son were still living there, and they had turned the place into a cattle ranch." That night the whole village celebrated Otto's visit, drinking beer and talking. "The granny was crying, she was so happy, and the young girl was grown and had kids."

In 1984 Professor Matthew Schott from Lafayette, Louisiana, began researching World War II POW camps in his state for a book to be entitled *Bayou Stalags: German Prisoners of War in Louisiana.* In his search for eyewitnesses he visited all the former campsites, and from prisoner lists he contacted those still living in Germany who had been imprisoned there. After a trip to Germany, Professor Schott arranged for a group of ex-prisoners of war to come to the United States and spend two weeks on a special tour of the south. Otto Dietz was one of seventeen who made the trip, later declaring that they were treated like visiting dignitaries.

Riding in ten rental cars with German and American flags flying,

Otto and the other former POWs paraded through the town of Ruston, and the mayor presented them with the key to the city. A television crew was there, filming the event for the news. "Our old POW camp was grown up with young trees," recalled Dietz. "You could hardly see where it was, and only one barrack was still standing."

From Ruston, the motorcade drove slowly along the highway, stopping in each town. "Every place we went, the sheriff came out to meet us." Otto and friends continued to Memphis, then down to the World's Fair in New Orleans. "The German consul was there, and he and the New Orleans police guided us through the fair. We even rode on an old paddle wheel called the *Natchez,* and another submariner and I got to go up on the bridge and talk to the captain. He told us that in the Gulf of Mexico a German U-boat had been sunk" (U-166, south of Houma). Otto thought everything was "very nice, with a Dixieland band playing on the boat."

Dietz's next destination was Chicago, where he stayed for six weeks enjoying the delights of America. A newspaper reporter discovered him and wrote a story for the *Chicago Tribune* with Otto's picture, captioned, "Otto Dietz, age 59, from Fürth, Germany." His story touched many people, and after his return to Fürth he received two hundred letters from Americans inviting him to come and visit them.

"I picked out several people and made the visits. First I flew to Buffalo where a lady had a big farm, and I stayed a week, then another guy had invited me to San Jose, California, and he showed me San Francisco and everything for another week." Next, Otto traveled to Slidell, Louisiana, and visited for a third week. Almost forty years after picking cotton and eating sparrows, Otto Dietz had become a hero.[1]

10   Tom Poser, U-222

■■

"On Sunday, January 27, 1924, when I was born, it was snowing in Bremen and times were bad in Germany," wrote Tom. Poser's parents, Friedrich ("Fritz") Poser and his wife Alice, christened their baby son Heinrich Friedrich Karl, but at the age of four the child announced that his name was now "Tom," and so he became. Young Tom was always looking for a laugh, but his antics, such as letting loose june bugs in the schoolroom, frequently got him into trouble. "We put a wet sponge under the teacher's seat, so my parents sent me away to the military academy in Potsdam when I was twelve years old." One day in 1936 Hitler came to pay a visit to the boys, and Poser never forgot his impression of the dictator. "I was already against him because our family had supported the emperor. But he had such power in his eyes that if he had told me to take out a gun and shoot myself, I would have." [1]

■■

At the ripe old age of sixteen, Tom Poser, whose father's ancestors, the Wellfs, had been officers in the King of Hannover's army, entered the engineering branch of the navy. After a short stay in boot camp he went to Flensburg Naval Academy to further his naval career in the submarine service.

One day a note arrived from his mother, telling him that she was on her way to Gotenhafen to see his father, who would be leaving soon

Tom Poser

on the new battleship *Bismarck*. Confused about what to do, Tom conferred with instructors and the head of the academy, who agreed the message was probably telling him he should meet her in Gotenhafen, even though the ship's location was top secret. (The *Bismarck* and her sister ship *Tirpitz* were the two most powerful battleships in the world.)

After a specially arranged trip to East Prussia on the *BdU* train, Tom arrived in Gotenhafen, where he inquired on various ships about his father, but to no avail. Next he went to the office of the port commander and was showing his mother's note to the duty officer when Herr Poser, former captain of luxury liners for North German Lloyd, entered the room. Recognizing his son, Poser immediately instructed him to go down the hall—that he would see him later. "While I was waiting, my father was asked if anyone in his family knew which ship he was on, and he said no. Even his own brother, a *Korvettenkapitän*, did not know." With that, the duty officer burned Frau Poser's note, and Fritz Poser came bursting out of the office. "He gave me hell," said Tom, "and not until that afternoon did I understand why he was so upset."

A couple of hours later Tom went to the boarding house where his parents were staying and asked the landlady where he could find them. She told him they were expecting to meet him on a certain walkway near the harbor. As soon as Poser saw his son he gave him two cuffs on the head, yelling, "You're not supposed to be here!" Unable to understand his father's intense anger, Tom stayed to talk and found out his father assumed that naval authorities had interrogated Tom to find out if Poser had divulged any secrets. "I want you to take the first train back to Flensburg, and you'll have to pay your own way," Poser barked at his son, but after a few moments he softened, telling Tom he could stay for one day and that he would pay for half the train fare.

"The next day my mother and I went to Danzig to get my train ticket, and I was shocked when my father told us, 'Look well at Danzig, look at everything, because who knows if we will ever see it again. The officers have all been discussing the fact that everyone seems to know all about the *Bismarck,* and we're extremely worried about it.'" Poser asked his son to take care of his mother in case anything should happen after he departed.

On 19 May the enormous, elegant, "unsinkable" warship, Hitler's pride and joy, sailed out of Gotenhafen to decimate British shipping. Eight days later, after destroying the British battle cruiser *Hood,* the invincible *Bismarck* was sunk—discovered and chased to her end by British aircraft and warships. The entire crew of 2,200 men (except for three) perished, bearing out Fritz Poser's premonition of disaster.[2]

Tom was transferred to the submarine school at Pillau (East Prussia), and he was "very proud of that," as service in the U-boats was reserved for an elite few. "But when they discovered that I was not one hundred percent *kriegsverwendungsfähig* [fit for war duty] they transferred me again. They found out that I had been wounded because my mother wrote to the Admiralty requesting I be transferred to another service, since I was the only son and my father had died." The news brought great disappointment to the younger Poser, who had his heart set on being a U-boatman.

As sometimes happens in wartime, fate intervened, for Poser's life would have ended had he continued his submarine career. His assigned boat, U-222, on a training cruise in the Baltic Sea in February 1942, collided with another U-boat while submerged, and every crewman on U-222 was killed.

Newly assigned to the freighter *Ost,* Tom went out on convoy duty with a group of former freighters taken over by the navy and converted to heavy artillery carriers, operating in the Baltic from Finland to Latvia and Estonia. In the winter, when most of the northern Baltic was frozen, "we were busy in the English Channel."

"At twilight one evening we were having a bad storm, and the lookout shouted that some Russian torpedo boats were coming after us. We got ready and started shooting in that direction, then realized that we were firing at a Finnish lighthouse, and the storm waves made it look like boats."

A few months later the convoy was again attacked by Russian speedboats and planes, and "our ship went down with the loss of some of our men and several officers." Two of the other freighters rescued Tom and the rest of the crew and took them to a navy hospital in Latvia.

After recovering from a shrapnel wound in his head, Tom launched into another military career, this time in the *Marine Nachrichten,* the navy signal corps, communications division. Poser was retrained and transferred to Paris, where he served on the admiral's staff of occupation forces, deciphering coded messages to and from ships and submarines at sea. "This was the secret stuff [using Enigma machines], and we transferred the messages on to Berlin. We also broke some of the British codes, as well."

"We weren't very popular with the army 'chain dogs' [military police] in Paris, because of our informal attitude. For instance, when we went in small groups to do something, we were not supposed to march, but we loved to get those chain dogs upset." Tom and friends would march along the streets singing "some good old navy songs that were especially disliked by the army guys and the SS."

Often they were stopped by a group of four military policemen, who wrote down the name of the navy "leader," and reported him. But Poser's commander always interceded and stopped any trouble. "My uncle, Hans Poser, who served on the meteorological staff, didn't think that was funny."

In those days, rules for the German military in France required strictly correct behavior. One day Tom and a friend were walking down the street, and a passing soldier saluted them. "Suddenly we heard a girl scream, and here came the military police, like lightning. They asked the young French woman what had happened, and she, probably not liking Germans, said that the soldier had pinched her. The poor guy would have been nailed, so we verified that he had saluted us and could not have done such a thing."

Tom heard a story about two U-boat sailors who were on their way home on leave and had to change trains in Paris. They had imbibed a few drinks on the train, and having a little time to kill in the city, went to a local bar to have one or two more. "The bartender, aware that the navy men might get into trouble with the military police, told them that they should not have any more drinks. One of them became belligerent, pulled out his pistol, and told the bartender not to refuse, but while this was going on, a barmaid called the chain dogs. Here they came in an instant." Seeing the sailor's pistol lying on the bar, the police hauled the two crewmen outside and shot them dead. Then they took a piece of paper, wrote a big sign saying that the German military was supposed to behave correctly in a foreign country, and pasted the sign on the bar window above the two dead U-boatmen.

Poser and friends thoroughly enjoyed the local French diversions, and many evenings they went to the Folies Bergères, where they gave the waiter "plenty of cigarettes" in return for box seats. During one of the numbers, twenty-eight chorus girls paraded down a ramp twirling umbrellas, each umbrella showing a letter of the alphabet. Audience members could guess what name they were going to form, and whoever won could come up on stage and give a girl a kiss. "I never saw a

German military man come up, even though they would have loved to. It was always a Frenchman. But *we* did." They had bribed the waiter to tell them the young lady's name. Tom and his cohorts also sent notes to the dancers telling them they would meet the girls later at a certain place. "We ran like hell to escape from the chain dogs and met them, and we always had a great time."

At Tom's headquarters there were many attractive young German women working for the military, and Tom had one favorite, who was doing an outstanding job. "One day a friend and fellow officer told me that I should be on my toes because people were saying that I was having an affair with her, which was strictly forbidden," he explained. "This was not true, so I asked him what I should do, and he advised me to be a little tough on her."

So the next time Tom was on duty he bawled her out for some insignificant mistake, and she burst into tears. "But something unforeseen happened. My commanding officer was standing in the next room, and the door wasn't closed all the way, so he saw what took place. When the girl started sobbing, I took her into my arms to calm her down." That did it. The colonel burst in, Tom saluted, and his superior curtly informed him that he would never make a good officer, and that he would have to serve as a "front pig," referring to a common soldier without any class.

"So there it was. I stood at attention and asked him to go ahead and ship me to the [Russian] front. And to my surprise, several of my men stood up and asked to be transferred, too. This was like a revolt." Tom said the situation was similar to one where a submarine commander was stripped of his rank and sent to fight in Russia because he had refused to go out on an impossible war mission, fearing for the safety of his crew. In all the cases Poser heard of, the whole crew elected to go with their captain, though they knew death awaited them in the Soviet Union.

In short order, Tom and several of his loyal men were transferred to Hungerburg, Estonia. "We boarded the military train to go to Reval and then to the Russian border. After leaving Paris we first went to Hannover, where my mother and grandmother met us, and I gave them some coffee, which meant a lot to them."

On the way to their next stop, some of the men asked Tom if they could get off to visit their families, as it had been such a long time since they had seen them. "I said I would see what I could do, but they had to promise on their word of honor to return after one day, and they agreed." It so happened that the night they arrived in Berlin a huge air raid hit the city. Tom told his men they were free to go see their relatives, but at all costs to avoid the military police, who would arrest them for desertion.

"While they were gone, I went to see some of my friends. The next day, as planned, we all met again. Some of them had had a rough time making it back at the correct hour because of the bombs. Then we boarded the train to go to Russia."

The ride seemed interminable, across Poland, through sections of Russia, and up into Estonia. For a year and a half, Hitler's forces had been fighting a losing battle in the Soviet Union, their numbers decimated the previous winter as they tried to survive the brutally cold weather without adequate clothing, food, or equipment. German General Friedrich Paulus' last major attack on Stalingrad was beginning, with vicious fighting and heavy casualties on both sides.[3]

"It was still in the early stages of the war [November 1942], and the ride was very interesting. Sometimes our train would stop to let other trains pass, coming from the front, and they were loaded with prisoners and some civilians. Whenever we saw a train stop with our troops from the front, we went over to them and handed them cigarettes and whatever we could."

After a few days they arrived at Hungerburg, where they received orders to proceed to an outpost near Leningrad, where they were to function as navy signal corpsmen, sending and receiving messages in Morse code. "They told us that our quarters were in the former summer residence of the czar, a beautiful old castle. We had no sooner moved into the castle when shelling from Russian battleships and artillery on the coast started. It was so regular you could set your watch by it."

Poser and comrades, trained for sea duty, had never experienced war on land. Each time the booms started, they had to scurry to a nearby air raid bunker, where they were safe and had communications equipment. "We learned to run and duck, and the first time we were lucky we didn't get hit on the way to the bunker."

The signal corps group somehow survived for two years, and in January 1944 the Allied offensive started. German General Ferdinand Schoerner and his troops, fighting southwest of Leningrad close to the Baltic, found themselves surrounded by the Soviets. "The general called me and ordered me to set up a signal station to tell him where to attack, so they could get out. I told him the best thing to do was to set up a portable station in a truck, because staying in one place would be fatal—they would find us." Schoerner replied to Poser: "We are the army and you are the navy, and you will do what we order. You will stay in one place."

Tom carried out the general's directions and set up the signal station; thirty minutes after they had it functioning, the Russians located them and started shelling. "We got several full hits with *Stalinorgeln* [multibarreled, artillery-sized rocket guns that fired nonstop]. Out of my fifteen men, only four of us survived—we were wounded and unconscious. When I woke up I was in a Soviet field hospital."

"They put four of us in two beds pushed together, one of us up, one down, and so on. If someone had a broken arm, they cut the arm off, and if the arm should have been taken off, they left it on, so he died. I nearly got hysterical because the guy next to me died, and I knew that he could cause infection in my stomach wound."

When Tom and his three men were somewhat recovered, the Russians transferred them to a prison in Leningrad for interrogation. "They realized I was navy signal corps and intelligence, and they wanted to find out what I knew. We had agreed not to say *anything*. When I told them that, they said, 'Okay, if you don't cooperate, you'll have to go into this room.'"

The guard put Tom into a box with his head sticking out through a hole in the top, and every minute a drop of water fell on his head. "You can do that forever," Poser told them, "and I won't talk." For an hour the drops fell, and then "I broke down." Poser answered their questions, such as, "Did you know this, did you know that?" He just said "yes," whether he knew it or not. "I didn't care. Whatever they wanted."

Some of the men endured the Chinese torture for hours and hours, and they lost their minds. "We had one SS guy and an air force officer, and they went crazy because they held out for too long. They were shot."

The Russians had another special treatment for those who refused to talk. The prisoner was led into a small cell with blinding lights. As he sat tied to a chair, hot water gushed out of pipes, filling the room until it reached his neck. Then the water was drained out and cold water filled the room, then hot, and so on. "It didn't come so high that you would drown," Tom explained. After several dousings, if the prisoner still refused to talk, the guards came in and put clamps on his hands and squeezed the bones until he broke down.

After the interrogation the Germans were shipped to a slave labor camp, or gulag, between Leningrad and Moscow—one of many throughout the Soviet Union. Since the 1920s the Communist regime had been building a massive penal system, where hundreds of thousands of Russian political dissidents, poets, writers, convicts, war prisoners, and others were forced into hard labor. Everywhere, conditions in the camps were so brutal that prisoners would almost certainly die. During the trip, many Russian villagers, in defiance of the rules, ran up to the train, threw food to the prisoners, and ran away. When they reached the camp, the other internees told them, "Boy, you sure do look good. Just wait until you've been here a few months, and you will look like us." Tom thought he was smarter than they and could fare better, not knowing what lay ahead.[4]

The men were put in work parties of a hundred, and since many of them knew each other from Leningrad, they agreed, "Okay, we'll figure out a way to get to them." In the early mornings the group had to go into a field, where some of them dug up clay and others formed it into bricks. Then the bricks were loaded on little trains, like the ones in coal mines. "We had to unload them and arrange them in big piles so that the wind could dry them, and we had to do a certain amount in order to get any food. If you did a bit more, you got a little more food."

"It didn't take long before we thought up a good idea. A couple of us started talking to the guard and telling him jokes, getting him into a good humor. We could talk some pidgin Russian with lots of gestures." While the conversation went on, Tom and friends quickly put some wood planks in the bottom of the cars and loaded bricks on top. "This worked well, and the guard marked us down for extra loads, so we started to get more to eat. But then we overdid it."

Meanwhile, the camp commander had studied the reports and was pleased that so much work was getting done; he could see himself in line for a big promotion. One day the commander decided to take some of his commissars on a tour of the brick-making area, and when they appeared, the prisoners thought the jig was up. "We were lucky because we were able to kick the planks under the cars, right there as they were standing around." But it did not take long for the commissars to figure out something was wrong, because the number of bricks supposedly manufactured didn't correspond to the few piles they saw drying. "They yelled, 'Sabotage! Sabotage!' and then threw us into the calaboose for fourteen days without anything to eat except watery soup. After a while we started to look like the other bunch."

"Why did you cheat on us?" the commissar asked them. "You should be happy to work for us, because we bring happiness to the world." Tom thought to himself, "What in the hell do you mean?" The commissar went on: "All of you were born with silver spoons in your mouths. You eat with silver forks and spoons that burn your tongue, so we will give you wooden utensils and you won't have to say, 'Ow, it's too hot.'" Poser and the others were dumbfounded at this supposed logic.

A short time later Tom and some of the others were shipped to a prison in Moscow, and there they were put to work on the subway, spending months digging, installing marble, and doing other backbreaking labor. "That was built with many German prisoners—that famous subway. That's why it still works today." And nowhere in the world does another exist with such lavish decoration—elegant chandeliers, marble benches, and colorful paintings of Stalin receiving flowers from children.

"One day Stalin was going to appear at a public festival. Here came a parade of thirty cars, each one exactly like the other, and all of them had a chauffeur and a Stalin look-alike passenger in the back seat. Then all the cars went off in different directions." Of course any saboteur would be unable to tell which vehicle to blow up.

Tom's next destination was a copper mine in the remote Ural mountains. "It took us days and days on the train to get there, riding in boxcars, and many died along the way. There we had to live in old broken-down barracks, and we didn't have anything to eat but soup with rotten potatoes and old cheese, so we caught rats, barbecued them and ate them. That's why I always clean my plate now."

One day the prisoners were working away in the copper mine, chopping with picks and drills. "It seems to me that this is a stupid way to do mining," Tom remarked to a young officer. "What do you mean?" the Russian asked. "You can get a machine to do the work of three hundred of us, because we are very slow," replied Poser. And the guard explained that they were afraid of using a mining machine because they feared sabotage. "If three hundred people decided to wreck a machine, we would put a hundred of them against the wall and shoot them, and the other two hundred would have to go on working," the guard said.

At the end of a grueling day, one of the trucks hauling the prisoners back to camp broke down. Because it was cold and they wanted to hurry, Tom got out, looked at the engine, and recognized the problem. He went around to the driver and whispered to him that the carburetor needed a certain part. "I talked softly so that the captain, who was walking nearby, wouldn't hear, because he would have shot the driver for not knowing what was wrong."

"We were all getting colder and colder sitting there, so I asked the captain, 'Why don't you stop one of the military cars?' and he told me, 'They won't stop.'" Tom urged him to go ahead and try, so the captain got out and started waving at the passing vehicles, but they just waved back and kept going. Finally one of the trucks pulled over, and a sergeant agreed to give the prisoners and Russian driver a ride to the camp. "He put a guard in the back with us so we and the driver wouldn't steal anything from the truck."

Every day the prisoners made a grueling trip to the mines, rattling and rumbling along for two or three hours, depending on how much snow and ice covered the road. "In four months we went from ten thousand people to four thousand. Six thousand died. They died like flies." Food rations were insufficient and medical treatment was non-existent, yet Tom survived there for a year and a half.

"In 1948 some of the first ones were allowed to leave, because the Russians wanted to make a nice gesture. They let several go, but they were the ones who could hardly walk anymore. All of them had to ride in boxcars."

In the camp there was one American of German descent from Pennsylvania—Hans Noble. He and his parents had gone to Germany to visit his ailing grandfather shortly before the war started and were unable to get out of the country. They were interned, and after the war the Americans released the elder Nobles and detained Hans. "When the Russians took over East Germany, they put millions of German civilians in Russian camps, and most of them died there. I heard terrible stories about thousands being killed in one of them."

American and British soldiers were incarcerated in Poser's gulag as well. "After we were released, we were not supposed to tell anyone who was there. And some of them had disappeared." Those still in the camp wrote notes to their relatives and gave them to the ones who were leaving, telling them they were still alive and hoping the messages would reach them. However, the guards had forbidden anyone to carry papers out and searched every departing internee. If anyone was caught with a message, he was returned to prison. "So the prisoners ate the papers, but the Russians were not stupid and they caught on to that, too. They gave them castor oil so they had to shit, and then the guards could find the papers."

Then the departing prisoners started memorizing names and towns. "It didn't do any good to remember streets, because so much had been destroyed, so you memorized, say, 'Ingrid Poser, Bremen.' Then they could find out where the parents or close relatives were." The Russians shipped them back in boxcars, and it took many weeks. When the guards found dead bodies, they just threw them off the train.

"I got out in December 1948 and went home the same way everyone else had—in a boxcar. It took nearly a month, and about forty or fifty percent of us died from cold and hunger. They only fed us a little thin soup and old bread."

In postwar Germany efforts were being made to restore life to the shattered, burned, and devastated cities. There were few places to live and little to eat. "In the beginning, many died, and people were still on rationing cards. When the relatives came back, their families fed them lots of food, and their bodies weren't used to it, so they died right away." When Tom arrived home, the British hospitalized him and the others for two weeks and fed them like babies to help them return to normal.

After Poser recovered he was happy to get volunteer jobs at A. G. Weser and Vulcan shipyards in Bremen. From there he went to work for Neptune Lines, became an engineer, and went back to sea on Norwegian ships. With his earnings, Tom acquired a master's degree and won a scholarship to MIT in the United States. At the age of thirty-one he left Germany to live in America.

When asked how he survived the ordeals of Russian gulags, he says that most of the people who died were either quite old or very young. "They had not been in war like us. And let's face it, Uncle Adolf trained us rough, and we were used to tough times. I was young, I ate food nobody else would eat, and I survived."[5]

11   Wolfgang von Bartenwerffer, U-536

■ ■

Outside the von Bartenwerffers' house in Essen, a Japanese cherry tree, covered with pink flowers, brightened the street. My visit coincided with its brief, once-a-year blooming, and it seemed a lucky sign. Frau von Bartenwerffer served homemade apricot cake, tea, and many delicious meals for the two days I was there interviewing her husband. Wolfgang spoke admirable English, and with my bit of German we put together the story of his remarkable voyage to Canada. Afterward, when we went to visit their son and family, Herr von Bartenwerffer and his three-year-old granddaughter took their positions on the swing set and had a contest to see who could go highest.

■ ■

By September 1943 the outlook for U-boats was distinctly gloomy: the German Metox could no longer pick up radar from attacking planes; Allied fleets of carriers, corvettes, and bombers were growing rapidly; mid-Atlantic air attacks were decimating the U-boats; and the subs were now carrying doctors. In the summer of that year patrol aircraft were destroying three out of five boats in the Bay of Biscay. Circumstances could not have been worse for U-536 to undertake a long-distance mission.

"In the beginning, we did not know where we were going. Only Commander Schauenburg knew because he had been in Berlin with Dönitz," recalled von Bartenwerffer, executive officer of U-536.

Wolfgang von Bartenwerffer

Admiral Dönitz had just assigned the boat a rescue mission—picking up "Tonnage King" Otto Kretschmer and other U-boatmen on the coast of Canada. Kretschmer and his prisoner of war compatriots had been tunneling their way out of Camp Bowmanville near Ontario, with the intention of traveling to the distant east coast, where U-536 would take them aboard. By fall 1943, with the Allies gaining supremacy on the seas, Dönitz had every reason to want Kretschmer back in action; he had been in prison camp for two-and-a-half years, unable to help his country.

Korvettenkapitän Kretschmer, captain of U-23 and U-99, had accumulated an astounding number of sinkings: forty-four ships (266,629 tons) before his boat, U-99, was sunk in March 1941. (For the rest of the war, no other commander equaled his record.) Still a leader of his men in Canada, Kretschmer formed an escape group called the "Lorient Espionage Unit" at Camp Bowmanville. Lacking detailed charts, the captain used a school atlas to find a rendezvous place and chose Maisonette Point, on the western coast of New Brunswick, where there was access from the Gulf of St. Lawrence.[1]

When they had reached the mid-Atlantic, Schauenburg informed his crew of their mission. "I was very glad to have this task," said von Bartenwerffer. "It was a special honor for us to rescue Kretschmer and his comrades." At Lorient, before departing from the U-boat base in September, a dinghy with motor was loaded onto U-536. "This was unusual, and we didn't know what it was for. We tried to guess why we were taking it along."

In the middle of the Atlantic Schauenburg also pointed out that they were going to a dangerous place, Chaleur Bay, which was only twenty-five to forty meters deep. The U-boat would have very little room to maneuver and escape detection, and therefore could be easily captured or sunk. "I was the torpedo officer, and in case we were about to be taken over, my job was to blow up the boat before it could fall into the enemy's hands, after the crew had abandoned ship, of course." U-536 was ready for the worst.

At Camp Bowmanville, the escape group had received Admiral Dönitz's assurances that he would have a submarine ready to pick them up on 27 or 28 September 1943. His messages reached them in ordinary correspondence from relatives, wherein the German navy had inserted the "Ireland" code, a complicated system using Morse code and letter substitutions.

The U-boatmen were making good progress on their one hundred-meter-long tunnel, but while they were feverishly hauling loads of dirt, Canadian naval intelligence broke the Ireland code and uncovered their plot to escape. In addition, the crime detection lab, examining some books sent to the prisoners by the German Red Cross, found a map of the eastern Canadian coast and other items sealed inside the binding of one of the volumes. Now armed with a map indicating where a U-boat was to land, the Canadian navy made plans to capture U-536 intact. However, a bit later they decided that the idea was too farfetched and instead gave orders to destroy the submarine.[2]

U-536 sailed into the Gulf of St. Lawrence about the sixteenth of September, with the crew looking forward to meeting the escapees in Chaleur Bay on the twenty-sixth. "We entered the bay without seeing any ships. We were supposed to go along the coast back and forth at night looking for the prisoners, and we hoped to find Kretschmer and the others quickly. Dönitz had told Schauenburg back in July, 'In Bowmanville they dug a tunnel, and if it succeeds, twenty, thirty, or fifty men could get out.'"

"Our orders were to patrol off Maisonette Point, looking for a light signal. Once we spotted it, we were to signal them back and send our dinghy to fetch the men to the U-boat. If we were unable to do that, the prisoners were supposed to try to capture a fishing boat and to row out to the submarine." When they arrived at their rendezvous location, they looked through the periscope on Saturday the twenty-sixth, and "We could see cars driving around, houses, even people, and we had the impression that all was very peaceful."

That night they carefully scanned the coastline and observed nothing out of the ordinary. "We saw only streetlights, lights in people's homes, and the lighthouse at Maisonette Point, and we hadn't noticed anything on the water at all when we came through Cabot Strait." The entire bay was devoid of life—no fishing boats, no navy ships, not a vessel of any kind. The waters were strangely deserted. "About ten-thirty or so, the northern lights brightened the sky, and to avoid being seen from the coast we had to dive and wait until darkness came again."

"Just after going under, we heard propeller noises, and this was surprising because everything had been so quiet." The screw sounds seemed completely out of place, when no sign of the enemy had been present. "Schauenburg had a democratic style and summoned all his officers to the mess. He asked each of us what we thought about the situation, and we all said, 'Something is wrong. We have a bad feeling, and it looks like a trap.'" Von Bartenwerffer said they waited a few hours, then took the boat up again, where they observed that the northern lights were now much dimmer, and at that point they decided to give up the search for the escapees.

"We had a very good map of Chaleur Bay, and we saw that the water depth was mostly twenty-five or so meters, but there was one place where it went to forty meters. Since we needed at least thirty meters for cover, we decided to lay up in the deeper part and wait." That was the night of 26 September.

Early in the morning of the twenty-seventh they went to periscope depth and Schauenburg took a look around. "He saw eight or ten warships across the horizon. They had us blocked off, and we were imprisoned in Chaleur Bay, so we had to try to get out without any damage."

U-536 immediately dived to the bottom and stayed flat on the sea-floor. Then suddenly they heard propeller noises and depth charges exploding. "That was lucky for us because those bombs showed us that they knew we were inside the bay." The next morning Schauen-burg could see that the ships were patrolling, so they dived again and waited another day, until the morning of 28 September. "We went again to periscope depth to look, and the same situation. We had no fresh air in the boat, and the crew needed to get out, because without air we would start feeling sleepy and die. So that morning we decided to risk escaping from the bay."

In a scant thirty meters of water, the U-boat crept along with only a few feet of clearance. "We could hear with our own ears the pro-pellers of the ships going over our boat, and we guessed that in the coming seconds depth charges would explode and sink or damage us, but nothing happened. We were standing in the mess—the second watch officer, the doctor, and I—and we said to each other, 'Our last hour has come.'"

As U-536 sailed directly below the enemy corvettes, the men held their breaths, expecting to be blown to pieces at any second. Some-how, by a miracle, they moved along untouched and at last emerged from the deadly trap.

The boat had now reached the Gulf of St. Lawrence, and as they traveled submerged, "All was very quiet, but suddenly overhead we heard a loud winch noise." U-536 had become entangled in a fisher-man's nets, and the trawler was trying to haul in the U-boat. "He thought he had a big fish in his net, and that fish was us. We later found half the net draped over our tower, and each of us cut off a piece as a souvenir."

WOLFGANG VON BARTENWERFFER, U-536 129

One morning a few days later, while they were still near Cabot Strait (off eastern Newfoundland), Schauenburg saw shadows at a distance of about four or five kilometers. "We shot two torpedoes in a fan shot, then dived because it was getting light. It was two destroyers, and we thought we had sunk them. We couldn't see them sinking, but we heard the explosions."

Just after U-536 came out of the Gulf of Saint Lawrence, Schauenburg sent a message to *BdU* informing them that their mission, codenamed *Kiebitz,* had not worked because Kretschmer's plan had been discovered by the Canadians. Headquarters accepted U-536's message, and in return ordered them to proceed into the Atlantic and fight the enemy. "So we did, from the beginning of October to our sinking in November."

"Our only other success was a Victory ship of nine thousand tons. By then our fuel, oil and food were running out, and we were told to come back to Lorient. But on the way we found a big convoy from Gibraltar to Liverpool." After giving them the location of an enormous group of ships, *BdU* ordered U-536 and two other U-boats to get together and position themselves in a row, directly in the path of the oncoming armada. This formation, called a "stripe," allowed the U-boats, while defending each other, to attack the convoy en masse. German submarine losses were drastically increasing in the fall of 1943, and new tactics had come into use.

"We were positioned as the center group in three stripes of U-boats, about one day's march away from the enemy. We had only one torpedo left, and on the evening of 19 November a German reconnaissance plane radioed us the convoy's exact location. We then realized that we were standing just in front of the mass of ships." As the convoy plowed toward them, they waited. "Then we dove to a depth of forty meters or so to meet them." Heading up the convoy, a support group of two corvettes and a frigate roved the waters, scouting for German submarines.

Churning along at about ten to fifteen knots, the three escorts discovered the submerged U-boats at ten o'clock. "We heard asdic on our boat—*tinc tinc tinc tinc tinc.* The support group had picked us up and started dropping depth charges on us." U-536 had been waiting at about forty meters and immediately dived to 180 meters. "The charges were hitting closer and closer, and at somewhat after midnight a series of concussions came almost onto our boat, exploding deeper than they had before. We thought that 180 meters was a safe depth, but at that time, in November 1943, the British had depth charges that exploded at two hundred meters." The explosive waves coming up under the boat were far more dangerous than the ones bursting over their heads. "That was a new thing for us, that the charges were exploding so deep."

U-536, a large type IXC boat, had extra tubes for reserve torpedoes in the upper deck, and the barrage of depth charges caused the reserve tubes to start leaking badly. Soon the stern became excessively heavy, and the whole submarine went into a vertical position, catapulting downward to about 220 meters. "Commander Schauenburg, to save the crew, brought the boat back up, right in the middle of the three ships. This was after midnight, and we lay on the surface. Then he gave the order: 'Leave the boat and sink it.'"

With that, the firing began. "The frigate and corvettes started shooting with artillery and machine guns at us and didn't stop while the boat stayed on the surface. Most of the crew were getting off as fast as possible, and many were being killed as they tried to leave. I personally didn't get off the boat until a bit later." The engineer in the control room began final preparations to scuttle the vessel by opening the valves. "When it started going deeper and deeper and the deck was just going under, I sprang into the water."

Von Bartenwerffer was wearing no life jacket, having given it to one of the young sailors who had forgotten his own. "I had to try to swim to the *Snowberry,* and it was difficult because the seas were heavy and I had on my shirt, trousers, and socks. When the bomb attack started, we took off our shoes to keep from making any noise." After a thirty-minute struggle, von Bartenwerffer made it to the *Snowberry* but was too weak to climb the ship's ladder. Two Canadian sailors came down and lifted him to the deck, pulling him under his arms. "I had no special feelings," he remembered. "I was not angry, just glad to have survived."

When von Bartenwerffer appeared on the *Snowberry,* eleven of his men were already on board, and they said, "Ah, here comes the first watch officer." The Canadians gave them each a towel, a cigarette, a drink of cognac, and a small parcel with simple clothes. "When I was warm and somewhat settled down, I was asked to list the names of the sub crew who were on board the corvette, so I did this for them, putting each man's rank and the town he came from. This was for the British, who would publish the names of the prisoners on the British radio."

The German officers were then taken to quarters in an area apart from the rest of their crew. That night a boat arrived, bringing an intelligence officer to question the prisoners about the U-boat—which number, where it came from, where it was going, and so on. "We didn't tell them. I said I was a German officer and would not talk about such things."

The next night after their sinking, the *Snowberry* sailed past another U-boat stripe, and there were several alarms on the ship when the submarines tried to attack the convoy and its support group. "We heard depth charges and gunfire, but the U-boats didn't sink any ships, because the escorts were too good. It was very difficult to attack, because many destroyers and battleships were there—even an aircraft carrier. The protection was so strong that it was very nearly impossible for a U-boat to get into the convoy." Von Bartenwerffer recalled that it had been much easier for the subs to operate in 1941 and 1942 and that this convoy was the first one that U-boats had attacked since May 1943, six months earlier.

The *Snowberry* landed at Plymouth, England, and the German crewmen were transported, under guard, to an interrogation camp in London. "I noticed while I was there that the British were very informed about our patrol. They knew Schauenburg's name and what he did before taking command of U-536; they knew the number of the boat; they knew when we left Lorient and so on—all the details, plus the fact that we had sunk the Victory ship and torpedoed two destroyers in the Gulf of St. Lawrence. But they didn't know that we were going after Kretschmer, or at least they did not mention it."

At the London interrogation camp von Bartenwerffer was put in a small room by himself, where he was "prepared" for interviewing. "We couldn't talk to anyone, and they wanted us to feel depressed so we would tell them more. But I did not reveal anything."

"A couple of weeks later Schauenburg and I were sent to a prison camp in northern England, but the British could not feed all the prisoners, so they sent a couple of thousand of us to Canada. Our engineer and the doctor had died in the sinking, and the second watch officer was wounded in his knee, so he had been transferred from the *Snowberry* to a ship that had a physician."

Schauenburg and von Bartenwerffer were sent to Canada in February 1944, to a camp near Montreal called Grand Ligne, remaining there for one year. Then the Canadians transferred all younger navy, air force, and army officers to a camp between Banff and Calgary in the Rocky Mountains. "It was nice of them to send us to the Rockies. We had a very good time at that little camp; it had small huts for eight men. On the train from Montreal to Calgary we ran into Kretschmer and the prisoners from Bowmanville who had dug the tunnel, and we all ended up in camp together. They told us all the details of 'the escapees who couldn't escape,' and we told them our story about coming to get them in Chaleur Bay. That was the first time we all knew what had happened." Kretschmer and friends explained that they thought U-536 had been destroyed in Chaleur Bay—they were unaware that the boat had been sunk close to the Azores on the way back to France.

Fifty-one years after his U-boat went to the bottom of the Atlantic, Wolfgang von Bartenwerffer flew to Canada to see what was left of his old POW camp near Calgary. "I had the best of impressions of Canada, with beautiful weather—a real Indian summer," he wrote. "For seven days we drove across British Columbia, more than three thousand miles, and arrived at my old camp Seebe. The camp itself didn't exist, but a 'Captain's cabin' and one watchtower had been left there." Von Bartenwerffer and friends found inside the little cabin some mementos of the war days: a model of the old camp buildings, some photographs, bottle ships, letters, newspaper articles, and a few other things. "It was very interesting to me, and I took many pictures."

Looking back on his navy days, Wolfgang summed up by saying:

"My memories of the time in the *Kriegsmarine* are very good, and the standards for an officer helped me later in civilian life—qualities such as a sense of duty, reliability, endurance, loyalty, and comradeship." After the war Wolfgang went home to Essen, became an engineer, and worked for Hochtief AG, a large construction firm, for thirty-four years.[3]

12   U-682 and U-735

■ ■

Near midnight on 28 December 1944, a wave of bombers flew over Oslo Fjord, Norway, unleashing two hundred bombs on U-682 and a second submarine, U-735. U-682 crewman Herbert Wodarz, believing that the planes were American, wrote to me in an attempt to get in touch with the squadron that had made the massive attack. "Our U-boat comrades want to invite several of the American pilots to our May reunion and to thank them for their bad aim," he explained. U.S. Air Force records showed that no American planes had made bombing raids over Oslo Fjord that night, and Wodarz subsequently learned that the squadron had come from England. In the spring of 1994 several nervous RAF pilots and their wives flew to Germany to meet their former enemies, and there they received a hearty welcome in Zeltingen-Rachtig, a picturesque village on the Mosel River. Both sides shared fascinating experiences, compared maps, clinked toasts, and reconstructed their amazing story of the December air raid over Norway.

■ ■

As the year 1944 drew to a close, U-boats were being bombed and sunk so frequently that the German navy, in a desperate attempt to keep them going, began to install schnorkel devices (air masts) on them so the boats could travel underwater indefinitely, using their diesel engines and recharging their batteries at the same time. An excellent idea, but it came too late in the game.

On 23 December 1944, as the Reich's defenses crumbled and Allied planes leveled city after city in Germany, U-682, equipped with radar to detect enemy aircraft, sailed from Kiel at midnight and traveled with escorts to Frederickshavn, Denmark. Two days later, the boat departed from Frederickshavn and sailed to Horten, Norway, on the west side of the immense Oslo Fjord. Years earlier, in 1941, Germany had established small naval bases around Norway, and U-boats were able to safely practice maneuvers in the deep fjord waters. U-682, under the command of *Oberleutnant zur See* Sven Thienemann, arrived at Horten the day after Christmas at 10:20 P.M. and anchored at the entrance to the harbor.

All day on the twenty-seventh Thienemann and his crew practiced with their schnorkel, trying to deal with the somewhat tricky new device. Similar to a periscope, the tube extended above the tower, but each time a wave went over the schnorkel, the diesels created a sudden vacuum, causing the men to feel as though their heads were exploding and ears bursting. Nevertheless, with a few trial runs the annoyances could be conquered.

At 7:30 that evening U-682 was anchored at the harbor entrance alongside several German merchant ships and another U-boat, U-735. Hearing the wail of an air raid siren from Horten, the watch on U-682 spotted two or three planes in the distance traveling northward. "We did not shoot because they were too far off," wrote Thienemann in his log book. However, they could hear the bursts of German antiaircraft guns on shore.

Another warning sounded, and again single planes flew by, still too remote for U-682 to shoot. Since these were somewhat closer, Thienemann ordered the 3.7-centimeter gun crew to stand by. At 9:00 that night, "We saw single four-engine planes twice, probably [U.S.] 'Fortress II' types," noted the commander. "During this time we did not see them drop any bombs, so I assumed we were dealing with attack planes returning from Oslo."

Sirens wailed again to warn of approaching aircraft. At 11:28 several planes came toward them at a distance of four or five kilometers. "I suspected . . . that they were going to attack the ships lying near Horten, so I decided to heave anchor and head west, traveling close to shore at slow speed."

Bombers buzzed overhead, now within gun range of the U-boat. "We are dealing with several planes, but to keep from giving away the submarine, we do not open fire." The German navy had issued orders that all U-boats were to shoot at planes flying either overhead or away from them, so that once the pilots had seen the flak, it would be too late for them to drop their loads.

First came the flares and target markers, floating silently through the night air and casting an eerie glare on the sea and the ships. "The whole fjord is lit up almost like daylight. . . ," remarked Thienemann. Bellowing explosions followed, and "our boat catches a bomb very close to the bow on the starboard side." Shock waves from another burst hit them from the port side, throwing tons of water over the deck and tower. "Our bow is deep in the water . . . bent approximately five degrees toward starboard."

Reports from every area of the boat indicated water was coming into the bow torpedo room and that diving cell five was damaged. "I give orders to slip [cut] the anchor. However, since the mechanism is bent, we have to heave anchor." When efforts to pull up the burdensome attachment failed, U-682 limped westward, dragging the anchor and 120 feet of chain.

Bomb blasts were lashing the boat from every side. "They are probably aiming at a tanker about 500 meters on our right. . . . The 3.7-centimeter gun is malfunctioning, and I am firing it at half-automatic." When the gun stopped working altogether, the crew began to haul the rubber dinghies out of the deck containers to have them ready for abandoning ship.

At this point Thienemann could see the tanker sinking and several dinghies drifting on the water close by. More bombs spewed the water where the ship had disappeared. "We don't see any survivors now," he wrote. Then, as though there were no end to the barrage, a new series of blasts came, some quite close to the boat. As the bombs rained down, ripping the sea everywhere, Thienemann fired his two-centimeter antiaircraft guns at the planes flying over them. "We are finding pieces of bombs on the bridge and tower, and we figure they are 500-kilo [one-thousand-pound] bombs." He was right—they were.

Thienemann noted in his log that the behavior of the crew was quite good during the battle. They had been able to fire about a hundred shells with the big gun and six hundred shots with the antiaircraft guns, hitting several planes with their flak.

At 12:20 A.M. silence prevailed, and as German rescue boats searched the wreckage-filled waters, the crew of U-682 started cleaning up their littered deck. Attempts to contact U-735, out for schnorkeling maneuvers that day, brought no response. U-682, severely damaged and unable to make a rapid escape, cut off her anchor with a blowtorch and headed into port.

Two hours later, when the boat had tied up in Horten harbor, the commander assessed his damage: water was pouring into the forward torpedo room at the rate of four to five tons per hour; tubes one through five were completely out of alignment and leaking; and port diving cell five had burst from top to bottom. At any rate, the engines and batteries were in fairly good shape.

In dry dock the next few days for repairs, U-682's good periscope was given to a new boat, U-1018, in exchange for their useless one, since Thienemann's battered craft was now headed home. And so, with a bent bow, four torpedoes stuck in the tubes (disarmed except for one), extra diesel fuel removed, and a nonfunctional periscope, U-682 departed on 3 January 1945. Grateful to be alive, the entire crew made it back to Kiel at midnight on 5 January. Two months later at the Hamburg shipyards, U-682 was completely wrecked by a massive air attack.[1]

U-682 had managed to escape Norway, but the second U-boat in Oslo Fjord experienced a different fate. "We were at Horten . . . to test our new schnorkel," recalled Herbert Hermann of U-735, under the command of Hans-Joachim Börner. "On the morning of 28 December 1944 we sailed out on a test cruise, came in about 6:00 P.M. and were searching for a suitable place to drop anchor. Our long delay ultimately became our doom."

Making schnorkel test runs that day, U-735 had lost a great deal of

John Whiteley,
RAF captain
and pilot

compressed air. While Hermann and other crew members worked to
replace air supplies, ten of his comrades went ashore to take a break.
It was to be a trip that saved their lives.

The crew's attempts to refurbish the boat's air were hindered by
the malfunctioning of the diesel compressor, forcing the mechanics to

use a slower electric compressor. "It took about three hours to reach a reasonable pressure in the compressed air bottles. This lasted until 9:30 P.M., when we heard the air raid siren."

"Now things became urgent. The commander ordered us to drop anchor and save the little air we had." When Börner instructed the engineer to get the diesels ready for starting, low air pressure made it impossible, and at the same time, the crew heard the far-away drone of planes. As a last resort, the chief engineer transferred compressed air from the torpedoes to the diesel air bottles, and at 11:30 the engines were ready to go.

During their delay, the wireless operator was continuously reporting large numbers of bombers over Horten Fjord. Börner shouted orders to sail and for the gun crew to man the deck guns. "All men stood by awaiting further orders," said Hermann. "At this time I was stationed in the central control room, where I could observe everything that went on."

U-735's diesels, now functioning, propelled the boat on a course away from the center of the fjord just as the first bombs erupted around them. Börner immediately ordered a zigzag course, but as the boat began to turn, an explosion hit nearby, throwing a fountain of water over the sub, across the conning tower, and down the hatch. One of the gunners on deck was thrown overboard, and the captain yelled for a diving plane operator to take his place.

"I took the planesman's station at the rudder, which lasted only a short time, as a terrible detonation threw me against the wall of the tower. It didn't knock me out, but I was bruised up. My immediate impression was that the boat had taken a direct hit, and this turned out to be true."

Heinz Meier, engine mechanic, came staggering into the control compartment, badly wounded. "Water in the engine room!" he shouted. Smashed by the bomb in the diesel area, the boat was sagging steeply at the stern, making pumping impossible. Commander Börner, seeing a disastrous situation, ordered everyone on deck and off the boat.

"Everybody jumped overboard, as we were heading down fast. It all happened within one minute. My first thought was to distance myself from the sinking boat, so I would not be pulled under by the suction."

"I was dressed very warmly, wearing a turtleneck pullover, thick underwear, leather gear, and a life preserver. The most important thing was not to make any swimming motions, because that would allow the ice-cold water to get near my skin. When I jumped off the boat, my watch stopped, and it seemed as though I was in the water for a very long time. I estimate I waited for about thirty minutes."

Floating in the icy sea, Herbert had no thoughts of dying, confident that help would come in time. The bombing had ceased, and all was deadly quiet, completely dark. "There were no flares or markers in sight. All I heard were yells and cries for help in the blackness."

As he waited, motionless, Hermann could see spotlights in the distance start to blink and wheel in a circular pattern. "Whenever the light came close to me, I raised my arm, then finally the beam caught me." At last one of several German search boats arrived and pulled Herbert Hermann from the water, the only crew member found alive from U-735.

After the air raid, diving crews recovered twenty-six bodies from the submarine; twelve more were missing, and ten crewmen had gone to shore. Shortly thereafter, on 5 January 1945 at the war cemetery in Oslo, the men of U-735 were buried, the same day that U-682 dragged back into Kiel.[2]

When Herbert Hermann and the thirty-one crew members of U-682 greeted their RAF guests a half century later, they learned the story of the air raid from the British point of view. John Whiteley remembered it well.

"I was based at Royal Air Force, Strubby, a bomber airfield near Mablethorpe, a small seaside resort on the east coast, and the afternoon of 28 December I was told that I and four other crews had been selected for operations that night." Whiteley, as pilot and captain of Lancaster Squadron PG-H, summoned his men to the operations room at 3:00 P.M. to get instructions. Knowing that a limited number of aircraft would be used, as well as a certain type of armor-piercing bomb, Whiteley suspected they would be going on a special mission.

Herbert Hermann

The station commander pulled back a curtain covering a large map and pointed out their destination: Oslo Fjord near Horten, Norway, twenty miles south of the city of Oslo. After explaining that the mission would include sixty-seven Lancaster bombers with leading Pathfinders, he outlined their routes to and from the target and described the tactics to be used. A short briefing from the intelligence officer gave them scant information about German flak, searchlights, or possible night fighters, and the meteorological officer predicted clear skies over the North Sea, explaining that clouds would be building over the mainland of Norway. With airborne radar, the leading Pathfinders could locate the unseen targets and drop colored marker flares to show the Lancaster crews where to unload their bombs.

"Our primary objective for the Horten operation was destroying the German light cruiser *Köln*, believed to be in the Oslo Fjord," said Whiteley, "but whose exact position was unknown." Anxious to eliminate the cruiser's threatening presence in the Atlantic, the Royal Navy had asked the RAF to put her out of action. If the pilots could not locate the *Köln,* they were to bomb any German merchant vessels they saw.

Three hours before takeoff, the pilots grabbed large flasks of coffee and supplies of sandwiches, as well as money belts and escape packs in case they were shot down. Pathfinder crew member R. E. N. Porrett said his pack included rations, fishing lines, tiny compasses, flare matches, revival drugs, cigarettes, maps, and small files to aid escape.[3]

"I took off at 1950 hours and flew on a compass course roughly northeast, at a height of one thousand feet above the North Sea, in order to avoid being picked up by German radar, until we had almost reached Norway," Whitely continued. About ten minutes before the squadron arrived at the southern side of the fjord, Whiteley's group started a rapid climb at a thousand feet per minute, up to their operational height of seventy-five-hundred feet. "The next twenty-five minutes or so we spent flying up and down the fjord looking for the *Köln,* but without success. As we passed Horten, on our port side . . . it was quite obvious from the none-too-friendly reception we received that there was German shipping in the harbour." Antiaircraft flak spewed upward around them, fortunately missing Whiteley's plane.

In one of the leading Pathfinders, bomb aimer Porrett, watching his radar screen, picked up Horten, and as they flew closer, he saw two small blips of light indicating a couple of fairly large ships, possibly the cruisers *Köln* and *Emden.* Realizing that his red marker had to be accurate, Porrett concentrated on perfect timing, as a few seconds could throw everything off. The main squadron had only three minutes to do its job. "Bombs gone!" shouted Porrett, banging the marker release switch. He watched the marker dropping down toward the thick cloud layer below; then "a great red glare lit the clouds . . . and we made a tight climbing turn to get above the Lancasters as they came in. We could see them as sharp silhouettes against the glare of the markers on the clouds, perfect targets for night fighters. The flak was coming up thick and fast now, meaning that there were no night fighters in the vicinity."

Captain John Whiteley (center) with the crew of his RAF Lancaster bomber. Crewmates include John Hurst, Jim Garrett, Bill Adams, Jock Joughin, Larry Rigden, and Freddie Jones.

Porrett emerged from his cramped quarters, walked into the main cockpit, and looked out the canopy at an unforgettable scene: "The marker threw out bright red festoons of fire as it drifted lazily downwind with the markers dropped by other Pathfinders, and a row of white flares acted as guides for the aircraft pouring in. Great flashes of light indicated the explosions of bombs, and vivid splotches of flame betrayed the bursting shells sent up by the enemy." Tracer shells appeared as "tiny coloured balls of light that . . . appeared to float gently upward, but as they came on a level with us, gathered speed and burst in angry splotches." Occasionally a "spoof" popped with multicolored lights, intended to mimic an aircraft going down in flames.

Whiteley's bomb aimer informed him that he had spotted a ship below and instructed the captain to direct the plane so that he could keep the target in his bombsight. He then told Whiteley to open the bomb doors and at the right second released seven one-thousand-pound blockbusters. Whitely turned, made a second run, and dropped the rest of the load at 11:54 P.M. "I cannot remember seeing another Lancaster over Horten," the captain noted. Scheduled to arrive at varying times, the planes had flown in groups so as not to appear in one bunch. "The only sound I heard was the purr of my own Rolls Royce Merlin engines. . . . and from a height of seventy-five-hundred feet, we did not hear or feel the explosions."

"My immediate job now was to get away from Horten as quickly as possible, because the Germans were being particularly unfriendly!" Dropping the plane to a thousand feet, Whiteley flew back to Strubby, landing at 2:30 A.M. on 29 December 1944. "We had been airborne for six hours and forty minutes."

Shortly after the Lancasters landed, a WAAF intelligence officer held a debriefing. She asked the crews about weather over Horten, German night fighters, flak, searchlights, and whether they had seen any aircraft shot down. "Why were you not able to find the *Köln?*" she demanded, and, "Did you make a thorough search of the Oslo Fjord?" By then it was three in the morning, and "bearing in mind that I had been in the pilot's seat for at least half an hour before take-off and fifteen minutes after landing, and having flown the Lancaster for six hours and forty minutes without the use of an automatic pilot, I was feeling somewhat irritable and rather hungry," said the captain. "When she asked my bomb aimer if he could tell her the number of masts on each ship we had bombed, this rather stupid question was too much for him. His reply went something like this: 'Madam, if we had been a hundred feet lower, I could have given you the bloody names of the ships!'"

Debriefing for Porrett and his crew was followed by an operational supper, "steak and eggs as always—a rare delicacy in those days," he said. The Pathfinder crew, having observed a huge glare on the cloud tops evidently caused by bomb fires, considered their mission a success.

Fifty years later Whiteley and the other Lancaster crew members were surprised to learn that two German U-boats had been among their targets at Horten. "Until I read my 'Squadron Association Bulletin' for September 1993, I had no idea that U-boats were present in the fjord."[4]

At the 1994 reunion of RAF pilots and U-boatmen, Commander Sven Thienemann explained that the bomber pilots had not been able to find the *Köln* because the German navy had hidden her in a remote inlet on the Swedish side of Oslo Fjord. The *Köln's* war diary revealed that the cruiser had dropped anchor at Horten roadstead on 13 December, where she met the tanker *Udvär*, and the two ships lined up side by side to transfer fuel.

Before transferring could start, an air raid siren began to wail and brilliant lights from marker bombs illuminated the ships. The *Udvär* immediately cast off and the *Köln* fired her antiaircraft guns. Bomb after bomb exploded close to the cruiser, accompanied by machine-gun fire—a twenty-minute raid that damaged the antiaircraft guns and diesel engines, but caused no crew injuries or deaths.

After quick repairs, the *Köln* weighed anchor and left Horten roadstead. Fifteen days later, on 28 December, when RAF bombers again tried to destroy the cruiser, she had retreated to the far side of Jeloya Island, close to the opposite shore of the fjord. An hour and fifteen minutes after she arrived, at 8:00 P.M., an air raid warning screamed, and the crew watched as a bomber was shot down over Horten. A second warning sounded, and twenty Lancasters roared over the ship, as the *Köln* fired her antiaircraft guns. Red and green markers brightened the waters, followed by bomb bursts, some around Horten, some near Jeloya Island, but no impacts came near the cruiser. Then at 11:51 a Pathfinder dropped markers three hundred feet from the *Köln*. In a blaze of light the captain weighed anchor as quickly as possible and moved his vessel northward through an extremely narrow passage to Drobak, where he anchored.[5]

Many years later, when the five Lancaster pilots asked U-682 commander Thienemann to explain what happened to the *Köln*, he showed them her secret location on a wartime chart. This mystery settled, the old enemies sat around the hotel bar sipping German beer and exchanging reminiscences of their December encounter. Several days later, after a convivial dinner, Lancaster pilot Tom Gatfield marched out wearing his old leather flight cap and gas mask, and U-682 crewman Paul Herden appeared in his ancient skintight sailor's suit, to the wild applause of all. At the end of the evening, John Whiteley, medal-winning RAF captain, and Herbert Hermann, single survivor from the sinking of U-753, looked at each other for a few seconds, then shook hands.

13   Oskar Kusch, U-154

■■

"As I remember," said Paul Otto, crew member of U-154, "Oskar was blonde, strongly built, a Germanic type, and a very good sportsman. He was somewhat quiet and serious, unlike most of us." Heinrich Lüdemann recalled that Kusch was a Catholic and had kept a small crucifix on the wall of his quarters, as well as a miniature altar that opened up to show the Last Supper. Victor Nonn remembered his commander as "a quiet friend who could express his opinions well." To Heinz Wolff, Oskar was extremely intelligent, sensible, and never standoffish. "I liked him, and I was very sad about what happened later."

■■

Born in Berlin in 1918, handsome young Oskar Kusch spent a few years in the Hitler Youth, and at age seventeen decided to leave the organization. Oskar entered the German navy in 1937 as an officer-cadet, was sent to submarine service three years later, and by February 1943 had made his way up the ladder to become commander of U-154. On Kusch's first enemy patrol in May through June of that year, he sank two ships and torpedoed two more near the coast of Brazil, winning Iron Crosses Second and First Class. In November and December his second mission to the waters off French Guiana brought no successes, but by that time U-boat effectiveness was greatly dimin-

Oskar Kusch
Heinz Kuhlmann

ished by Allied destroyers and aircraft using radar, and only one in seven submarines was returning.

On U-154 the top members of the crew were Dr. Ulrich Abel (first watch officer), Heinrich Meyer (second watch officer), Chief Engineer Kurt Druschel, and a physician, Dr. Nothdurft. Although Kusch had never joined the National Socialist Party, some of his higher staff were ardent members, and they observed their commander's every word and action. When U-154 arrived in France after her second patrol, Ulrich Abel reported his commander to naval authorities for "subversion of the military" and "listening to foreign radio stations."

As is typical of every despot, Hitler demanded unquestioning obedience and worship from every man, woman, and child in the country. However, in the first years of the war, the German navy had managed to stay clear of party dogma, and U-boat officers usually shared their opinions freely while at sea. Unfortunately, Oskar Kusch did not get away with it.

Abel and Druschel testified at Kusch's secret court-martial in Kiel that one of the first things Oskar Kusch did upon taking command of his boat was to ask the two of them to relocate the portrait of Hitler in the officers mess because Kusch did not want to have any "idol worshipping." Kusch requested that they hang a seascape he had painted in its place, and the two officers did as they were told, but they moved the portrait to another spot in the room.

Conversations in the officers mess were carefully monitored by all the officers, and they reported Kusch had made many remarks to the effect that "only Hitler's fall and the end of the National Socialist Party could bring peace to the German people and give Germany cultural development." They went on to say that Kusch expressed the view that the population was suffering badly under the government's pressure and needed to overthrow the regime, so that other countries could make peace with Germany.

Another unforgivable and illegal statement, they swore, came from the commander when he announced he did not believe in the "final victory" Hitler was proclaiming. He thought the enemy's dominance was increasing, for their raw material sources had grown larger. To this Abel argued that the Germans had many secret projects that could win the war, but Kusch replied, "You may think so, and I hope it is true, but I do not believe it."

During the second enemy patrol Kusch was talking to the boat's physician, Dr. Nothdurft, and asked him why he thought they were fighting, but he answered the question himself: "Only because this megalomaniac wants to swallow the whole of Europe. Why don't we stop the war?"

Once Kusch told his men a silly joke, and without his knowledge they published it in the boat's newsletter. In court the joke was repeated as evidence: "Question: What's the similarity between the German people and a tapeworm? Answer: They are both surrounded by brown stuff and both are in serious danger of being killed."

Many conversations in the officers mess, according to the witnesses, centered around Hitler and the Nazi Party. Kusch called the fuehrer a crazy utopianist and said he had heard from people close to Hitler that the fuehrer sometimes had seizures, falling to the floor, writhing around, and tearing curtains off the windows. Kusch thought that the dictator had wanted to make war since the day he came to power in 1933.

Furthermore, continued the witnesses, Kusch advised them that they should not believe any of the propaganda they heard, that they ought to make up their own minds. For instance, slanted news broadcasts were proclaiming that Allied bombs were intended to kill innocent civilians, but Kusch believed that they couldn't help hitting people. Abel and Druschel had argued that they thought all the Jewish people in every land were going to join forces and try to rule the world and that all Freemasons were dangerous, and to that Kusch replied that he thought the power of those groups was grossly overestimated. As to the *BdU*'s radio messages to the U-boats (code-named Rose), encouraging them to keep fighting in spite of all odds, Kusch believed these messages were "a slavery whip, to keep us going on and on."

Listening to foreign radio broadcasts by U-boat commanders was allowed, but only to obtain information about their situation. Kusch was known to have tuned in to stations in Mexico City and New York and to have shared the reports with his officers, telling them that what he had heard was completely different from the German news and that they should be aware of it.

Abel and Druschel made excellent impressions on the court and sounded believable. Others who testified against Kusch were Second Watch Officer Heinrich Meyer and some of the other crew members, who stressed that Kusch's words were exactly as they remembered. However, Oskar Kusch asserted they had twisted and exaggerated his words at times when he was merely trying to make them think and to realize that Germany had problems to solve.

Kusch's defense counsel pointed out that he had been a fine naval officer with willingness to fight, had a good record of sinkings, and had been awarded two Iron Crosses. "Kusch gave his comments in the officers mess only to make the conversation a little more interesting," counsel pointed out. The defense admitted that the commander had broken two laws by criticizing the military regime and by listening to foreign radio broadcasts, but that he had expressed his opinions in private and never intended to undermine crew morale.

After listening to both sides, Chief Judge Karl-Heinrich Hagemann came to the conclusion that Oskar Kusch was guilty of subversion of the military and of illegally listening to foreign news, and furthermore, that he had expressed his opinions "in public, because the U-boat was a public place, where Kusch's comments were overheard by the cook and the hydrophone operator." In the cramped quarters of a U-boat, the officers took their meals in the midsection passageway, between the sound room and the galley.

The judge also wrote in his summary that the defendant had shown "liberal tendencies" as a young man by getting out of the Hitler Youth. Later, when Kusch's officers on the boat had tried to change his mind by arguing with him, the commander refused to budge. The judge did admit that Kusch had been an honorable and successful officer, but Hagemann thought Kusch's record did not excuse him from his major crimes. As punishment for listening to foreign radio stations, the judge gave Kusch one year of prison, and for military subversion, death. All civil privileges would be lost for life.

When given a chance to ask for clemency, Kusch refused. True to his Catholic religion and moral principles, the courageous commander chose to die. Sentencing took place on 26 January 1944 and less than four months later, on 12 May, a firing squad shot Oskar Kusch to death.

The same day as the execution, the court wrote a letter to Heinz Kusch, Oskar's father, with the word "*Geheim!*" (secret) stamped in large letters across the top. It stated that because of Kusch's "crimes," he had been court-martialed in January and executed on 12 May. "Death notices or obituaries in any newspapers, magazines, and so on, are forbidden. Signed, J. A. Meinert, Navy Staff Judge."

In Kiel, where Oskar Kusch was shot, no news of his trial or death appeared in the local paper, and no records ever have been found concerning the details of his execution. On 21 January the command of U-154 went to Gerth Gemeiner, and the boat was sunk on her next mission.

"I was the last crew member to say good-bye to Oskar Kusch," recalled Heinz Kuhlmann, "and that was January 1943. In July 1944 I was sent to a training course in Bremerhaven, and there I found out that Kusch had been shot because of cowardice before the enemy." For Kuhlmann, the news came as a shock. "All of us in the crew, except the officers, thought we had an outstanding commander, both as a soldier and as a human being."[1]

When the Allied Control Commission signed a law in December 1945 to punish all persons guilty of war crimes, Oskar Kusch's father felt he now had a basis for action against the court-martial judges. On 9 May 1946 Heinz Kusch filed charges of murder in the high court at Kiel against Chief Judge Hagemann and his two assistant judges, and against Abel, Druschel, Dr. Nothdurft, and two other military court officials. In the beginning, Herr Kusch asked the prosecutor to arrest Hagemann, but the court denied the request, stating that a high degree of guilt for murder could not be proven. One of the assistant judges, a former submarine commander, was being held in a British prison camp at the time, and the hearings were delayed until 1947. When the matter finally came into court, it was decided that the three judges had not acted outside the law.

Then in May 1949 Judge Hagemann was accused of "crime against civil rights" for sentencing U-boat commander Oskar Kusch to death. When Hagemann received a "not guilty" verdict, the prosecutor objected, sending the case to a higher court, and in September 1950 the case was retried in Kiel. Hagemann admitted that he had condemned Kusch, but that he had followed the military law that a soldier was supposed to obey all orders, and furthermore, Kusch had showed no signs of regret. Again, the court judged Hagemann not guilty for the same reasons, saying that a commander was prohibited from undermining the morale of his men, a law that remained in effect in 1950.

Eighteen years later, between 1968 and 1970, German submarine veterans installed handsome bronze tablets on the walls of the U-boat memorial at Möltenort showing the names of all commanders and crew members who died in World War II. The name of *Oberleutnant zur See* Oskar Kusch headed the listing for U-154 as commander, restoring his place with his comrades and in history as a valiant soldier who met death courageously.[2]

14   Siegfried Koitschka, U-616

■■

The story of U-616 came to me by way of correspondence from Dr. Koitschka, who ended each letter with, "Calm seas and gentle winds, Siegfried Koitschka." Any U-boat commander who lived through World War II has a right to calm seas for the rest of his life. Koitschka, born in 1917, joined the Reich work corps in October 1936 and in 1937 signed up with the navy. At the end of 1940 he served as second and first watch officer on U-552 with the well-known Erich Topp, then went on to command U-7, a training boat. In October 1942 Kapitän-leutnant Koitschka was assigned to U-616 and became a successful commander, making eight patrols in the Mediterranean at a time when the odds were totally against him.

■■

Out of six missions with Erich Topp, one particular incident stood out in Koitschka's memory. In 1941 Topp, in U-552, crossed the path of "a very big steamer" at a distance of about two thousand meters and found himself in an excellent position for attacking. "Topp was a crack shot," Koitschka declared, "and he fired three torpedoes." When all three missed the target, Koitschka and the rest of the crew fumed about it for a while and attributed the failure to bad luck. However, the German torpedoes in those days were known to be unreliable in many cases.

Later, when the U-boat reached port, they learned more about the incident. "The name of the ship was the *Ile de France*, and the passengers were about two thousand children bound from England to Canada." For unknown reasons the British had not registered the voyage with a central agency in Switzerland, so that the great ship could safely travel unescorted. "Without a doubt, we were glad our torpedoes missed. It is unimaginable what would have happened. The big thumb of God lay between the *Ile de France* and us."

U-552's crest, a "serious-looking red devil holding a torch," looked like a lean, mean, Olympic runner with horns, hooves, and a long tail. "When we brought U-616 into service in October 1943, we felt that we would be losing the war in the not-too-distant future. There was no choice other than cynical heroism, so we created our own little red devil." Armed with a big black pistol, Koitschka's short, pudgy character, with one hand on his hip and a leer on his face, was "a mésalliance between the imperious devil of U-552 and a French prostitute of Toulon."

For his second patrol in U-616, Koitschka was to operate in the Mediterranean out of the U-boat base at La Spezia, Italy, but in order to do so, he had to sneak through the narrow entryway at Gibraltar, where warships and aircraft swarmed. Successful in this harrowing enterprise, Koitschka arrived at his new port in Italy. (Between September 1943 and May 1944, twenty-seven U-boats attempted to break through the heavily guarded Straits: fourteen succeeded, seven were sunk, and the remaining six turned back.)

From La Spezia, Koitschka sailed forth in August 1943, patrolling for convoys—all well protected by fast escorts—and after three weeks at sea he received orders to head for another U-boat base at Toulon, between Nice and Marseilles. The Allies, on 10 July, had landed on Sicily, and Italy would fall by 3 September. The time had come to move the U-boats out of Italy and into France.

"When we arrived at the approximate vicinity of the harbor early one morning there was fog everywhere," said Koitschka, "and we could not find any landmarks." During their trip through the Mediterranean the navigator had been unable to calculate positions from the stars or sun because the sky was cloudy and enemy planes often forced

Siegfried Koitschka

them to travel underwater. The boat's present location off the coast of France had been gained from dead reckoning. "There was deviation from the course by wind and sea, and our reckoning was not exact."

So the crew waited impatiently for the fog bank to lift, but nothing happened. Suddenly they heard noises of a diesel engine, and a few minutes later a fishing boat appeared on the scene. "We trained our four-barreled antiaircraft gun on the fishermen, who felt they were at death's door and flung up their arms. Our second officer yelled through a megaphone in French: '*Où est le port de Toulon?*' [Where is the port of Toulon?] With that, the fishermen's faces relaxed, and they called, pointing in the direction they had come from, '*Ici.*' [Over here.]"

"We responded very politely, 'Merci, messieurs!' and turned our gun back." U-616 started forward through the heavy mist, and after a short trip arrived at the harbor entry of Toulon. Later, Koitschka reported details of the patrol to naval headquarters in Berlin. "*Gross-admiral* Dönitz looked at me in an expression halfway between seriousness and a grin and said, 'Lousy navigation.'"

In September, U-616 was operating in the Gulf of Salerno, south of Naples. "It was a typical Mediterranean night—misty, with a sea as smooth as a duck pond. Suddenly the radioman reported that our position had been fixed by radar." Shortly afterward, Koitschka heard a destroyer in his wake about three thousand yards away, closing in rapidly. "We feared that they were about to depth charge us and kill us, and we were in a calamitous situation. With the destroyer behind us, showing her smallest silhouette, there was no way to hit her with a conventional torpedo. That was called 'position zero.'" Then they remembered something that might be their salvation.

"In Toulon we had taken aboard a *Zaunkönig* [acoustic torpedo] that we had been ordered to test. It was the first one, and we did not trust it, but we had the fish in tube five in the stern, ready to go." Koitschka ordered, "Fire!" and the torpedo zipped off, with everyone doubting the results.

"At four minutes and fifteen seconds, we saw several huge jets of flame, then a two-hundred-meter-high column of smoke." After a few minutes of puzzling, the crew realized that their torpedo had ignited the armed depth charges carried by the ship, causing the strange flames and billowing smoke. "It was a terrible sight. The ship was the U.S. destroyer *Buck,* and eleven officers and 150 men were killed by their own war weapons."

In December of 1943 Koitschka's boat had been assigned to an area of the Mediterranean near the toe of the Italian boot. "We were operating not far from the volcano Stromboli, which was spitting out a column of smoke every few minutes. It was a very nice sight through the periscope—the blue sky, the calm sea, the puffing Stromboli." After enjoying this "wonderful area," Koitschka decided to take a look all around with his periscope. "I was really alarmed when I saw a gray wall with the number H26. I was sailing alongside a grown-up British destroyer." Through the eyepiece Koitschka could see a sailor practicing knee bends near the bulwark.

Within seconds the destroyer crew spotted their friendly escort and let loose a volley of depth charges. "But we were sailing so close together that the canisters hummed over us and caused no serious harm. I was not able to fire any torpedoes, so I dove as quickly as I could. The destroyer left as fast as possible, too."

To relieve the horrors of battle and to "prevent the sailors from getting too wild and having trouble with the military police," Koitschka used the old navy remedy, a lavish party in home port. Every crew member was to show up well shaven, hair neatly cut, and wearing his best navy dress uniform. "There was lots of food," said the commander, "and of course *quantities* of beer. Our purpose was accomplished, because the sailors were destroyed for three days, and after that their behavior was satisfactory."

On one occasion, after a princely dinner, the crew put on a show, directed by the quartermaster. A sailor named Kasperzak came out dressed as a Spanish bullfighter, with black toreador pants, black hat, and red jacket with gold buttons. Armed with an unloaded tommy gun, the "pistolero" blasted away at an empty bottle of champagne on a desk, assuming various contorted positions—firing between his legs, over his shoulder, and in other absurd ways.

In front of the curtain sat the desk with bottle, but hidden behind the curtain was the quartermaster, holding a popgun in one hand and a hammer in the other. While the pistolero pretended to fire his tommy gun, the quartermaster popped his toy pistol and quickly hit the bottle through the curtain so that it fell over (the wrong direction). This uproarious entertainment went on for half an hour, loudly applauded by the beer–happy audience, but near the end of the act a slight mishap occurred. "While aiming over his left shoulder in the backward position, the pistolero pinched his ear with the tommy gun breech, causing blood to run, so he yelled, 'Stop this damned shit-shooting.'" However, the quartermaster emerged from behind the curtain, calmed him down, and the show went on.

By the time Koitschka went out on his eighth patrol in the Mediterranean, the Allied commanders had organized the "Swamp Operation." By keeping U-boats submerged at great depths for a prolonged time, they would be able to starve the boats of air supplies and battery power, force them to the surface, and then destroy them. By this means they intended to wipe out every last U-boat in the Mediterranean.

Some of these antisubmarine operations required many warships, planes, and considerable time, but they paid off. Code-named Monstrous, one particular Swamp operation set the record for World War II, lasting over three days.

"In May 1944," said Koitschka, "we were sailing along the African coast one night at a depth of one hundred feet when the hydrophone man reported low noises. I ordered the boat to surface, and we were damned surprised to find ourselves right in the midst of a huge convoy." In the bright moonlight they could see ships in front of them, behind, and to the right and left. Unfortunately, the ship lookouts spotted U-616 as well and let loose a barrage of gunfire. "What to do now? We had to disappear fast, but before we did that, we fired two acoustic torpedoes, and both of them hit." He had sunk the *G. D. Walden* and the *Fort Fidler*.

Seven destroyers, along with Air Squadron 400, set out to find Koitschka and arrived on the scene to discover another destroyer already delivering depth charges. This armada of eight warships plowed up and down, intent upon catching the deep-sea predator, until one of the planes reported a radar contact thirty miles westward. To this point they raced, then spent an entire day roving the area, listening. Early that evening another plane made radar contact well to the north of the search area, signaling the warships with flares and bringing forth yet another charge toward the fleeing fox. The *Ellyson* threw some depth charges, then lost contact, but the next morning a long oil slick lay on the surface, indicating that their quarry was wounded.

For two more days and nights the great search and bombardment continued, and then one of the planes spotted Koitschka's boat speeding along on the surface about thirty miles from the destroyers. Again the armada charged forward, found the U-boat, flashed a searchlight on it, and fired a few rounds before U-616 crash-dived. Four of the destroyers spent all night throwing depth charges at Koitschka, who then finally gave up.[1]

"With the batteries exhausted and all lights out, it seemed as though the end had come," wrote Koitschka. "We surfaced and saw the destroyers circled around us, shooting out of all buttonholes like a fire brigade." Within seconds the crew abandoned the boat, leaving Chief Engineer Nieke and Control Room Mate Gruber to open the diving tank valves, letting water into the tanks to cause sinking. At this point the two men and Koitschka jumped overboard to join the others swimming in the Mediterranean. When the destroyers saw that the survivors were struggling in the water and that their boat had gone under, they ended the barrage.

The *Ellyson* and the *Rodman* fished the entire crew out of the water and transferred them to Mers el Kebir, Algeria. "A fortnight later we became guests of the United States in the military jail in Norfolk, then we went to camps in Mississippi, Oklahoma, Texas, and Arkansas." In September 1997, fifty-three years later, Koitschka and friends attended their first reunion with the crews of the *Rodman* and *Ellyson* in Atlantic City and Washington. "We spent some great hours with them—indeed, we became good friends—friends you can trust. The ceremony for the deceased crew members of the *Ellyson* was very impressive and touched us to the heart."[2]

15

Hans Georg Hess, U-995

■■

*U-995, one of two restored German submarines in the world, sits on
the beach at Laboe, Germany, near the towering navy war monument.
Inside the control room former commander Hess tells a group of friends
about life in a U-boat. With a background of six successful patrols on
U-995 in 1944 and 1945 and a Knight's Cross for outstanding performance, he knows his subject well. Delighted with the audience, Hans
Georg steers the group through "his" boat, describing the intricate
mechanisms, engines, torpedo tubes, and living arrangements. "Each
valve handle," he points out, "has a different shape so that it can be
identified in the dark." We are spellbound listening to him—he is still
the commander after fifty years.*

■■

Early in his navy career, *Oberleutnant zur See* Hess served as second
and first watch officer on U-466 with *Kapitänleutnant* Gerd Thäter.
In the summer of 1942, before air attacks were a major hazard, the
men sometimes went swimming in the Atlantic. One peaceful afternoon as Hess and his friends were splashing in the dark blue water
near the Azores, they noticed several sea turtles swimming below them.
"I thought we should capture one of them, because turtle soup was a
delicacy."

Hans Georg had heard it was important to catch a turtle just after
sundown, so the men reboarded the boat and waited until the proper

Hans Georg Hess

time. As the sun was disappearing, Commander Thäter ordered slow speed and the U-boat crept forward. "Then we stopped the engines and drifted close to the turtles so as not to disturb them." A crew member jumped overboard with a rope and swam to one of the large creatures, turned it upside down, and tied the rope to its leg. He then pulled the turtle to the boat, and the cook loaded it onto the marine deck.

"The cook had never slaughtered an animal in his life," Hess went on, "but he finally succeeded, carefully cutting the meat into pieces for the soup. Some of us cleaned the shell, and we gave it to the first watch officer as a trophy to take home."

Hans Georg took it upon himself to explain to the crew that turtle soup was a special treat, because he knew the men had never heard of it and would not want to try it. "So I, like Frederick the Great, went from compartment to compartment telling them all that the soup was delicious, taking sips, and urging them to eat it. I had to motivate them."

In early 1944 Hess left U-466 to attend captains school in Neustadt and Gotenhafen for three months. Then in October of that year, the lanky young man, a mere twenty-one years old, was given command of U-995. Realizing that he would have to deal with a tough, older, and more seasoned crew, he worried about how to instill respect in them. "I will not try to be a buddy," he vowed. He also determined to use some subtlety, by being strictly proper in his attire. Traditionally, the commander wore a regulation white officer's cap; however, most of the captains put a slight fold in the upper part so as to look more dashing. Not Hess. "I made my first visit on board wearing my cap the correct way." And apparently this strategy worked, judging by the young leader's successes on almost every patrol.

In mid-October 1944 Kiel, Stuttgart, Munich and Innsbruck had been heavily bombed, Hamburg was devastated, the British had made it to the lower Rhine, and the Americans had arrived in Aachen. With little hope of success, U-995 took off from Narvik, near the northernmost tip of Norway, to patrol the Barents Sea above Norway and Finland. U-995 spotted a large convoy headed toward Murmansk, a strategically important port on the western edge of Russia, near Finland. Britain and the United States were shipping crucial war supplies to this destination on what was then called "The Murmansk Run," a hazard-laden trip. It was the only Russian port ice-free all year and had rail connections to Leningrad.

Hess could see a group of planes flying above the convoy and an aircraft carrier alongside, and he conjectured there were probably more warships at the rear. With the assumed safety of distance, he drove the boat on the surface at full speed for five miles, then submerged and attempted to get within firing distance, but the convoy zigzagged away, and U-995 could not catch up. "For a short while the next day I saw smoke trails on the horizon, but I could not make contact with the convoy a second time."

Two weeks later U-995 and several other U-boats were following a convoy when they heard the *ping* of sonar hitting them one night. Hess cautiously went up to periscope depth and peered through the eyepiece, where he barely made out the silhouette of a destroyer about two miles away, then three more escorts. "It was apparently a submarine raiding party," observed Hess. Flares from four escorts looped through the night skies and drifted downward, illuminating the warships as though on a stage. It was midnight. Hess unleashed one "eel," then another. "As I drove the boat down at full speed, the boom of a hit rumbled nearby. Hydroplane operator Alfred Ottine reported hearing only three screw noises, and two detonations followed, therefore, it can be assumed that even the other 'tin fish' has reached its target." For the rest of the night the crew endured a nerve-wracking attack, lashed and shaken by a barrage of explosions. Just before air supplies in the sub were about to run out, the destroyers departed and U-995 surfaced.

When U-995 had crash-dived the first time, there was an unexpected racket inside the boat. A prized barrel of kippered herrings, lashed to a ladder in the forward torpedo compartment, broke loose, and smashed into the torpedo tubes. Pickled herrings exploded all over the men's bunks, food supplies, floors—the entire room. Even though the crew thoroughly scrubbed the disaster area, the reek of fish assailed their noses for the rest of the voyage. "The torpedo tubes had never been so spotless," chuckled Hess.

Times were bad for German subs: their glory days were over, and most were meeting a watery death. Convoy protection, with great numbers of cruisers and escort ships, made U-boat attacks extremely difficult; however, Hess managed to hit a merchant ship in convoy on 4 December. Shortly afterward, U-995 let loose a torpedo that became a dreaded "circle runner": instead of heading straight for the enemy, it turned and headed back toward the U-boat. "We could tell by the noise. After it exited the tubes and became quiet, the noise started to get louder. We killed the engines and waited with baited breath for a few terrifying minutes until we heard it explode some distance away. We did not want to get in its path."

Twenty-four hours later, on 5 December, the young commander rammed a Russian fishing vessel, although a U-boat was not designed for ramming. "We took a chance that it could damage our rudders, but we got away with it. Before we could back off, one of the Russians jumped from his deck over onto ours, and we allowed him to remain on U-995."

Shortly afterward, the hydrophone operator picked up the sound of pistons forty miles away, and U-995 went in pursuit. In the darkness Hess torpedoed a Soviet auxiliary minesweeper, and as the boat sank he told the crew: "We are not going to dive; I want to save all the survivors I can. Move forward slowly, and three men go to the forecastle with heavy lines." Wireless operator Richard Schwedhelm remembered that they picked up just one Russian, who was swimming for his life, close to the boat. "Our deckhands took good care of him, and he recovered well. He was only seventeen years old." During his short stay on the German submarine, the young man expressed heartfelt thanks to the crew and later, when he and the other "stowaway" were put ashore at Tromsö, Norway, they bid the crew a friendly farewell. For his outstanding performance in sound detection, hydrophone operator Alfred Ottine received an Iron Cross First Class.

On 23 December Hans Georg announced that he had approved First Watch Officer Schröder's idea of exploring a small island called "Maliikii," two miles off the Russian coast, near Murmansk. If unoccupied, the island might provide a hiding place for observation of convoys traveling from west to east. Hess sent Schröder and *Bootsmaat* (Boatswain's Mate First Class) Josef Klapf to do the job, and Klapf explained: "I went on this mission not decked out in a fine blue uniform, but dressed in leather, and the first watch officer and I rowed over to the island in a rubber dinghy. I felt as though mice were jumping in my stomach, fearing that there would be Russian soldiers on the island or some dangerous animals." The two men, after a brief exploration, saw neither man nor beast on the desolate land.

"We knew our U-boat was out there under the water waiting for us, but it wasn't easy getting back. I had to push the dinghy from the beach, and then jump in. Once out, we made very little headway because of the strong, freezing wind," said Klapf. "When we finally got to the boat, they pulled us aboard, and we were as stiff as pokers. The submarine felt like a palace."

"At first I was worried, because I wasn't sure anyone was on the island," said Hess. "I waited offshore, submerged, as we had an agreement that after twelve hours the two men would come back, which they did." Hess decided not to use the area as an observation location and continued patrolling.

But now it was Christmas Eve and time to have a small celebration. Hans Georg gave the men a short Christmas talk, and the radio operator played carols on the speaker system. For dinner the cook made a holiday feast: "Berliners" (pastries filled with jam), along with a portion of red wine. Such brief festivities helped the men forget about war and gave them a moment of peace in their tin tube three hundred feet down in the sea.

By February 1945, three months before the end of the war, the Russians had occupied the port of Kirkenes, Norway, a short distance from Murmansk. Hess, remembering Prien's surprise attack at Scapa Flow and sinking of the *Royal Oak*, determined to sneak up on the new Russian base. On a freezing night, 9 February, U-995 crept cautiously into the fjord (mined by Germans), submerged except for the tower, and settled on the bottom next to the shipping lane. The next day the U-boat headed toward the harbor and suddenly crashed into something. "We had run aground near the shore on a steep rock and were in danger of sliding off. This would have seriously damaged our screws and hydroplanes."

Afraid to attempt any movement, the commander decided to wait until dawn. To the crew he announced: "If anyone is scared, it is I, and I am also afraid for you; therefore you needn't worry. It's better to be courageous than to eat sandwiches in a Russian prison camp." The crew seemed to take heart from their captain's words, and all went well that night.

The next morning, after a twelve-hour wait, U-995 maneuvered off the rock and went to periscope depth, where Hess could take a look at the situation. "I grew extremely apprehensive when I saw a Russian guardhouse and two patrolling sentries about a hundred meters away from us. To calm myself and the men, I told them exactly what I was seeing. It was important to be frank." With electric engines barely making a sound, U-995 started out of the fjord, but before exiting the harbor, Hess unleashed a torpedo at the only ship at the dock, Norwegian freighter *Idefjord*. "We managed to torpedo the only ship at the pier," said Hess, "at a distance of two thousand meters." U-995, unobserved by the Russians, reached the open sea and made her escape.

A few days later news came from U-boat headquarters that Hans Georg Hess, youngest U-boat commander in the fleet, had just been awarded the Knight's Cross. The last months of the war were bringing record losses for German submarines: twenty-one sunk in February and thirty-four in March, then sixty-four in April and forty-one in May. Hess was one of the few to survive and to achieve success in overwhelmingly deadly circumstances.

U-995 went out on one last patrol in March 1945, sinking a Soviet subhunter and damaging the freighter *Horace Bushnell.* Forced to go ashore for repairs and have a schnorkel installed, they arrived at the German base at Trondheim, Norway; before the work could be completed, they were told that Germany had surrendered. U-995, unable to travel, was ordered to stay in the dock rather than depart for England in "Operation Deadlight," where the U-boats were being given over to the Allies. Hess and crew found themselves prisoners of war in Trondheim for four months, then were allowed to go free. "I traveled on the train from Trondheim to Oslo in full uniform, with medals and all. People didn't know what to make of me," smiled Hess. "I enjoyed it." The youthful Hess, who liked Norway, remained near Oslo for a year following the end of the war, then returned to his homeland.

U-995, after sitting idle for seven years, was commissioned by the Norwegian navy, renamed the *Kaura,* and set to work as a training vessel. Then, as a gesture of goodwill, the Norwegian government presented the submarine to the German Federal Navy, stipulating that the boat be preserved and displayed to the public. The German Navy League, after many difficulties and years of fund-raising, succeeded in placing U-995 in a seaside park at Laboe, overlooking Kiel Fjord.

Occasionally Hans Georg Hess has a chance to visit his old tin friend and still enjoys telling people about the war days. "When we first went out on patrol, we needed a few hours to forget about the good times on shore and to get ready for the fear and the cat-and-mouse games. This mental change was necessary every time we went

Led by Commander Hess, the crew of U-995 marches through the streets of Trondheim, Norway, in early May 1945, while their boat was being fitted out with a schnorkel. *Theodor Sterzinger*

out, and during the first days at sea we didn't talk very much until we got used to the bombs and attacks." Hess said they also had to become accustomed to the "overwhelming narrowness" of the boat, the engine noise, the terrible odors, and their mates.

In order to survive, it was essential that each crew member perform his particular tasks quickly and carefully, for one mistake could mean death for all. "Every one of them had something to give," explained Hess, "and it was important for me to assign places according to talents." As for watch duty, this was a crucial task requiring continual searching of the horizon with binoculars, even in treacherous seas, rain, and snow. "We made a competition out of it, and I rewarded successful lookouts with a prize."

One of the customs U-boatmen most enjoyed was choosing an insignia for their boat. As soon as U-995 embarked on her first cruise, word went out that the commander wanted everyone to come up with ideas for the emblem, but rules disallowed anything associated with war or fighting, such as bulls, swords, lions, and so on. "My idea was to put a cheerful insignia on the conning tower and the crew's caps, and so we staged a contest. The winner came up with a picture of two children playing *Fang den Hut,* or 'Catch the Hat,' an old German game where one child ran after another and tried to snatch the cap off his head." This image appealed to the youthful commander, who could see that the game was similar to the one U-995 was playing in the northern seas. And so the crew painted two romping youngsters on their conning tower, a symbol that was to become well known. "I think they were more proud of that emblem than they were of the pennants showing how many tons we had sunk," grinned Hess.

Along with their *Fang den Hut* crest, the U-boat crew, like many others, enjoyed singing, and one of their favorites was "The Merry-Go-Round," an old boating ditty. It went like this:

> "Let us have one more drink
> Because tomorrow we may sink.
> They have sent us north without any hope,
> And in a funeral group goes our boat.
> Boy, boy, what a life."

"We often sang in miserable situations. The main thing was to keep the men's hopes up."

"As for discipline, I only had one problem with the crew, and that had to do with food. In those days, our meals and drinks were far superior to anything that the folks in Germany were having, and there was temptation to take some of it home for a wife's or mother's pantry." Hess admitted that two of his noncommissioned officers stole a huge supply of edibles and stored them in a locker. The commander found out about it and had them court-martialed, because "without obedience in minor things, we might not have total cooperation in dangerous situations."

Many people ask the former captain about the political atmosphere on U-boats, and he explains that freedom of thought and expression in Germany was severely limited at that time. "We dared not give our true opinion about the party and state, although inside the boat we could be more honest. We felt that by serving our country, or 'fatherland,' it didn't mean we necessarily identified with those in power. We were not Hitler's mercenaries, but German navy men with much the same love of our country as the enemy had of theirs."

"Very few U-boat captains cared about all those dogmas of the Third Reich," Hess explained. He recalled that the renowned and highly decorated Teddy Suhren came into Saint-Nazaire in 1942 after a successful patrol, where crowds of admirers greeted him at the pier. "Are the Nazis still in power?" he yelled at them. "If so, then both engines full back."

Hess's former crew member Rudolf Müssener added: "Nobody appreciated the Nazi party. We openly expressed our dislike of it when Admiral Dönitz visited our base." Richard Schwedhelm commented, "We were twenty to twenty-five years old and educated as idealists." He explained that words like "fatherland," "duty," and "solidarity" were empty words for them. "None of my comrades wanted that war —it was terrible."

"Whenever I return to U-995, or *Fang den Hut,* as we call it, the boat becomes alive," Schwedhelm continued. "As I walk through it, the old events come back to mind. Our fears and sorrows of the last months of the war are still there in the boat."

"The senses, too, have a strong memory," mused Hess. "Certain sounds remind me of battles at sea, and when I smell oil on the road, I can't help but think of destroyers in the night."[1]

16 Walter Tegtmeier, U-597, U-718, U-997

■ ■

Longtime friends Walter Tegtmeier and Hans Georg Hess were unaware of each other's existence during the war, though their submarines were part of the 5. U-Flotilla at Kiel and each boat made numerous patrols in the North Sea and Arctic Ocean. Tegtmeier's U-997 and Hess's U-995 even attacked some of the same convoys during the last months of the war, and they could hear each other's radiomen reporting hits or misses to headquarters. "Today," said Walter, "we talk about our escapades in the Arctic Sea quite often, and we can remember Korvettenkapitän Möhle bidding the submarines farewell on 25 April 1944 as we set out for enemy operations in the North Sea."

■ ■

"I enlisted in the navy in 1937 based on a certain spirit of adventure, for I was hoping to travel to foreign lands and get to know the countries and people in them. After serving on the cruiser *Königsberg,* I volunteered for the submarine service in 1940 and trained on U-6." Before it was all over, Walter served on three U-boats and lived to see the end of World War II—but no sightseeing.

"In July 1942 U-597 had been patrolling in the North Atlantic in a ten–U-boat group named Wolf, looking for convoys," said Tegtmeier, who served as petty officer third class with Commander Eberhard Bopst. Just after they had been depth charged by a destroyer, someone noticed a rattling noise near the galley hatch. "We surfaced, looked

Walter Tegtmeier

around, but could not find any damage." Walter was then sent up to the deck, where he strapped on his safety harness, hooked the rope onto the antenna wire, and began to investigate the situation. "That day the seas were rough, and I was supposed to open the grating over the galley hatch. I had only been working there for about five minutes, tying down loose equipment to the deck, when a big wave hit."

Before he realized what was happening, the wooden grating lid slammed shut and Walter was swept overboard, but in the process his right thumb was cut off at the middle joint. "It hurt horribly," he remembered, as the crew hauled him back onto the deck. In those days of 1942 submarines had no doctors, merely a pharmacist's mate;

however, commanders took a medical course as part of their training. "When the accident happened, the captain looked at my hand and said, 'Come on in, my friend, and I will look in the book and see what to do.'" With that, Bopst applied a dry plaster bandage and ordered Walter to bed in the chief petty officer's room. Shortly afterward, the boat experienced an air attack and crash-dived. "While we were down, the commander continued reading his manual and realized that he had some pain shots on board. He said, 'Walter, turn around, take your pants off, and here it is—bingo!'"

The shot helped Walter's pain and should have put him to sleep, but, "I was afraid that if something happened to the boat and everybody abandoned ship, I would be inside sleeping. I kept awake." Realizing he had a serious problem to tackle, Bopst sent a radio message to *BdU:* "Control room petty officer right thumb is torn off. Urgently need a doctor." Soon an answer came back: "Cut off the loose flesh pieces and put castor oil salve on the wound."

Several days later, Tegtmeier was suffering a high fever as U-597 made her way to a rendezvous near the Azores for refueling from supply boat U-461. "During the fuel transfer a doctor came over from 461 and examined me, then they moved me on a rubber dinghy to the large submarine. The doctor put me on the operating table, and when I woke up, my boat was gone, and I was left on the milkcow."

Eight days had elapsed between the time of Walter's accident and the surgery—too long for the doctor to get the skin completely sewed together—and an open, infected place remained. "My grandma once told me to wash wounds with soap and water and to apply sugar to extract the dirt, and that's what I did."

"On board there were five wounded men, including me. One had fallen down the conning tower and broken his leg; a second one was very sick and could not be diagnosed; and a third, working in the aftersection of the submarine, was hit in the back by a torpedo that fell out of the tube while they were diving. He could not lie flat, but the supply boat crew, using small steel pieces from their riveting equipment, made a support for his back so that he could lie down. And a fourth man had venereal disease."

Back at Saint-Nazaire, Tegtmeier was transferred off the U-tanker and placed in the hospital near La Baule. He learned that U-597, his former boat, had landed at Brest the same day. "After the crew took a forty-day vacation, they went out again and never came back. It was sunk in the North Atlantic by a Liberator bomber, and a total loss— no survivors." Tegtmeier had been unable to rejoin the crew because his injury had not totally healed, even with Grandma's remedy.

Assigned to observe construction of his next U-boat, U-718, Walter went to Hamburg with the rest of the team to familiarize himself with every detail of the new sub. At the beginning of November 1943 the boat began the usual tactical training in the Baltic, near Gotenhafen. "We were with ten or fifteen submarines, practicing attacks on a fifteen-ship convoy. It was 11 November, and at four-thirty in the morning we were outbound, in a big snowstorm, and another sub was inbound. In total darkness, we collided at full speed on the surface. They hit us in our engine room." Walter, at that point, was supposed to have been on duty in the diesel room, but instead had been assigned to the central control room. He was one of the three who managed to scramble up through the tower and escape. A few others were already on the bridge.

Since Baltic maneuvers were extremely hazardous and many accidents had occurred, all the crewmen were wearing life vests. "As we were sinking, the bridge was full of people. I didn't know what was going on and I thought maybe it was best that I jump into the water, but then I realized I was already in the water." Walter, dressed in leather pants and a shirt, had an easier time than the others from the bridge, who were wearing heavy suits. Commander Wieduwilt attempted to organize the struggling men, but they quickly drifted apart, and choppy waves made it impossible to see them. In the blackness, with snow swirling down, Walter tried two methods of blowing up his life vest but could not manage to get any air into it. Seeing a light in the distance, he gave up trying to inflate the vest and swam in the direction of the beacon. "There's one," he heard from far off.

"The submarine that hit us, U-476, aimed a searchlight on the water, and the front of their boat was all bent, with the torpedo tubes going upward. I heard them yell, then the boat moved away, and I thought they were going to leave me there. I was very afraid." But the boat

Example of U-boat (U-259)
with bent bow.
Bundesarchiv, Koblenz

had turned to get the floating sailor on its lee side. U-476's crew rescued Walter and six others, and, after forty-five minutes, finally located
Wieduwilt. "Somebody jumped from the submarine and picked him
up. He couldn't even move any more."

"On this tactical exercise, the last one before a boat goes off to
combat, they lost twelve submarines," said Tegtmeier. Without radar
or means of communication, the subs had no way to detect each other,
and forty-seven people died on U-718. It was customary to have an
investigation and court hearing of every U-boat accident, and the collision was officially looked into; however, the court decided that no
one was guilty, and Wieduwilt, after a few months, was put in command of U-262. "The other commander, who hit us, continued on his
boat and was later sunk in the Arctic Ocean."

For his next assignment, Walter joined the crew of U-997 in March 1944. "Our *Obermaschinist* was arrested in a Königsberg restaurant because he kicked a military policeman, and they sent him away to prison for four months. They called me in to take his place." Their assignment: the Arctic Sea, to attack convoys headed for Russian ports.

Patrolling in the "Icemeer" brought difficulties for a submarine, in that each time they surfaced, "everything started to ice up—the antennas, tower, weapons, and so on." With extremely low temperatures, the rough seas and fierce winds threw moisture over the men on watch, freezing their clothes hard. When they came down from the conning tower, they broke the ice off themselves and tried to warm up. "When we were cruising on surface, the guns froze and we had no defense against airplanes. The only thing we could do was dive." Their worst enemy was the elements.

Luckily, Tegtmeier did not have to stay on the bridge, to be frozen stiff. "But the engine people did have a chance to go up into the conning tower for five minutes to get some fresh air." Nights being almost endless, the men sometimes ran up to catch a glimpse of the sun.

The Gulf Stream kept northern harbors like Narvik open. "So the convoys from America departed from Halifax, stayed close to the ice border, and went a different way each time, to fool the submarines. We did not get into substantial ice barriers because we were hunting for convoy ships, and they were avoiding the ice. Actually the Gulf Stream, coming from Texas, saved submariners' lives."

In April 1944, less than two months before D-day, Walter's boat was sent, with twenty others in a group called Mitte, to Kristiansand, Norway, and from there to Egersund. Lehmann's war diary explained that they were supposed to "help deter an invasion if one took place," and there they waited from 2 May until 14 May. Naval higher-ups felt an Allied invasion of the continent was imminent, but they did not know when or where it would come. Nothing happened, so U-997 went with three other boats to Narvik and were sent from there by *Fregattenkapitän* (Commander) Suhren, commander of Arctic Sea Flotillas, to patrol between Norway and Jan Mayen, an island west of Norway. U-997 attempted to attack a carrier group but had no luck and headed in to Hammerfest.

In mid-July, with U-425 and U-362, they went out to make a search for convoys, but heavy attacks by aircraft caused their return to base. Small groups of merchant ships were sailing with the protection of many escorts and carriers, making attempts by the U-boats to attack the enemy close to unthinkable, and a majority of the boats were being sunk or seriously damaged. Only one out of five submarines was making it back from missions, and Walter's boat was spending a great deal of time in port for repairs. During one forty-eight-hour period U-997 had been forced to dive twenty-three times. Compelled to endure many hours of bombardment at dangerous depths, the U-boat crew's nerves and spirits were taking a hard beating.

Lehmann's boat, along with Hans Georg Hess (U-995) and Günther Unverzagt (U-965), was sent out to operate against a PQ convoy on 13 October 1944. At the edge of the ice line and in semidarkness, U-997 surged toward Murmansk. Along the way, Lehmann received "the questionable order" from *BdU* that all U-boats were now supposed to fight enemy aircraft on the surface and not dive. "Thank goodness," remarked the commander, "that no planes are in sight."

The inevitable then happened. A Thunderbolt observation plane saw the boat, called for help, and a group of destroyers soon arrived, depth charging them for twelve hours. Two nights later came another lashing from above, lasting seventeen hours. With that, Lehmann was told to return to Narvik.

At the end of their fifth patrol, and having fought fiercely and accomplished almost nothing, the crew headed back to Narvik and celebrated Christmas on the *Black Watch,* a ship with crew living quarters. The boat was outfitted with a new schnorkel and the crew was given brief training with it in the Trondheim harbor before they set out for Harstadt—in extremely rough weather. "About five o'clock in the morning we were ordered to go to schnorkel drive, in spite of a very heavy sea astern. Sometimes we cut under and were submerged for a minute. When the schnorkel mast went below water, all the air was sucked out of the boat, and the crew had to quickly cut off the diesels." On one occasion the starboard diesel suddenly conked out, and ten to fifteen tons of water poured into the diesel room through opened air intake and exhaust valves and the schnorkel mast. "We tried to drain the water out of the diesel into the bilge, then we tried to clear the port diesel, but it wouldn't start, either." Meanwhile, carbon dioxide and exhaust smoke started to fill the boat, and almost every crewman, unable to grab his breathing device, started gasping and choking. Commander Lehmann brought the sub back to the surface as fast as possible, trying to overcome the problems of sick crewmen who could hardly function and fifteen tons of water in the diesel room bilge.

Once more on the surface, the water was pumped out, engines started again, and U-997 began to recharge her batteries. Then a fuse box caught fire, thick black smoke billowed out, and to top things off, the gyro- and magnetic compasses failed. During this bedlam, the bell screamed, and U-997 dived, pitching forward at a sharp angle, and *Bootsmaat* Sachse fell overboard. When Lehmann surfaced again, he was unable to find his crewman.

The sixth patrol of U-997 in March 1945 took her in the direction of Murmansk in pursuit of a convoy, and after attempting to sink a destroyer, a barrage of depth charges damaged the boat so much they had to cut short the mission. Ten days later they were back in Narvik. On their seventh and last patrol, U-997 encountered two merchant ships escorted by ten destroyers, plus a large number of aircraft. Lehmann got off seven torpedoes, and in return received about 480 depth charges, but was able to get back to Narvik on 25 April 1945.

"When the war ended we were close to Murmansk, and the order came to take down the German flag with the swastika and put up a black one, then proceed to Murmansk. We all said, 'They must be nuts.' So we put up a black flag and went to Norway." No German wished to be subjugated to his deadly enemy, Russia. At an assembly station in Narvik, U-997 met thirteen other boats in the group Nordmeer, including the weather ships. "We wanted to go to Trondheim, because it was our point of origin," said Tegtmeier, "and we had all our possessions in storage there, but the Canadians said, 'No, the submarines go directly to Scotland.'"

Guarded by five Canadian corvettes, the fourteen U-boats headed for Scotland, and on the way one of them was forced to stop to make some quick repairs. Explained Walter: "The Canadians signaled the

U-boat with lights, saying, 'We can't believe that a sub has technical problems. It's not German-like.'" The U-boat replied that yes, they actually had trouble, and so the one boat remained there, guarded by a corvette, while the rest proceeded with their journey.

At Loch Eriboll, Scotland, a small group of British soldiers boarded the submarines, a few U-boatmen debarked, and the trip continued to Londonderry, Northern Ireland. "Here we joined a group of forty German U-boats tied up in groups of five." More of the crew were taken off, including the commander, leaving fifteen or twenty men, including Walter, to unload provisions and weapons and take care of the engines of the five-submarine row.

After the subs were emptied, the most advanced boats, types XXI and XXIII, were separated. The older, standard types were collected for distribution between the Russians and the British.

In the months before negotiations took place, Walter—a trained mechanic—and some of his crew remained on board U-997 as maintenance men. "Under guard, we were escorted once a week to a nearby camp for showers, then we were taken to see a movie about the liberation of a concentration camp, and when we came out, they asked us what we thought about it. I said, 'I saw the same thing in a German movie when they opened up Katyn [Poland], and found a group of top Polish officers murdered by the Russians.'"

After three weeks, many more U-boats had arrived and there was no more space on the pier, so U-997 was transferred to the Bay of Stranraer, Scotland, and tied to a buoy. "We were sitting on the empty boats and couldn't do a thing. Our only duty was to start the diesel engines once a day and keep them in good shape; the rest of the long hours we were loafing, so we made kites and started to fly them." Walter said that the kites disturbed the pilots of British planes, so they had to stop the fun. "Then we built a wooden cage, or trap, connected by a rope to the conning tower, and as soon as a pigeon went in it, we closed it, caught him, put a nylon string around his neck and let him fly. This was something to do, and we were relatively young. I was twenty-five."

Walter had never smoked, but he had saved up some cigars, and

Fifty-five U-boats taken by the Allies at the end of the war, at Londonderry, Northern Ireland, 6 June 1945. U-997 is next to the pier, second row from bottom.

U-Boot Archiv, Cuxhaven

knowing that the others liked to puff, offered a reward of three stogies to whoever would jump into the water. "There were plenty of takers," he chortled. "You know the old German proverb, 'If you start loafing, trouble starts.'"

In December 1945, seven months later, the Russians arrived on a cruiser and held a conference about division of the submarines, demanding they get some of the newer types. "The negotiations took a long time, but the Allies didn't allow them to have any except the standard ones, and so they took six back to Russia." Then in January 1946 the British sank all the rest—110 U-boats including U-997, in Operation Deadlight. Two-hundred-twenty-one commanders had scuttled their own boats rather than give them up, and 156 surrendered.[1]

Walter Tegtmeier spent another nine months "as a guest of the King" in a prisoner of war camp in Scotland, regaining his freedom on 29 September 1946. In serving on three submarines, he escaped death on the first because of an injured thumb, survived an accidental ramming on the second, and lived through seven patrols on the third. "My former boat, U-718, is still down in the Baltic sea in about eighty meters of water."

In summing up his experiences, Tegtmeier says: "Although I experienced very difficult and dangerous situations at sea, I enjoyed the camaraderie on board, so I would enlist again today. Our many good relations with our former enemies in America and England mean a lot to me and my friends."[2]

17   Josef Matthes, U-963

■ ■

*Matthes survived nine missions, spending three hundred days on U-963
under three commanders. While provisioning for war patrol in 1944,
his captain,* Oberleutnant zur See *Karl Baddenberg, carried a small
stack of wood onto the boat. On the sixty-seven-day trip, between torpedo shootings and depth charge attacks, Baddenberg built a baby
cradle for his first child, soon to appear in the world. U-963 arrived
back at Brest with the newly constructed "Wiege" sitting on the bow of
the U-boat, and the crew chose the child's bed for their tower emblem.
For many years afterward the baby cradle passed from one crewman
to another, as each announced a forthcoming family member.*

■ ■

The first trips on a German submarine for Josef Matthes involved a
great deal of searching for Murmansk-bound convoys. As soon as the
lookouts spotted a mass of ships, they radioed headquarters, who in
turn sent out wolf packs to try to sink as many merchantmen and
escorts as possible. "We had a lot of opportunities to attack, but our
torpedoes weren't very good," explained Matthes. "We had specially
constructed ones, built so that they were attracted to noise. But the
Americans and British knew about them, so they dragged a long rope
with a gadget behind their ships, and it was noisier than the engines,
so the torpedo went to the gadget."

When Germany surrendered to the Allies in May 1945, all U-boats were ordered to raise a black flag and turn themselves in. "We were in the Irish Sea at that time and were supposed to head for a port in England. But we didn't do that. As we left the Irish Sea, Commander Wentz asked the crew, 'What should we do?'" Mulling over their dilemma, the crew concluded that they had only two choices: go to British prison camp or get back to Germany somehow. "The commander said that neither was possible and that we would head south, maybe to Argentina, and although we had sufficient food supplies for that long trip, we did not have enough fuel."

With South America out of the question, they decided Spain would be a good destination; however, when they listened to the radio, they heard that the country was having economic and political problems. "Our only possibility at that point was Portugal. We made it to the coast of Portugal and sent up some SOS flares, but when the Portuguese answered by radio, they said they would rescue us only on condition that they could take the submarine." With no intention of surrendering U-963, "we got busy and destroyed everything on the boat, including the engines. We had to jump into rubber dinghies to get away, because our commander had set timed explosives on the U-boat. When we were far from the boat, we heard a big explosion and our submarine disappeared into two or three hundred meters of water." When a special Portuguese navy towing ship arrived at the scene, all the boat engines were useless, and the sub was half-submerged.

Safely ashore in the village of Nazaré, the relieved crewmen marched quietly with their guards to the fire station, where they were arrested. "There was a long discussion between Commander Wentz and the Portuguese officers, then they took us to a local hotel, where we were served a nice fish dinner with excellent wine, and we even had fresh flowers on the table. The hotel was too small to accommodate us, so the guards drove us down the coast to Peniche, where there was a little fortress, and there they put us in jail."

Next morning busses arrived, and U-963's survivors rode into town. Along the way, local Portuguese yelled, "Viva Germany, Heil Hitler." Josef said they complained to the authorities that prisoners of war were not supposed to be held in jails, but their protests went unheeded. "We were then taken to Lisbon, expecting to go to a place that they had said would be very nice. It was surprising to see all the lights in the city, after having such complete darkness all during the war." Passing through Lisbon, the bus continued to the coast, where Josef's crew arrived at a former summer camp for children of Portuguese soldiers. "It was a super place, and we had toilet articles and everything—even vino." Everyone could order what he pleased for meals, but no one was allowed out of the area. A five-foot-high wall surrounded the compound, guarded by Portuguese soldiers, who marched around it only at night.

Each evening a committee of officers counted the crew members to make sure no one had wandered off. "Every time, before the Portuguese commander left, he would say to us, 'I want you to sing a German Nazi song for me.' A chorus of voices always answered: 'No! We only sing sailor songs.'"

"We were there about three months," recalled Matthes, "and it was like paradise for us."

Paradise could not last, however, because the British insisted on taking the German prisoners, as Portugal had remained neutral during the war. "A British ship came, and the sailors were really afraid of us, even though we had no knives or weapons of any kind." After roll call, U-963's crew was escorted aboard the vessel, with armed sailors standing on all sides, ready to fire. "We had to go to the bottom of the ship, where they fed us supper, and afterward we had a friendly meeting with our guards. It was an amazing situation, because we said to the British, 'Please show us how they trained you with gun handling in parades, and so on.'" Obligingly, the British crew performed their gun presentation, then offered their weapons to Josef's group, saying, "Now show us the German way." And so several of the U-boatmen presented arms with their enemy's loaded guns.

"We were allowed to go up on deck for about an hour each day, and sometimes, with special permission, we could walk through the whole ship—a corvette. We asked which direction we were going, but the sailors didn't know." As Gibraltar came into sight, the ship headed toward the big rock and landed. There the U-boat crew was marched ashore and confined to a military jail for interrogation. "Some of the British officers were Jewish, and they beat us. Two of us at a time were taken into a little cell for questioning, but our commander had told us what to say and what not to say. The hearing, conducted by a British officer, went on for several days." When asked how they happened to be in Portugal, the crew all replied that "British bombs sank U-963."

In the cells, one tiny window allowed a bit of light, and there was one large iron door. "We were allowed to smoke, but we had no matches." Somewhere in the jail they could hear a British prisoner playing the bagpipes, and gradually they grew somewhat used to their quarters, even though the jail was full of insects. "The bugs plagued us, so we pulled the necks of our turtleneck shirts up over our heads to protect our faces. It was terrible. One of my friends was badly bitten."

Conditions soon improved for Josef, as the crew was shipped to England and housed in villages outside London, where they helped with the crops. Matthes ended his prison time working in a farmer's fields and occasionally looked after the farmer's two children in the evenings. "It was a really nice experience," he smiled.[1]

18

Helmut Wehlte, U-903, and Günther Thiemrodt, U-1205

■■

Helmut Wehlte came from a family of merchant mariners, and one of his uncles, a ship captain, wore a splendid blue uniform. "All the girls went wild over him," said Helmut, "so I figured this was the way to go." At seventeen Wehlte volunteered for submarine duty, serving on U-963 (with the baby cradle emblem) as Maschinenmaat. *Günther Thiemrodt, a* Maschinenmaat *on U-1205, and Helmut Wehlte took part in a little-known and terrifying rescue mission at the end of the war.*

■■

As the Third Reich's war efforts crumbled, Russians launched a major offensive on the eastern front in January 1945, causing hundreds of thousands of German citizens and soldiers to flee from eastern German provinces toward the west. "The U-boat campaign was no longer the Navy's most important task," wrote Admiral Karl Dönitz in his memoirs, "and I therefore transferred large portions of the fleet to assist in the defense of the eastern front and to rescue German nationals from the Russians." His use of part of the navy, merchant ships, and every other available vessel for evacuation created an intense drama that caused Dönitz's delay in surrendering at the end of the war.[1]

"It was unusual for a submarine to carry passengers. There were many reasons, and confidentiality was one, for there was a lot of equipment that we didn't want anyone else to see," explained Wehlte. A

Helmut Wehlte

second crucial factor was space: U-boats had barely enough room for fifty or more men, who shared bunks and one or two minuscule toilets. Helmut's boat participated in a highly dramatic refugee evacuation called Project Rescue, orchestrated by Karl Dönitz.

Conditions could not have been worse in Germany at the beginning of 1945: there were no munitions reserves, weapons, food, or fuel left; communications did not exist; Italy had surrendered; and troops in East and West Prussia were being overwhelmed by superior Russian forces. Dönitz determined to use every available ship "of any size or kind" to evacuate fleeing people and wounded soldiers to western Germany. Filled with visions of rape, murder, and enslavement, great masses of men, women, and children were hastening by any possible means to safety behind American and British lines. Thus, U-903 was pressed into rescue duty.

Günther Thiemrodt

"Transport boats were leaving from Königsberg, Pillau, Danzig, Gotenhafen, Elbig, and so on," explained Wehlte. "At the end of 1944 U-903 was in dock to be overhauled and repaired for one more mission to the front. While we were tied up to the pier, we got a bunch of 'Christmas trees' [marker flares dropped by bombers] and some bombs, but fortunately, no damage."

When Russia launched her campaign on the eastern front, submarine headquarters ordered U-903, along with two other submarines, to go to a small town called Krantores to generate electricity for the city of Danzig (now Gdansk, Poland). "We were in shock at having to do this, because the only result would be that we were either sunk or taken prisoner." Helmut said that when Germany appeared to be beaten, sailors started saying: "Enjoy the war; peace is going to be horrible." However, instead of generating electricity, U-903 was called for duty as a transport boat, and the crew heard the announcement with great relief. They were more than ready to leave Danzig, knowing that the Russian army had reached the city suburbs.

"One evening, and I do not remember the exact day, but it was not the thirteenth [an unlucky day for sailors], about twenty civilians, including some children, came aboard. They were from different parts of East Prussia. We hardly had room for the crew, much less a group of passengers, especially those who might suffer from claustrophobia. And the enemy would be unaware that ours was a rescue mission and would not hesitate to attack. Boy, what a trip that was."

On the night of their departure in January, the weather became ferocious, with torrents of rain and howling winds. As the sub left, "everything that wasn't nailed down was tossing around in the boat, and we even lost part of the deck." The passengers attempted to keep out of the way by huddling in bunks where the crewmen on duty had slept. The children, used to dangerous and frightening situations, sat still and behaved well. As the submarine traveled toward Kolberg in the darkness, the violent rocking and rolling caused many to become seasick, and others suffered bruises when they were thrown against metal objects.

"We were supposed to try to be somewhat invisible, without submerging, and the big storm was an unexpected ally, helping to keep us out of sight of the enemy. A lot of water came in through the tower hatch, and everyone in the control room was busy trying to pump it out." With all kinds of objects flying around in the boat, a paper sack of noodles landed in the bilge. The sack dissolved and the noodles were sucked up by the bilge pumps, clogging the filter. "With all our other problems, we had to take the filter apart, remove the noodles, clean up, and get the pump ready again."

A second concern had to do with the boat's trim. "Every day one of the guys put together a weights and trim table so that he could tell if the boat was in the proper trim and the right weight for submerging. It was almost impossible to dive because we never knew just exactly what our weight situation was." Expecting enemy attacks at any moment, the submarine plowed onward for four days.

U-903, with thankful crew and passengers, succeeded in reaching her destination, although the other two U-boats were sunk. "We deposited our precious cargo, with upset stomachs and lots of black and blue marks all over their bodies, at Kolberg and then went on to Lübeck. I wonder whether anyone is alive today who was on our submarine for that fateful trip. I do not know of any," Wehlte concluded.

Günther Thiemrodt, machinist's mate on U-1205, experienced the great exodus as well. In April 1945 his boat was sent to the Bay of Danzig for front training, and with the dreaded Russian army drawing closer, their mission became one of rescue. "We had to bring aboard about thirty boys from the ages of ten to fourteen, and one of them insisted that he take his bicycle along, which of course did not fit into a submarine." Obviously, it could not go down a hatch, so the crew lashed the vehicle to the railing of the antiaircraft gun.

"We asked the youngster to take the air out of the tires," explained Thiemrodt, "but he refused, saying he did not have a pump to pump them back up. During the trip to Warnemünde we had to submerge several times, and the pressure on his bicycle tires was so great that they exploded." Discovering this, the boy cried bitterly, for the damage was irreparable. The crew was not too happy, either, for the young boys had lice, and all the men had to go into Kiel to be deloused. At least, though, everyone was alive.

In the hectic months of January through May 1945, evacuation operations were wholly dependent on sea transportation, as the land routes either were blocked by the Russians or being bombed. During this period 2,022,602 people from Courland, East and West Prussia, Pomerania, and Mecklenburg were sailed to safety through the Baltic Sea. "The evacuations had been carried out under constant attack by British, American, and Russian aircraft, by Russian submarines . . . and through waters repeatedly and heavily mined," said Admiral Dönitz in his memoirs. Four thousand refugees died on the ship *Wilhelm Gustloff*, seven thousand on the *Goya*, and three thousand on the hospital ship *Steuben*. However, 99 percent of them made it to western Germany, thanks to the supreme efforts of Dönitz's navy men.[2]

19
Peter Petersen, U-518

■ ■

With the fiftieth anniversary of the capture of U-505 rapidly approaching, the staff of the Chicago Museum of Science and Industry conceived the idea of firing up one of the engines of the old German submarine for the big event. To help in consulting efforts, they enlisted Peter Petersen, who had served in the engineering division on U-518 and lived in a neighboring state. Many sub veterans considered the plan farfetched, but Petersen and others thought it could be done. On 4 June 1994, as newspaper and television crews readied their cameras and crowds waited with anticipation, a museum staff member yelled "Now!" and Peter, dressed in coveralls in the engine room, started the diesel with a mighty roar. Everyone cheered and yelled "Hooray!" One German lady cried.

■ ■

Peter Petersen is alive today simply because of luck: shortly before his U-boat was sunk in 1945, the navy transferred him from U-518 to officers' training school. A previous narrow escape had occurred when U-518 patrolled the American east coast in the fall of 1944. "We were going along underwater, when the captain stuck up the periscope to have a look around. All he saw was the gray wall of a destroyer passing us. I was with him in the tower, and he yelled, 'Get down!' We heard the loud WHOOM, WHOOM of that thing going by." They were

Peter Petersen

so close to the destroyer that its prop wash shook the U-boat. "I guess the sailors on that warship were just looking the other direction."

On another occasion they were cruising along submerged, and the helmsman, sitting in the tower by himself and bored to death, started to play with the flare pistol. "We used the gun for recognition signals, and it had two big barrels. All of a sudden the helmsman accidentally fired both barrels, sending a galaxy of red, blue, and green balls down into the control room. We slammed the hatches shut, ran for the fire extinguishers, and went chasing after those things, because if one of them had gotten into the battery compartment, we would have blown up and been gone, and nobody would have ever known what happened to us."

Realizing that it had been an accident, the commander meted out punishment accordingly: he made the helmsman serve as steward to the petty officers for the rest of the trip. "And that was the worst punishment there was."

In 1944, U-518, bound for a secret rendezvous with a Japanese submarine in the mid-Atlantic, had brought three people to be transferred to the Japanese boat as pilots to bring them into Lorient. "We approached the other submarine very slowly and carefully, then exchanged recognition signals. And when we got closer, we could see their crew members standing on deck with some kind of knee-length pants on. We thought that was funny."

When the moment came to connect the two submarines, the Japanese attempted several times to heave a line to U-518, without success. "We saw that they were having trouble and used our line gun to fire one over, and when they heard the BANG, they thought we were shooting at them. It really scared them."

U-518 delivered the three crewmen, with some radio and navigation equipment, to the Japanese sub, which was bound for France. Weeks later in Lorient, Petersen met the three Germans and asked them about their ride with the Japanese. "The food was terrible, and the boat was dirty and smelled bad," they reported. "It was a horrible experience."

Discipline of U-boatmen in the German navy was harsh, sometimes resulting in the death penalty. "Whenever we were getting ready to go to sea," said Peter, "we placed all our private belongings in small lockers in a storage facility on shore because we certainly couldn't take it all with us. If we didn't come back they would send everything to our parents or relatives."

The storage building was heavily patrolled around the clock by guards whose only duty was to protect the submariners' possessions. However, six or seven of the guards yielded to temptation and broke into some of the lockers, helping themselves to suitcases and seabags. "Well, they were caught and arrested, so the next time we were due back, the authorities planned a court-martial."

"To show us that they were looking after us and to impress us, they ordered us to attend the hearing. We had to wear our best blue dress uniforms." Peter recalled that the culprits received different grades of punishment, and some of them were sent to prison. Four received the death sentence, and after the announcement, one of the young seamen facing prison walked forward and said to the judge: "Your honor, I cannot live with this shame. My brother died for his country in Russia, and I'm the only son left in the family. I prefer to have the death penalty."

As the judge considered this request, a U-boat commander in the courtroom came forward and addressed the court: "I would like to have this sailor on my submarine." Apparently, the well-known commander was held in high regard by the judge, and the two debated for several minutes. In the end, the commander was granted his request, and the errant sailor joined the crew. However, that particular U-boat was subsequently sunk, and the shame-filled seaman had his wish.

"The execution date for the thieves did not take place immediately," recalled Petersen. "It happened at a later date, but I found out from other crew members that they were ordered to attend the execution by firing squad. We thought the death sentence was cruel punishment, but those guys should have known better. Theft from a comrade was probably one of the most despised crimes a sailor could commit."

As for furloughs, the U-boat crews were given four or five weeks of vacation after every patrol so they could go home. "We had our own train, called the *BdU* train. It was a fast one that ran from southern France to the major cities in Germany, and only submarine crews rode on it." Peter said they always enjoyed the trip, sleeping on fresh sheets in private compartments, eating excellent food, and getting away from the war.

"One time I had gone home to Husum, a little town on the northern coast. It was afternoon, I think, and I was sitting out in the sun in an easy chair trying to catch a few winks of sleep. I remember that my four-year-old brother, Karl Heinrich, was there in the yard, as well, playing." Suddenly Peter heard a strange noise, as though someone were throwing pebbles, trying to awaken him. "I looked all around, and on a dirt road about twenty-five yards away, I saw little sand fountains popping up. 'That's funny,' I thought. It was strange, and I couldn't figure out what it was."

Something made Peter look up at the sky, and instantly he realized what was taking place. "There was a giant air battle going on way up there, too high for me to hear the engines of the airplanes. But they were shooting at each other, and the cartridges and spent ammunition were making the popping noises on the road."

Realizing the danger, Peter grabbed his little brother and ran into the house. "We had a couple of repairmen working on the roof, and I hollered at them to take cover. But they, too, saw what was happening, because by then we could hear the faint sound of airplane engines and see smoke trails. It was really a big fight, and pretty soon some of the airplanes came screaming down in slow motion, spinning crazily to earth." Petersen watched as Allied bombers and German fighters fell from the sky and crashed, with huge explosions and fires. "It was a horrible noise, just like you hear in the movies—the diving to earth and exploding, screaming like heck. Parachutes came floating down, too, and pretty soon some German army trucks came to try to round up the ones who had parachuted down, taking prisoners or helping the Germans get back to their bases."

For Peter, the sight of the air battle was quite an unforgettable experience. It happened that his parents lived at the entry to an air corridor where big Allied bombers entered and departed from Germany. Huge groups of planes, a thousand or more, arrived fully loaded, flying to Berlin, Hamburg, or Hannover, and there was little antiaircraft defense against them. On their way out, the bombers sometimes jettisoned bombs to avoid transporting the heavy loads back across the North Sea. "They tried to drop them into the ocean, but sometimes it was dark, and they didn't know exactly where they were. The bombs exploded in the countryside around Husum, and sometimes on a house."

Occasionally Peter could see antiaircraft guns firing along the coast, and with the whole country blacked out, the sight of the shells streaking up into the sky was spectacular. "It almost looked like fireworks, but of course it was deadly. You could see the lights from miles away."

"The whole country was dark. The few cars running had tiny slits for the lights so that no aircraft pilots could see their targets. But they found them anyway." All the windows had black shades, and civilian patrols marched through the neighborhoods nightly. The patrols were made up of very old or young people, and they criss-crossed the countryside looking for various infractions, such as slivers of light shining through curtains.

One inky-black night Peter had ridden his bicycle to a New Year's Eve party at his favorite hangout. "This place was kept in reserve for us when we came home on furlough, and the local people always dug up some booze for us." After the celebration, Peter, feeling no pain, started pedaling home in the early morning hours. "Suddenly I crashed into somebody on a bicycle going the opposite direction. After we picked ourselves up, we looked at each other in the darkness, and it was my best friend, who had just come from another party."

Expecting to find everyone asleep in his house, Peter was surprised to see that lights were on. "My brother had unexpectedly come home from the Russian front and had just taken a bath and was ready to go to bed. He was overjoyed to see me, and it was quite an exciting occasion, both of us being home at the same time. My parents were really happy about it, and that furlough was wonderful." The Petersens never knew when their sons were going to show up. They just appeared.

Hitler had forbidden German citizens to listen to foreign radio broadcasts, on penalty of death, but many people did it anyway, in the privacy of their homes. "Every now and then my parents would tune in to the English stations and listen to what they had to say about the state of the war. One time [in June 1944] I was home on vacation, and they said to me: 'There are going to be problems: the invasion has started. The Allies are entering France.' And sure enough, the German radio later officially announced that France was being invaded."

The same day as the announcement, a telegram arrived instructing Peter to return immediately to his U-boat, by any means possible. "Keep in mind that I was in the northern part of Germany, and my boat was in southern France, at Lorient. That was quite a trip. I had to go partly by train and truck, some of the way by bicycle, and partly on foot. I said my good-byes with only half my vacation gone." Peter hopped on a train in Hamburg, went to Holland, and when the train stopped, was loaded onto one of the military vehicles headed in the direction of France.

"There were lots of other guys trying to get back. We rode along in the back of this open-air truck and stopped in a little forest for a rest. Food was so scarce that I don't think we had anything to eat." Sitting at the edge of the woods, the men saw two planes fly by. "Hey, look at the Messerschmidts—aren't they nice looking," remarked Petersen. As they started to discuss how much fun it would be to fly one, the two "German" planes wheeled around and started straight toward them. "All of a sudden their noses dipped and their wings lit up. Each plane had eight machine guns, so there were sixteen machine guns firing at us. They were Spitfires, but we hadn't recognized them, and we charged into the woods to get away."

"There were maybe a hundred of us guys there, and when they saw us standing around, they took a shot at us." Whizzing machine-gun bullets denuded the trees above as Petersen jumped into a nearby creek and huddled under a bridge in water up to his waist. "Fortunately no one was hurt. I can still see those blinking flashes of the guns on the wings."

Peter made it to the boat, but "it was a horrible trip back." In July, a month after the Normandy invasion, General Patton's Third Army was sweeping eastward, and as U.S. VIII Corps troops advanced on Brest, Lorient, and Saint-Nazaire, the French Resistance closed in on La Pallice and Bordeaux. After incessant heavy bombing for three years, the U-boat port cities had been devastated; nothing much was left but the massive concrete submarine bases, impermeable to bombs or artillery shells. Shortly before the Americans reached the outskirts of the blackened city of Lorient, U-518, one of 188 boats still functioning, embarked on a patrol, strangely enough, to eastern U.S. waters.[1]

As customary, the crew put their belongings in the storage lockers. While they were patrolling off Cape Hatteras, word came from headquarters that their bases in France had been taken by the enemy and that all the French-based boats were to go instead to Norway. "As a result, we lost all our private possessions—many photographs, jewelry, watches, our good tailor-made uniforms, shoes, and everything."

Peter's trip to America brought almost no results: damage to one freighter, the *George Ade,* which was sunk while being towed in a hurricane. When the boat landed in Norway, word came that they were to go to a ship repair yard in Stettin. Petersen, destined for officers school, left the boat. Then U-518 went out on one more war patrol in March 1945 and was sunk by American destroyers *Carter* and *Scott.*

At Itzehoe, near Hamburg, Peter had just begun his studies when the school was closed, requisitioned for German troops returning from Norway and Scandinavia. At Wilhelmshaven the same thing happened. "It was obvious that the war was going to be over quickly, so they issued us rifles. We were supposed to go out into the farm-lands and defend against the British, who were getting closer and closer."

While they were quartered for a short time in farmhouses and barns, the sailors had to forage for their own food. "We caught a cow and killed it and roasted it on a spit and things like that. Fortunately for me, the war was over a day or so before the British would have reached us, and we didn't have to fight. Again, I was saved, because navy men were not supposed to be in the trenches."

When the official announcement came that the war was over, Petersen and friends went back to the school and threw away their gas masks, rifles, and steel helmets before the British arrived. "We were very curious to see what they looked like and what they would do to us, so we stayed in our rooms and looked out the windows when they drove up in their jeeps and trucks. They talked to our officers, and then we had to abandon the school because they wanted to take it over."

"We were given much nicer quarters—on a giant ocean liner, the *Europa,* and we lived very well there until the British came and told us to get the heck out. I recall exploring the ship and climbing inside the huge smokestack. It was very clean." Only about three feet in diameter, the smoke pipes were encased with larger funnels, creating a more attractive appearance. One could enter by a doorway and climb upstairs to the top, to the rim. "I remember one morning we climbed up and sat on top of the smokestack in the sunshine, and even now when I see pictures of the *Europa,* I think about that day."

After their ship stay, the prisoners went again into the country to a prison camp that consisted of a fenced-in area with no tents or food supplies. "The best we could do for shelter was to dig holes in the ground, but they never mistreated us in any way, like beating us. In fact, they treated us correctly except for food and shelter. They didn't care whether we ate or not, so we did the best we could by scrounging." The Germans were then assigned to various farms, and there they bought some sheep and a horse from the farmers and butchered them. No possibility of work existed, so they just sat around waiting for time to pass and occasionally went fishing. "There were too many people, and we were falling all over ourselves."

"There were thousands of us—all navy men. We were loosely guarded and could have escaped, but nobody did." None of them realized exactly where they were or what was going on, as there were no telephones or mail from home, no trains, and no traffic on the roads. Many had no way to find out whether their families were alive or dead. "Everything was shut down." Peter did know that he was only about a hundred miles from his hometown.

One day British officials came around asking if any of the men were farmers, as the food shortage in Germany was critical and the planting of crops was of major importance. "Since my father was a farmer and owned a farm, I said I was a farmer. Even though I detested the idea, I thought it might get me home." So Peter and some others were loaded onto British trucks and taken to the nearest town, Bielefeld, where they signed release papers stating that they were lawfully discharged from the armed forces.

Back on the trucks, the Germans rode to another town and registered; then they were dismissed. "My house was about fifteen miles away, and I walked. I was darn glad to get home, too. It had been about a year since I had been there." When Peter arrived unannounced, the family rejoiced: all seven children had made it through the war, including one brother who had been severely wounded in Russia and sent home.

With the British strictly enforcing curfew laws, the townspeople had to be off the streets between eight in the evening and eight in the morning. "Of course we knew the area much better than the English soldiers did, so we got around anyway. When we saw a patrol coming, we hid until they walked by, then went on our way."

More and more soldiers and sailors were returning to Husum, and "we were all young and wanted to start living again." They organized barn dances in the farmers' barns with accordion music and dancing all night, way past the curfew. "We didn't get home until the wee hours of the morning."

Gradually the curfews eased up, but even with the new freedom, confusion prevailed. "There were military people moving all over the place, and all the German bases had been abandoned. Trucks were left parked in the roads, soldiers had thrown away their rifles, and military equipment was lying around everywhere. Some things were valuable, like a truckload of underwear or uniforms." At an airfield near Husum, "you could have taken any of the planes discarded by the German air force if you had known what to do with it." Tanks were all over the place, and one of Peter's friends was driving around in a half-track.

One day Peter came across an almost-new BMW motorcycle and took it home. "Oh, what a nice machine! But I couldn't register it or anything, and we were not allowed any gasoline, but I sailed around on it for a little bit." Then the British issued an edict: under penalty of death, anything that had belonged to the former German armed forces had to be turned in by a certain date. "I suppose I could have hidden the motorcycle, but I would have had to eventually register it, so I turned the damned thing in. I was chicken. But I thought, 'I made it home safely, so why take a chance on a lousy motorcycle?'"

"Possessing any weapons was punishable by death, as well. So we took great care that we had none of that stuff."

With no jobs available, Peter lived at his parents' farm for six months. All the factories were closed, and what little money people could earn was worthless. With experience in machine repair and engineering from the navy, Peter became a journeyman machine repairman for a short while, then moved to Hamburg and worked for a construction company.

"It was not construction, it was destruction. We took down war-damaged buildings and dismantled them. Once I almost got killed." On one of the large buildings, workmen were in the process of ripping off what was left of the roof with a crane. "I was lying on top of the roof on my belly and feeding the steel cable through it from the crane. Suddenly the roof collapsed under me and somehow, I still don't know how, I caught myself on a beam with my left hand and hung there, holding my whole weight, equipment and all. I immediately reached up and grabbed the beam with my other hand and there I was, dangling about fifty feet in the air with a concrete floor below." Hand over hand, Peter hauled himself over to the next girder, where the men had pushed a ladder to reach him, and he climbed down, to be greeted by the foreman, who said, "Just sit down quietly and don't move." Much relieved, Petersen relaxed and lit a cigarette.

"Construction work paid pretty well, but there was nothing to buy because the stores were all empty. What can you do with money if you can't buy anything?"

Petersen quit construction and went to work in an oil factory that produced cooking oil, a valuable commodity on the black market. "Everything was black market. You had to have something to trade, and we had access to the oil, so we swiped some, whenever we could, took it to the black market and traded it for cigarettes and booze and whatever we needed. That's the only thing that made work worthwhile."

In 1948 came the currency reform. An announcement on the radio said, "Starting tomorrow morning the money you have in your possession is just paper. It is worth nothing at all. However, each person can now pick up forty new marks." And every person in Germany was issued new currency. "The richest man in the country was the one with fourteen children, because he received forty marks for each child."

"And then, like a miracle, the stores had merchandise again, and with the new money you could buy things. It got better and better. The next payday they gave us the new marks." Everything they had saved had lost all value; however, the government later gave people a fraction of their savings in new currency.

Things slowly improved. "You could get decent food, and there was a great surplus of women. I don't know what the statistics were, but it seemed there were about ten women for each guy. It was hogs' heaven." In Hamburg one of the dance halls had a "Widow's Ball," a safe and proper place for young females to go. When the band struck up a waltz, the ladies chose male partners for dancing or served them drinks. "We caught on to that fast. It was nice, and when a widow asked you to dance twice in a row, you had it made for the night."

"In thinking back on it, we had very mixed emotions at the end of the war, because so much was unknown. Would we be shot? Would we become long-term prisoners? Was there a future for us in Germany, with jobs?" Then in 1948, while working in Hamburg, something happened that changed Peter Petersen's life. On a trip back to his hometown of Husum, he met two visitors from the United States —Mrs. Lutz and her seventeen-year-old daughter Irma, who had come to see the elder Lutzes. Mrs. Lutz, who had emigrated to Ohio in 1928 and was the first outsider to come into Husum after the war, stayed for several weeks with her parents, the Petersens' next-door neighbors. When the two women went back to Ohio, Mrs. Lutz offered to sponsor Peter, if he wished to work in Toledo.

"I had always been fascinated with the United States and as a boy had read about Chicago, New York, Niagara Falls, the Indianapolis race, and the cowboys and Indians in Texas. When I had a chance to go there, I took it and went to Ohio in 1950." Three years later and happily working, Peter proposed to Irma Lutz. "Since we had an interesting story to tell, Irma and I were accepted to be married on a national television show in New York called *Bride and Groom*." Today Peter emcees a weekly radio show with German music and news, sponsors a German language-speaking club, and pitches in for the town's big annual Oktoberfest.[2]

20   Wolfgang Heibges, U-999

■ ■

In May 1995 the German newspaper Schleswig-Holsteinischer *published a special section devoted to end-of-the-war events in Schleswig-Holstein, northernmost province in the country, bordering Denmark. Photographs showed elderly refugees hobbling down a gangplank at Flensburg, bombs exploding in a Hamburg shipyard, starving children, British prisoners at Bergen-Belsen prison, and others. During those tumultuous last weeks of the war in Germany, twenty-two-year-old Wolfgang Heibges, commander of U-999, set out to sea with little hope of returning.*

■ ■

By March 1945, with major cities devastated, railroads and canals blown up, American army forces clearing the west bank of the Rhine, and the Soviets coming nearer and nearer to Germany's borders, Hitler still refused to surrender. Instead of saving what he could of industries, transportation, and food supplies, the madman ordered everything left to be blown up; fortunately, his orders were not carried out. Meanwhile, Admiral Dönitz continued with the navy's refugee rescue operations in the Baltic.

"When the Red army moved closer, and German U-boats had to leave the harbors of East Prussia, we boarded onto U-999 more than forty women and children, the youngest three months old, and a group of Hitler Youths, who had been building tank traps and could no

Wolfgang Heibges

longer get home. We sailed from Hela, Poland, submerging just out-side the harbor, and marched toward western Germany," explained Heibges. Because of the excess weight, underwater speed had to be reduced, causing the journey to go more slowly than expected. "It was not an easy trip, with all the children cooped up inside the nar-row confines of the boat. We finally arrived at Warnemünde, and our precious cargo went on shore, to their unknown destinies."

"From there we traveled to Hamburg, arriving on 1 April 1945 at the U-boat bunker Finkenwerder, where we were to have a schnorkel installed." Eight days later British planes dropped extra-large bombs on the bunker, breaking the massive concrete roof and damaging U-999 at the stern and rudder. "The next day we were working to get all the damage repaired before the English troops arrived at Hamburg. They were already advancing toward the city, and at that time the chances were slimmer and slimmer that we could get the boat into really good shape before they reached us."

Superficial problems caused by the falling concrete were patched up; however, time did not allow for the necessary work to be done on U-999's rudder and stern. "Just before the British army took over Hamburg we received an order on 27 April to leave and go to Kiel." Early the next morning, "completely alone, with no escort, U-999 crept out of the harbor in the darkness and traveled down the Elbe River, reaching Brunsbüttel Locks just after dawn." Heibges was convinced that the British troops, camped on the left side of the great river, would see them. "I stopped the diesel engines and ordered use of the quieter electric engines. The tension in the crew was worsening every second, but on the shore no one was moving: they were all asleep in their tents." Sliding smoothly along on the surface, U-999 sailed right past the British camp, and "it would have been easy for them to see a lonely U-boat in the early dawn light. Perhaps for the English soldiers the war had already ended. We went on through the locks and made the trip through the Kiel Canal without any problems."

At four o'clock that afternoon they arrived, feeling relieved, at the Holtenau Locks near Kiel, and moments later docked at the U-boat bunker in Kiel. On 30 April Heibges moved his boat over to the Deutsche Werke Kiel dockyards to get started on repairs, but nothing happened "because no one could see any sense in doing the work because the war was almost ended."

Almost the whole crew remained on board, and on 1 May they listened to the radio news of Hitler's "heroic death" (suicide) in Berlin and the proclamation that Grossadmiral Dönitz would succeed him. Two days later came an order to prepare for departure to Flensburg, as Kiel was to be surrendered to the British army at ten o'clock the next morning.

"At exactly ten o'clock we left Kiel, and with quiet seas and good visibility we traveled at high speed toward the north, 'escorted' by English planes, who more than once dove toward our boat but did not use their guns. With immense relief we reached Flensburg, but there we received an order to go to Gelting Bay [at the southern end of Flensburg Fjord] and wait there for the 'Rainbow Order.'" All German U-boats in the bay were to self-destruct.

"So," Heibges continued, "we made our way back to the bay, which we had passed only a short time before, and put out our anchor somewhere around two or three hundred meters from the beach. A lot of old and new U-boats, fifty of them, and many other different kinds of ships arrived just behind us." A few of the crew lowered a small motorboat, procured earlier by one of the seamen in Flensburg, and rode over to the beach, walked to several nearby houses, and asked the help of the farmers who lived there. "They were willing to keep our personal belongings in their homes, so we spent the entire next day, 4 May, ferrying the portable boat equipment and some of our possessions to shore. Sometimes British planes flew around above us, but they didn't care what was happening down below."

Heibges and crew were considering as to how they could best scuttle their boat, having had no previous experience at it. To sink the boat, it was necessary to have four men: one responsible for the electric engines, the control room mate, the torpedo man, and the commander. All others would have to leave the boat quickly.

"Time was passing since the Rainbow Order had been given, then a second message came in, forbidding the scuttling of U-boats. I was completely confused and did not know what to do. Was this opposite command really following Dönitz's orders?"

Nothing more happened during the night of 4 May to clarify the situation for the boats. Then came the announcement that German capitulation would begin at 8:00 A.M. on 5 May, and conditions of the surrender forbade the sinking, damaging, or destroying of any ships. "Only one thing was absolutely clear. Scuttling a ship after the surrender would act against conditions of the capitulation and would not be allowed in a few hours."

"I did not have to make any decision, because I was told that the first U-boat had started scuttling procedures, and I gave the crew orders to make preparations for sinking. At dawn on 5 May one U-boat after another disappeared from the surface of the sea, but we took our time." After the crew had left the sub, the remaining four started to do their job.

"We prepared the explosive devices so that after the boat sank, we could blow it up." Working calmly and efficiently, the three crewmen opened all the hatches to allow water to fill the boat. Suddenly the men in the stern compartment and control room shouted that water was coming in through the stern torpedo tube openings. "I ordered everyone to abandon ship. The first two quickly jumped into their life raft, and endless minutes went by until the torpedo mate stuck his head out of the front torpedo hatch and asked, 'Is it time?' He could not know, being in the bow, that a great deal of water was already in the back of the boat." Heibges yelled from the bridge: "The boat is sinking! Leave instantly!" The torpedo man, after some difficulty making his way up the sloping deck, went past the tower and jumped into the water.

"I quickly climbed down from the bridge, knowing that the motorboat could not pick me up at the stern. I ran to the bow and leaped into the water, and my only thought was to get as far away as possible from the boat, because of the suction." After the captain had swum a short distance, he looked back and saw the bow of his submarine rise into the air, then plunge with a bubbling noise into the depths. "At that point I realized that my jumping into the water and fast swimming had saved me from drowning, because otherwise I would have been sucked down by the boat."

Completely alone in the frigid Baltic Sea, Heibges saw that U-999 was the last submarine to be sunk. "I hoped that the motorboat would pick me up shortly. Then I spotted the little boat off at a distance, but it did not come to get me. I waved my white commander's cap, which I had not lost, surprisingly, when I jumped into the water, and tried to signal my men." Still wearing his uniform and boots, he tried to blow up his life jacket, but to no avail. "Waving the hat cost a lot of energy, so I started to swim the breaststroke, but the water was about ten degrees [45°F]. I don't know how long it took until I noticed the rescue boat starting toward me, but it seemed an endless time until it reached me. Probably it was only a few minutes." Heibges realized then that he was the last U-boatman in the waters of Gelting Bay. With yells of "Hello!" the crew of U-999 greeted their commander and hauled him aboard, eagerly explaining what took them so long to rescue him. "The motor wouldn't start," they declared. Heibges, worried about his three men who left the sub just before he jumped, asked where they were. "I was relieved when I heard that all of them had been picked up by the motorboat."

Aboard one of the crew pickup tenders, the *Donau*, Heibges and crew were taken into Flensburg and remained there a week. The British navy then ordered them to march inland to Schleswig-Holstein province, where all troops were surrendering, and they lived in various prison camps until July.

"After all the formalities for discharge were done, we were put on British military trucks and transported to a place near Bielefeld, and from there I went by foot to my hometown of Paderborn. I approached the town with much trepidation and hope, as I could see some of the ruins from far away. I was prepared for the worst, as far as my family was concerned." After marching across several large bomb craters, Wolfgang arrived at the house where his mother had lived and saw that the place had suffered only minor damage. Heibges soon found out that his mother and sister had survived the bombing raids, but that his mother had died of an incurable disease three weeks before his discharge.

"In the summer of 1947 my U-boat past caught up with me." The British stuck him in an internment camp at Neuengamme, where he stayed for several months behind barbed wire. "All former submarine commanders and chief engineers, for reasons never made clear, were taken before a Royal Navy review board for questioning and testing. They were especially interested in whether we had started or planned to pursue a different occupation." Heibges conjectured that military occupation forces were worried that the skilled former submarine officers might be receiving lucrative offers from Eastern bloc countries. Having been released and cleared by the British, the youthful sub veteran was then allowed to enter Göttingen University, where he pursued his law degree.[1]

21   Peter Marl, U-103, U-196, U-195

■ ■

Navy rules prohibited photographing or journalkeeping by sailors, but a few managed to smuggle cameras onto their boats or write secret diaries about their adventures. Perhaps they felt, and rightly so, that they were part of memorable historic events. One of these seafaring historians, Obermaat *(Petty Officer) Peter Marl, kept a comprehensive account of his long career on three U-boats, beginning in 1938 and concluding in 1945. Condensed slightly, his story went as follows:*

■ ■

"When German troops occupied Austria [1938], I watched a company of Bavarian mountain troops marching through my hometown of Krungl, and I was inspired to enter military service. I signed up for the German navy in April 1938." The nineteen-year-old Austrian was ready to get into action, but the German government assigned him to the *Reichsarbeitsdienst* (work corps) first. "I was very disappointed."

Dressed in a spanking-new khaki uniform, Marl built fences, moved earth, and erected barracks for a daily stipend of twenty-five pfennigs. To earn a bit more money, Peter charged his friends to take their photos with a camera his parents had given him for Christmas.

When construction work ended in March 1939, Peter reported to the naval base at Wilhelmshaven, Germany, headquarters for the North Sea Fleet. A local sailor met the forty-man group at the train station

Peter Marl

and marched them, suitcases in hand, through the town. "Halfway to the navy base we saw the fuehrer pass. He had just come from the launching of the battleship *Tirpitz.*"

At the base Marl was amazed at all the German dialects spoken by men from diverse regions of the country. Good-looking new uniforms were issued, and the enthusiastic sailors jumped into them, but, "We all had difficulty tying the silk necktie and narrow white band. *Bootsmaat* Klaasen showed us how to do it time and time again. It had to be perfect."

Basic training drills were "a hell of a pain," and the new recruits were confined to base at the beginning. "First we were sworn in and gave an oath of allegiance to the fuehrer. Later, we could go into town with a superior." Peter liked the city of Wilhelmshaven, full of beautiful sights, bars, and dance halls. "We were raw recruits, and if we asked someone to dance, she would usually say, 'I only dance with Mates.'"

Electrifying rumors buzzed throughout Wilhelmshaven and its large naval base, as probabilities of war mounted. "All countries were against us, as one piece of land after another was being retaken by Adolf Hitler into the German fold. It looked as if the situation were very serious."

At Wilhelmshaven docks, a fleet of warships had arrived to pick up munitions. Supply vessels *Dithmarschen* and *Westerwald* were there as well, filled with war materiel. Peter signed up for submarine service but was first put to work loading some of the ships, including *Panzerschiffe Admiral Scheer* and *Admiral Graf Spee*. "It was a very tense situation."

With five others, Marl was detailed to man the antiaircraft gun at the camp living area, then assigned to stand watch at the train depot. "There was a lot of traffic. Many people were being called to the navy and were leaving Wilhelmshaven. All of a sudden we heard on the radio that Adolf was going to make an address." Peter said that everyone ran to the loudspeakers just in time to hear Hitler say, "Force against force," meaning that the invasion of Poland had begun.

Soon thereafter, on 3 September 1939, France and England declared war on Germany. By then the submarines had departed, followed by the battleship *Scharnhorst*. "Some of the destroyers, plus all other available vessels, were being used to lay mines at the entries of British harbors."

"On 9 September I saw the *Admiral Scheer* shooting red tracers, then we heard loud bangs. All our guns were firing as an English plane flew right over us, then there was a big explosion. We thought the whole harbor had been destroyed." Marl remembered that "the joy was great when we heard that an English plane had been shot down and had landed on the stern of the cruiser *Emden*."

Hearing scuttlebutt that English parachutists might be coming, the young sailors started to feel totally confused. "We were afraid and doubtful about what to do, and we were still unable to go to sea. I resented the fact that the Luftwaffe pilots were lucky enough to be the first to meet the enemy."

Intensive submarine training kept Marl busy until spring of 1940. "When we heard about the invasion of Norway on 9 April, we were all a little hurt that we couldn't participate."

With other submariners, Peter watched construction of his new boat, U-103, at Bremen and met his captain, *Korvettenkapitän* Victor Schütze, former commander of U-11 and U-25. "He brought many experienced submariners from his old boat. Ours was a type IXC boat with the newest weapons and machines."

Peter noted in his diary that theoretical training at submarine school "didn't help me much at the beginning." He said that Petty Officer Deeken had to show him everything and that Deeken called him "stupid." "I was always doing something wrong."

At last departure day arrived. From Bremen they entered the Kaiser Wilhelm (Kiel) Canal, opened in 1895 to give the fleet an inland passage from the North Sea to the Baltic. "I really liked the trip through the canal, and it was a funny feeling to be on a submarine in the midst of green fields."

At Kiel the crew survived fitness tests, played games on the beach, then traveled on to Gotenhafen and Danzig. In Danzig they loaded torpedoes into the boat, a grueling job that left them covered with black grease. Next they sailed to Memel for night shooting exercises, and from there went to tactical training near Bornholm. "For seven days we practiced attacking convoys, together with *Kapitänleutnant* Möhle of U-123 and some of the other VIIC boats."

A short respite allowed Marl and friends to go into Rönne, where they ate themselves "big and fat for very little money." On the last night Peter and Fritz Zimmermann went to a dance hall and barely made it back the next morning before U-103 departed. "We had a lot of fun, and the *Bootsmaat* was happy when all his little sheep were together again to depart."

Back they sailed through the Kiel Canal, and arriving in Bremen, were quartered in a small hotel. "I had to function as cook and get up early in the morning to make our coffee." The civilian ladies who

Loading a torpedo into a U-boat. *Bundesarchiv, Koblenz*

worked in the kitchen taught Peter how to prepare meals, and they became his good friends.

At the end of summer 1940 they returned to Wilhelmshaven, and everyone worked hard to get U-103 loaded and ready for front duty. "One night at 2:00 A.M. we were having a late supper, and suddenly there was a big explosion that shook everything. The Tommies [British] had come and thrown some bombs around the harbor, near the boat."

"The next day we went out into the Baltic Sea with flags flying, but one of the diesels malfunctioned and U-103 was forced to return to Kiel for repairs." At last, in August 1940, "we went out against the enemy." That year had brought big triumphs for the U-boats in the Atlantic, and the crew must have felt keenly excited.

U-103, escorted by minesweepers, headed toward Kristiansand, Norway, a new German naval base. "We were dismissed from the convoy and now had free rein." North of England they proceeded into the Atlantic, and ten days later they sank their first tanker, the Norwegian *Nina Borten,* subsequently damaging another and sinking two more. They came across a convoy and charged after it, but "the destroyers dropped a lot of depth charges on our heads." U-103 reported the mass of ships to *BdU*, who sent out a wolf pack that included U-124 (Mohr), U-47 (Prien), U-99 (Kretschmer), and U-100 (Schepke). "They were an awesome team, and the convoy took terrible punishment from these guys."

U-103 headed west to carry out a special mission. They had taken aboard two weather buoys at Wilhelmshaven that could automatically record weather conditions and radio them back to Germany. "We put one of the buoys out at Rockall Bank [west of Ireland], but the other was water damaged in one of the deck storage tubes."

This done, U-103 headed southward for France, to the new German submarine base at Lorient. "I was really seasick, and that fit right in with my [lowly] status on the boat. I lost my confidence."

In the summer of 1940 and after the fall of France, the German navy had begun to build U-boat bases at ports on the Bay of Biscay. At Lorient, a pretty harbor town on the Normandy coast, crewmen found things in a strange state. "Everything was mixed up. The submarines were camouflaged with nets and tied up beside a funny old half-sunk steamship. We broke out a portable record player and put on *Denn wir fahren gegen England*, a popular navy song." U-103 docked near a power plant, where 2. Flotilla Chief Fischer greeted them. "Our quarters were miserable," griped Marl. "There were no tables in our rooms, and my pillowcase was not changed the whole time we were in the shipyard." Observing that the French navy had slept there in hammocks, Peter commented that it was a shame the "grand nation let their sailors sleep in such a primitive way." The sub crew had to march through the town in their dirty work clothes to take meals at the big Hotel Beausejour, where naval officers were billeted, and "we did not give the French people a good impression."

Marl said that submarine sailors were everywhere. "Alcohol was cheap, and champagne sometimes put us over the edge. The grand amour prevailed here, as well as at other bases."

While U-103 waited for spare parts from Germany, the crew enjoyed time off at Carnac, a resort near Lorient, where they luxuriated in excellent hotels, went swimming, and rode horses on the beach. Then in late fall of 1940, the boat headed out to sea, with success looking highly possible.

"On this trip the commander did not miss with a single torpedo, and even when destroyers blasted us with seventy depth charges, the boat remained intact. We were probably down so deep that the Tommies could not reach us with their bombs." Then, with eight ships sunk, U-103 turned south toward home. They seemed invincible.

About two hundred miles out of Lorient, the watch spotted a plane in the distance and the alarm bell screamed. "We jumped into the boat and closed the hatch. The chief opened the vents, and as we went under, water poured through the air vents into the boat—a lot of it. It looked like we were in a shower." Someone had made a mistake, causing U-103 to plunge downward at a frightening angle.

"We were plummeting with our terrible weight into the depths," said Peter. "Everybody to the back," shouted Schütze, and all the men struggled uphill to the stern. Righting itself, the sub became heavy in the rear, and everyone rushed to the bow. "But it didn't help."

"We could not make it through the electric motor room any more, because water had shorted out the motors and caused a fire. It smelled like burning paint and rubber, and the smoke was unbearable. Meanwhile, the boat was falling deeper and deeper." The chief frantically started up the pumps, but the boat had gone down so far that the water could not be forced out against the tremendous external pressure.

Deadly chlorine gas from the batteries began to fill the rapidly sinking vessel, and it seemed that they were in a death trap. "*Klar bei Tauchretter*," came the order, and the men grabbed their breathing devices. Then after a few minutes: "Surface. Blow the tanks." The boat began to reach an even keel, then slowly started to rise, and at a hundred meters she began to speed toward the surface. "The last thirty meters we could not even follow the depth gauge. Then there was a jump and a smack. We had reached the top but were tilting to one side." The crew opened the hatch and rushed out to man the two-centimeter antiaircraft gun.

At once they spotted the airplane they had seen before diving. "It came toward us and dipped its wings, and we saw that it was a German Condor. That whole shit was unnecessary." Still sloshing with seawater, U-103 limped with one diesel into Lorient.

"The reception was great, and some of us received the Submarine Front Medal or the Iron Cross. Our captain was awarded the Knight's Cross, and we were all very proud of him." Peter wore his new medal on furlough, feeling "as grand as a Spaniard."

On the next patrol in 1941 Marl's boat encountered a British freighter and fired several torpedoes that missed their target. The fourth hit home, set at a depth of just one meter. "We surfaced and watched the British crew abandon ship; then we were going to finish her off with the 10.5 cannon, but after we fired six shots, she returned fire." In amazement, the crew realized that the British seamen had rowed around to the other side of the freighter and climbed back aboard. "That was very brave of them. If every enemy sailor showed courage like that, we would have had a really tough time." Whacked with one last "eel," the fighting freighter went under.

Their next victim, a ten-thousand-ton tanker carrying aircraft gasoline, exploded with a deafening blast and burned with enormous flames. The skipper and crew, with dust and smoke in their eyes, left the scene, only to learn some days later that Lehmann-Willenbrock in U-96 had spotted the still-floating wreckage and finished her with a coup de grâce.[1]

Making ready to attack the next ship while submerged, U-103 was about to unleash a torpedo when her target blew up, broke in half, and sank. "Somebody else was already working on that one, and it turned out to be Möhle in U-123. He shot her right out from under our nose. We were very hurt."

In spite of their frustrations, the crew arrived safely in Lorient, where two military bands and crowds of friends and acquaintances from other U-boats cheered them in. "By now the base was built up and functioning. We had chairs, tables, and beds, and all those things that make life a little easier for a sailor."

Following an enjoyable stay at the base and a trip home, Marl reported for duty and received a new tropical outfit: khaki shirt, shorts, and a pith helmet. No information was given, however, about where it would be worn; they would be told once out at sea. U-103 crossed the Bay of Biscay, diving constantly because of enemy air surveillance, sailed past Cape Finisterre at the western tip of Spain, and started her patrol near the Canary Islands. "That was still fertile ground for the submarines. In the first days we sank six steamers, but unfortunately, we ran out of torpedoes and had to head for a supply ship near the South American coast."

At the rendezvous point they found U-38 waiting as well, and "there was a little disagreement between the two boats because each of them wanted to be first." This settled, the pair of submarines transferred ammunition, fuel, lubricating oil, and food into every nook and cranny. "As for the torpedoes, it was an ungodly amount of work loading them onto the deck, because we were not really equipped for such a maneuver. But in several hours the crew got it together and we did it."

U-103 crossed the Atlantic once again to patrol off west Africa. The radio operator, decoding messages from Freetown, noted departure times for British planes and ships, as well as the ships' cargoes. In one case Peter's crew was ready to attack a merchantman loaded with airplane parts, but she never appeared because another U-boat got to her first.

Out of fuel once more, Schütze made his way to meet a tanker near the Azores and was greeted by four other U-boats. After three days of waiting, they all gave up on the supply ship and exchanged a few canned foods. U-103's only alternative now was to head into a secret neutral port in the Canary Islands: Las Palmas, a Spanish protectorate. "During the night we ran submerged into the harbor, where we met the *Charlotte Schliemann,* a ten-thousand-ton German tanker." After securing the U-boat with lines, they worked "with the speed of wind" transferring fuel and keeping an eye on an armed British merchant ship lying nearby. "They couldn't touch us, and we couldn't touch them, because we were in a neutral country."

In two-and-a-half hours the job was completed, and U-103 moved out to sea, traveling swiftly on the surface, as daylight had not yet come. When the sun rose, they were "far from land."

After the rendezvous, "the food improved an awful lot. We even had white bread and chocolate, fresh fruit, beer and schnapps; we were really overjoyed and thankful to the men of the *Charlotte Schliemann.*"

A sailor decorates the tower of U-103 to celebrate Commander Victor
Schütze's winning of Oak Leaves to Knight's Cross, October 1941.
Bundesarchiv, Koblenz

The crew of U-103 hoped that the sailors of the supply ship could get
home soon, knowing that they had been at sea for years.

Back at Lorient, Marl's crew received a somewhat cool reception,
probably a mistake, considering that they had destroyed thirteen merchant ships, but "everyone knew that Schütze had sunk enough to get
the Oak Leaves." Then came news that most of the men would be
transferred to other subs and that Schütze would become a flotilla
commander. Many regretted parting with close friends, but Peter's
trip to Austria improved his outlook. "My brother and I climbed
Grimming mountain and went often to Fensterln." Following an old
German custom, a young man could go out late at night and knock on
a girlfriend's window, whereupon the girl would decide whether or
not to let him scramble into her room. If she slept on a second story
and he had big hopes, he would use a ladder.

At the submarine base once again, Peter learned his boat would be under the command of *Kapitänleutnant* Werner Winter. In the summer of 1941 they departed, traversing the mine-infested Bay of Biscay, and U-103 was forced to submerge "more often than ever," dodging RAF planes. Near the Azores they ran into a convoy and dispatched five merchant ships with six torpedoes, maneuvering on the surface. News of this excellent accomplishment reached headquarters, and a big celebration greeted the crew when they docked in France.

At Christmastime Peter visited his family shortly after 11 December, when Germany declared war against America. "We submarines were supposed to take it to the piers of New York. Hardegen, in U-123, was already on his way, and we left at the beginning of 1942 . . . as part of Operation *Paukenschlag* [Roll of the Drum], to hit the Yankees in the steamer lines."

Crossing the Atlantic they saw no other ships, but nearing America's shores, "it started to get lively." Peter was amazed that the ships were ablaze with lights, and there were so many merchantmen that deciding which to attack first was difficult. "The whole area was full of singly traveling freighters, and there was no defense of any kind. That was hard to understand." Off Delaware, U-103's crew could see light rays flashing in the darkness. "The whole sky was lit up with spotlights. Apparently the soldiers had never heard about the war."

After several days of U-boat attacks the ships turned off their lights and began to zigzag. Winter continued hunting in shallow water near the snowy, dark, New England coast and dispatched four merchantmen, using his last torpedoes. As the lifeboats of their final victim were being lowered into the freezing ocean, Peter sadly observed that the sailors were wearing only sport shirts and thin pants. "I felt very sorry for them."

With his mission completed, Winter transferred some fuel to Teddy Suhren in U-564 and headed home. A few days later the chief engineer, smoking a pipe on the bridge, happened to glance up as a plane came diving toward the sub. "Alarm!" he shouted, as he tried to jump into the boat. In a panic, the chief hit his head on the hatch, knocking himself out. The others lowered him into the boat and executed the diving operations without him, but before they could make it much below the surface, four explosions rocked the sub. "We all had stupid expressions on our faces," recalled Marl, "and from then on we exercised much greater caution on watches."

In Lorient Dönitz awarded Peter the Iron Cross First Class. His days of sea battles were adding up, as was the emotional stress. At the age of twenty-three the young sailor, whose hands were constantly trembling, felt almost like an old man. "Gradually I had become a bundle of nerves, like all submariners."

After a relaxing vacation in Austria and more training, Marl went to Bremen to join the crew of one of the largest German submarines in the navy, U-196, a type IXD₂. He wondered why none of the previous crew had wanted to stay on the boat, and "for me that was a sign that there might be some problems." At first everyone thought Commander Eitel-Friedrich Kentrat was a pretty good captain, but opinions later reversed.

Equipped with eighteen weeks of provisions, twenty-four torpedoes, artillery ammunition, and fuel oil, U-196 departed Kiel on 2 March 1943. At that time the Allies were making huge air raids on German cities, the Soviets had defeated Germany's 6th Army at Stalingrad, and the British were advancing in North Africa. In spite of all, the wolf packs were holding their own. "During those days almost four to five boats were leaving Kiel every day for front duty. We were facing a submarine war like the world had never seen."

A new gadget had been installed on the boat deck, "a funny looking wooden cross with an electrical connection that could warn us of enemy airplane radar." The Biscay Cross, as it was called, had to be handed down into the boat before every dive, but it alerted the crew that a plane was approaching.

Kentrat's discipline became harsh as the trip progressed southward toward the Azores. The commander ordered muster each day, something Marl had never experienced at sea, and at any excuse Kentrat and his officers threatened lower-ranking sailors with jail or court-martial. Many were sentenced to fourteen days in the brig when they returned to France. "I had never seen a man arrested on my previous trips."

Approaching the equator, the crew started to get "pretty good sunburns." Below decks, the heat was so intense that no one could sleep before two in the morning. "Admiral Trident" appeared, announcing that the "equator baptism" would soon occur and that "His Majesty Neptune, ruler of all oceans, seas, lakes, and ponds, would be coming on board to free the boat from the dirt of the northern hemisphere." Next day "Neptune" arrived with his "wife Thetis" and an entourage of unsavory-looking characters composed of crew members who had already made the crossing.

The "unsavory characters" forced all who had not been baptized to swallow large pills, covered them with dirt, then scrubbed them with brushes and threw them into the water for cleansing. During these hijinks everybody forgot about the war, and each received a certificate for his equator crossing. Wolfgang Lüth summed up the scene in December, 1943, saying: "I am of the opinion that young men should experience once in this life how much a healthy body can endure; the captain's duty is to see that the rough play does not degenerate into sadism."[2]

As U-196 sailed southward, cold weather and storms set in and tensions increased, making a difficult voyage worse. After rounding the southern tip of Africa, they arrived at their destination in the Indian Ocean, where other German submarines were already at work.

One day a destroyer came bearing down on them, and Kentrat yelled for a torpedo to be fired, but the "eel" became stuck in the tube with its motors running. With Kentrat shouting and cursing, they roared downward at a steep angle as the destroyer churned just above them, and the defective missile slid out. After this incident Kentrat ordered the entire torpedo crew to exercise for two hours every day, although they were not at fault.

With food and fuel diminishing, U-196 received orders to meet her old tanker friend *Charlotte Schliemann.* At the rendezvous, which lasted four days, Kentrat met U-mates Lüth, Gysae, Hartmann, Bartels, and Dommes. The commanders held a conference on board the big tanker and hopped on and off each other's boats to visit. "That seemed a little reckless to me," mused Marl. "What would have happened if the enemy had found us and attacked?"

U-196 headed north through the Mozambique Channel, between east Africa and Madagascar, observing nothing. Anxious for action,

U-196 meets ten-thousand-ton German tanker *Charlotte Schliemann* in Indian Ocean for fuel and supplies, summer 1943.

they fired a torpedo at a little sailing ship. "However, he was lucky, because the torpedo went under him."

The action started soon enough, though, when enemy planes spotted them and unloaded a rain of bombs. A day or so later, on a Sunday, the skipper ordered the men to transfer "eels" from the deck into the torpedo room with utmost speed, as they were surfaced and vulnerable. "After all the work was finished, the commander went into the galley and casually fried some eggs." The crew, puzzled as to why Kentrat thought they would be safe while transferring torpedoes in such a danger zone, asked their skipper how he knew that no enemy planes would attack them. "The British don't work on Sundays," he told them.

The respite was short, for thereafter the British bombed them unmercifully. "We were morally at an all-time low—I can't describe it," said Peter. "Besides that, there was the behavior of our superiors. It would have been better to hear the noise of ten bombs than the voice of the commander. Everyone shook when his words came through the speaker."

With dismal feelings the crew started home. Because German secret codes changed periodically, it was time for U-196 to obtain the latest codes, required for the last two weeks of her journey. Headquarters told them to meet U-197 (Robert Bartels) for the information; however, at the rendezvous point Wolfgang Lüth in U-181 appeared and gave them the new radio codes. "Lüth had received the Oak Leaves and Swords for his Knight's Cross, but Kentrat had been awarded his three weeks before that and tried to lord it over him. Lüth paid no attention to him."

As the rendezvous continued, U-196 received a message saying that U-197, sixty miles to the north, had been bombed by a plane and was in urgent need of help. Kentrat replied that he was heading south because he was low on fuel and could not transfer a sufficient amount from Lüth. Two days later *BdU* asked: "What is your position?" When U-196 explained where they were, headquarters gave them a tongue-lashing over the wireless radio, demanding that they go north to search for Bartels, and U-196 reversed course. "We went at full speed to the area where Bartels had disappeared three days before. Obviously we found nothing. I never understood why we went south instead of north."[3]

When they reached the Cape of Good Hope, frequent air patrols and ferocious seas forced them to travel underwater for hours at a time. At one point the commander surfaced the boat and climbed into the tower to check the situation, followed by Marl. Just as Kentrat opened the hatch a monstrous wave smashed over the submarine, pushing it nine meters under, and then, before the two men could move, the boat plunged again, bringing tons of water in on top of them. By a great stroke of luck, U-196 roared up once more, and they closed the hatch. "Afterward we each got a sip of cognac."

Continuing the long voyage back to France, Kentrat's boat unexpectedly encountered a submarine, and the boats approached each other warily. Signals revealed that it was Lüth in U-181. Kentrat had heard that Lüth had just been awarded the Diamonds to the Oak Leaves and Swords to the Knight's Cross, Germany's highest decoration, but offered no congratulations. Instead, Kentrat insisted on being the leader of the two subs on their trip home and attempted to give Lüth orders. After three days of discord, Lüth veered off to steer his own course.[4]

With enemy presence everywhere, U-196 made slow headway along the West African coast. "We surfaced only to charge the batteries at night for a couple of hours, so it took a long time to cover any distance, and the food was getting worse daily. We slipped past the Canary Islands and Azores like a fox." At last U-196 headed into the Gironde River and landed at Bordeaux. They had been patrolling for 225 days —the longest trip to that date made by a German submarine in World War II. Families of the crew members had thought their sons were missing in action.

"From day one, some of our men were thrown into the brig, and many had to appear at court-martials. Our watch engineer was sent to Paris to the mental hospital, and torpedo mechanic Boost had a terrible case of nerves." At the base Kentrat and Lüth took special care not to meet.

Marl enjoyed Bordeaux, with its excellent wines, movies, plentiful food, and girls. The fun was spoiled when he was stricken with a bladder infection and eye trouble, causing his removal from U-196 and an assignment to land duty, digging trenches and building massive submarine pens.

Marl and friends were losing faith in the German cause as the war dragged on, but the U-boats continued to fight. Marl did not realize that his next patrol—on U-195 with *Oberleutnant zur See* Friedrich Steinfeldt—would be his last. Before being converted into a transport vessel along with U-180, U-195 had been one of the swiftest submarines in the fleet, but now had all torpedo tubes removed for storage space. On deck were two 2-centimeter guns and a 3.7-centimeter antiaircraft gun for protection, as well as a new schnorkel that enabled them to charge the batteries while submerged.

"We worked hard loading stuff for the Far East below decks. In the deck tubes we put optical glass, and we stored mercury, steel rods, torpedoes, lead, light metals for aircraft construction, medicines, machine parts, communications equipment, and search devices in the forward and aft torpedo rooms. In spite of all this, it was still quite comfortable."

In the meantime, the Normandy invasion was progressing, with great disruption of the German rail system by the French underground, who were blowing up bridges as well. "Our leaders were having bad times in those days, and we sank only a few ships in the invasion fleet. In Bordeaux everything was still quiet, but after a few weeks the air raids started, first at the oil loading docks. The oil was meant to supply our southern front, and it burned for several days."

"Then came the attacks on the U-boat bunker. At first there was only a little jab at it; however, the munitions bunker blew up completely. The U-boats were still safe, and all returning subs had to come into Bordeaux because the other bases had been bombed and were surrounded by the Americans." Every bunker pier was filled with submarines.

As the great invasion progressed, Allied planes dropped hundreds of bombs on the submarine pens and around Bordeaux, leaving the pens intact, but creating a desolate, burning wasteland of the city. All civilians were gone. "The town was all ours now—we became kings of the vegetable gardens, and Paul Euler and I discovered a very nice vineyard, where we took some of the best grapes. In the canteen they were giving everything away, because our money had become worthless."

In their well-protected pens the U-boats awaited fuel, torpedoes, and food supplies, as well as various repairs. Some of them, like U-178, had come from East Asia with raw rubber and other scarce materials. All subs unfit for use were dismantled and the parts given to other vessels, then the stripped U-boats were blown up.

Suddenly, an order came: "Remove all cargo from U-195 and load it with dynamite for Brest or St. Malo." Peter's crew, appalled and worried, followed orders and converted their boat into "a gigantic powder keg." On August 3 the 6th Armored Division arrived at St. Malo, an old French stronghold, where a section of the division remained, and three days later the division vanguard made it to fortress Brest. The Germans, knowing that the Allies were intent upon capturing French ports, needed dynamite to blow up harbor facilities before the enemy could capture them.[5]

A few days later came a second announcement: "Everything back as before." Apparently the call for dynamite could not be expedited because of massive Allied land and air attacks at Brest. With immense relief, the crew carefully unloaded the dynamite and replaced it with the goods for East Asia. Space being limited, no schnapps was allowed on board, and all bottles had to be left on the pier for the enjoyment of the shipyard workers. "We were loaded like a pack mule."

With U-180 and two escort boats, they departed Bordeaux, headed out the Gironde and tied up to a buoy at Le Verdon, near the Bay of Biscay. A sudden air raid alarm caused U-195 to dive, and in their descent they discovered that the boat was too heavy, as was their companion, U-180. After throwing some unnecessary items overboard, U-180 and U-195 continued their journey through the mined waters with escorts.

In the Bay of Biscay they were greeted with enemy planes and crash-dived again. "We had a great deal of weight forward and went down extremely fast, at a steep angle. Then at eighty meters we crashed into the seafloor." Steinfeldt, attempting to free the boat, dumped most of the drinking water, but without result. Even the straining engines could not budge the pack mule. "Then we put some high pressure air in the tanks, broke free, and returned to periscope depth."

It was daylight, and a quick observation revealed three destroyers speeding toward them. "We did a fast dive and snuck along the bottom. That should have saved us, but the destroyers were listening to us and dropped some charges. Luckily, they missed by several thousand meters."

Submerged securely, U-195 slowly traveled southward. "The air in the boat started getting stale. We were still working hard, making repairs, and many of us were totally exhausted. Some were lying on their bunks sucking air from their breathing devices, and others had passed out in the aisles." Hannes Klein bravely ran among his stricken mates and replaced breathing boxes for them, an act for which Peter thought he should receive a medal, but none was awarded.

Fifty hours later U-195 surfaced to take in fresh air and charge the batteries. The next night they went to fourteen meters and for the first time used the schnorkel. Traveling along the coast of Spain, Peter wondered what the night fishermen in their boats might be thinking when they saw "a smokestack going by without a ship."

To the west of Cape Finisterre they received a radio message that U-180, their companion boat, had not reported. "Nobody ever heard from them again, and so once more we lost some good comrades. We are getting fewer and fewer."

After thirty-five days of underwater travel, U-195 began to run on the surface at night, in daytime submerged. At the equator they celebrated the customary "baptism," passed through the turbulent waters of the Cape of Good Hope, and entered the Indian Ocean with orders to proceed to the U-boat base at Batavia (now Jakarta), Java. As the December temperature grew warmer, the men celebrated Christmas with a traditional cake and received holiday greetings from the commander, who handed out little glasses of schnapps and rum.

"The last days of our trip the diesels were going full speed, and on 27 December Seaman Bänsch sighted land." Everyone who was free went on deck to see the coast. "We could smell it. A beautiful aroma came from the islands, sweet and rather spicy." As the boat drew closer and closer, the crew, with visions of a fairy-tale paradise, strained to catch their first glimpse. Entering the Sunda Strait, the first sailboats appeared, and small islands began to be visible in the morning sun. Coconut palms fringed the shores, giving the impression of tranquility. "However, our trained eyes observed that many of the small islands had been converted into fortresses by the Japanese."

To the surprise of the crew, a German Arado 196 flew toward the boat, gave the proper recognition signal, and escorted U-195 for several hours. "Allegedly there were many enemy submarines in this area. Then the plane landed on the water and the pilot came aboard. He told us that we could not stay long in Jakarta because yesterday a Japanese ammunition ship had been blown up—obviously sabotage." Hearing this, the men's spirits fell, as they had looked forward to a safe harbor.

A small boat with a Japanese flag approached, bringing a German officer and Japanese pilot to the U-boat. As U-195 neared the harbor, the crew donned new tropical uniforms and prepared to land. At the pier stood Japanese and German officers, including base commander *Korvettenkapitän* Kandeler. "All we could think of was some shore leave with fresh food and relaxation, with beautiful nights of sleep in real beds."

Several other U-boats had arrived before U-195, and their com-

manders greeted Steinfeldt straightaway. Along with the visiting captains, baskets of fruit arrived, and "we went at them like lions, especially the bananas." A bus took most of the U-195 crew into town,
leaving Peter and a few others on the boat to stand guard.

Intense heat and mosquitoes plagued the German sailors, who
sweated profusely and had a hard time sleeping. Peter, on his first trip
into Jakarta, was dazzled by sights of people bathing and washing
clothes in the Kali River and throngs of Indonesians in the city carrying exotic wares in baskets on poles. Japanese soldiers were everywhere. "They made a happy impression, wearing their short pants.
Many of them were holding hands, like little girls, and at first I thought
they were children, but to my surprise, they were about twenty years
old."

U-195's crew learned to use bicycle taxis to get around, enjoying
the bars, restaurants, and women. They celebrated Christmas again,
then were told they had a new mission to perform. U-532 (Ottoheinrich Junker) was heading home, along with two others, U-861 (Jürgen
Oesten) and U-510 (Alfred Eick), all three loaded with raw rubber and
tungsten, urgently needed by Germany. U-195 was to resupply Junker
at sea on a certain day in a specified large area, where it would be
extremely difficult to find the other submarine.

On 8 February Marl's boat arrived at the correct grid square and
roved the waters submerged, listening for engine sounds and searching after dark on the surface. Next day they spotted a shadow on starboard, which proved to be U-532. "The excitement on both sides was
great. We received a request list from Junker, then the two boats dove
and followed a prearranged course, so that the transfer could take
place that night."

On surface again, all off-duty men laid out the large rubber hose
for fuel transfer and piled spare engine parts, food stuffs, medicine,
and other items on deck. Steinfeldt ordered everyone to write a few
words to their loved ones at home, and after resupplying U-532, the
letters were given to them for delivery. With cheers from U-195,
Junker sailed off, and Steinfeldt returned to Jakarta.

"The war was looking bad for us. Even though the Anglo-Americans
were already on the Rhine, with Russians marching against our east-

ern frontiers and the Balkans cut off, our leaders were promising that some very special weapons would be forthcoming, but our enemies' great steamroller did not allow these plans to reach fruition."

When the crew learned that U-195 would continue to be used as a cargo boat in East Asia, they were badly disappointed, having been told that same day that they would be heading home. Instead, the boat traveled eastward to the supply base at Surabaya, Java, for repairs. There the sailors unloaded their vessel, then set about exploring the town. Peter described the population as a "fantastic mixture of people: Malays, Chinese, Arabs, Indians, Japanese, and Europeans." All Dutch citizens had been sent to prison camps years earlier.

In March, Peter spent his furlough in an attractive house with swimming pool and tennis court in the scenic resort village of Tretis. Some of the crew made a horseback trip to the top of Welirang, a sulfur-producing volcano, and from the peak they could see the island of Bali, "a wonderful view."

Back in Surabaya, repairs on U-195 were almost completed, and on 4 May 1945 base commander Joachim Hoppe called muster on the tennis courts. "The fuehrer is dead," he told them. "Enemies are all over the Reich, and Berlin is overrun by Russian troops. Some of our units are still fighting in the north, but that will collapse in the next few days." *Grossadmiral* Dönitz had signed a cease of hostilities with the British and Americans but hoped to keep fighting the Russians.

Next to U-195 at the dock sat a heavily guarded Japanese ship, the *Kitchitai*, where many officers in dress uniforms stood. "Nobody knew what was going on." Aboard U-195 the crew assembled on deck. "Following an order from the German ambassador in Tokyo, we are to lower our flag. We have lost the war," announced Steinfeldt. He continued to speak, reminding the men of the great struggles and battles Germany had endured. "Attention," he ordered, "Face the flag. Lower the flag." Peter remembered that he felt desolated as he watched the first watch officer haul down the red, white, and black banner, fold it, and hand it to Steinfeldt. With misting eyes, the commander accepted it, turned, and dabbed his eyes with the flag. As he walked toward the gangplank, the captain of the *Kitchitai* intercepted the commander and accompanied him back. "From now on, the submarine

U-195 belongs to Nippon Soukaigon. We are all sorry that you have lost this war and that you have made peace with our joint enemies. Today your armed forces are disbanded."

Then the Japanese sailors and officers from the *Kitchitai* marched on board, blew a trumpet, and hoisted the Japanese flag. "Our hearts were full of anger," said Peter, who glared at the bold red and white rising sun fluttering over his U-boat. In launches the men were taken back to their base, where they found the entire complex surrounded by Japanese guards with rifles: the submariners were now prisoners of their former allies.

"We spent three days locked up, and on the fourth day the port commander, Captain Futchi, sent us some chocolate and cigarettes. Some of the local girls threw more cigarettes, cakes, and cookies over the fence to us, too. Finally we were allowed to go downtown for a few hours."

A short time later, the German crewmen had to return to U-195 to instruct the Japanese in operating the submarine systems. "Language was a great barrier, but we formed many a good friendship with them." Slowly the Japanese were getting the boat ready for duty, but as yet they had not mastered the mechanisms. "Everything we tried to tell them had been for nothing."

Their base slated for abandonment, Peter and crew were assigned to work on a tea farm, and several of them, including Marl, went in advance to prepare their quarters. When the others arrived, they told their mates they thought Japan could not hold out much longer in the war. After about two weeks the Japanese did surrender, signing the capitulation papers aboard the battleship *Missouri.*

Local Dutch citizens were released from prison camps, but Indonesia was now struggling with internal problems. Two days after the surrender of Japan, the Republic of Indonesia was proclaimed and Sukarno elected president, but trouble was yet to come. "There were battles and skirmishes with the followers of Sukarno, who as far as we were concerned were nothing but pirates who went through the country plundering and robbing anyone they came across. All white people were their enemies." Representatives of the Sukarno government came to the German camp to try to persuade the men to side with them, but group leader Burghagen refused. Now facing Indonesian enemies, "We had to guard our fences with a meager supply of weapons: six rifles, two machine guns, and about thirty Mauser pistols."

A band of extremists attacked the officers quarters and cookhouse but were driven away, and in the nearby hills sporadic shooting could be heard. "Some Indonesians forced their way into a neighboring house, where several German women and two unarmed German officers were gathered, along with a few civilians. The Indonesians ordered all of these people to walk out the front door with their hands up, and they shot every one of them except my friend, Frau Huber, to death."

"Then the Singapore Gurkhas showed up and occupied Jakarta, as well as the surrounding suburbs." The sub crew, at the farm grinding grain and cutting silage for the cattle, could find almost nothing to eat, so Steinfeldt collected a kitty, and they were able to buy a few vegetables and eggs. "We would have had enough money for our return trip to Europe, too."

Exhausted and overworked, Peter fell ill with malaria and was forced to seek treatment in the hospital. Once recovered, he remained there as an orderly, and was surprised one day to see Steinfeldt being brought in. The commander, stricken with severe dysentery, died on 29 November 1945, six months after his country had surrendered.

To help protect the Dutch population, the U-boat crew was transferred to a British military barracks in another area, where shooting continued nightly. "With our binoculars we discovered Indonesians sniping in the palm trees. The next day we shot at them with machine guns, then it quieted down. When they came close to our camp we lit up the surrounding straw huts with gasoline, making great explosions, like fireworks."

"The British treated the German prisoners quite well," wrote Peter, and another Christmas passed for U-195's crew on foreign soil. Then, at the end of January 1946, they were taken to the "Devil's Camp" at Priok, on the Java coast. After spending a night huddled on the ground in pouring rain with their shoes disintegrating, the men boarded a dirty steamer, leaving suitcases behind for later transfer. "I was allowed to take my toiletries, guitar, and accordion." Arriving at Onrust Island, they were met by heavily armed Dutch guards, who herded them into prison buildings surrounded with barbed wire fences.

Seventy men slept together in one building on raw wood bunks and were given food that "smelled of burned hay and tasted revolting." At night the barracks were locked and latrines closed, and the building next to them housed seven hundred Indonesian guerrillas, including robbers and murderers.

When a few of the Germans went to work as cooks, the food improved, and everyone started to share his emergency rations, as well. But those who possessed a few halfway decent garments refused to loan them to comrades who had almost none, and friendships dissolved. Badly in need of their clothes, the men pleaded with the Swiss Red Cross representative and the Austrian consul; finally, after two months, the suitcases arrived. "Our bags were in incredibly bad condition. All our good things had been stolen, and what was left was tattered and full of dirt and feces. We were convinced that the Dutch had done it."

On Ascension Day, a religious holiday following Easter, the routine was relaxed, and it was announced that three men from every barracks would be allowed to go to a nearby island to fish, accompanied by two guards. This gave the U-boat prisoners hopes of making an escape, and they collected some extra clothing for the fishermen. When the sub group arrived at the island, they persuaded the guards to go off and shoot some ducks, while the three crept back to the boat and rowed away. By the time the guards realized their wards were missing, it was too late to stop them. However, the luckless escapees were arrested by street police in the city, brought back to camp, and placed in a heavily guarded prison.

"Things got worse for us. The food was hardly edible, except for the bread, and seven of us shared one loaf. We were all very thin—our ribs were showing." Mrs. Huber, the German woman who had escaped execution, sent Peter a small package of food, which he shared with his mates.

To kill the monotony of prison life, the men made kites, painted designs on them, and flew them in the afternoon breeze. An air force sergeant trapped a small bird and after a few days released him. That night the little creature returned to the compound and lit on the men's feet and hands, to their great delight.

Those with technical skills put together a radio receiver with five tubes, and after dark, when the electricity came on, the crew secretly listened to the news. Then, writing in tiny script, they produced a newspaper and smuggled it around the camp, telling others what was happening in the outside world.

On 5 July three former U-195 crewmen, who had escaped into civilian life, visited the prison and told their friends that they had been doing business in the black market and with the money had purchased houses and taken women friends to live with them. They said that after Japan's surrender, the Indonesians had seized U-195, but when the Gurkhas captured Surabaya, the British hoisted the Union Jack on the boat. Power plants had been blown up during the fighting, and German crew members were recruited to run the diesel engines, driving U-195's electric generators to make electricity for the city. A Dutch submarine did the same. When the task was completed, the British intended to sink the German sub and were towing it out of the harbor when the ropes broke. Six of the submariners then manned their old tin friend, steered her out of the harbor, and scuttled her.

Although the guards in the prison camp had confiscated all the crew's belongings, including postage stamps and treasury, conditions began to improve, and the prisoners were allowed to go outside the grounds to fish and swim. Even doors were no longer locked. "We could have a radio in our room, and the food was getting better every day." On the first of October 1946, when the crew heard by way of a Java station that the Nüremberg trials were in progress, they listened to the news with serious faces. Three weeks later the announcement came that they were to be shipped home. "The anticipation and joy of leaving this terrible island were immense."

Dutch navy boats picked them up and ferried them to the troop ship *Sloterdijk*, and on 5 November the voyage home began. "Everyone had his own bunk," gloated Marl, "and the food was unusually good, so good that it made some of us sick because we had had so little to eat." Past the coast of Arabia they sailed, through the Suez Canal, on through the Mediterranean, and past Malta and Sicily. "As old warriors, we had a hard time seeing battle sites as losers." On through the Straits of Gibraltar they went, around Portugal, and through the Bay of Biscay. "In Dover we took a pilot aboard, who guided us through the still-active North Sea minefields."

On 12 December 1946 the men of U-195 arrived at the spectral ruins of Hamburg, where they were put into cattle cars and shipped to a nearby concentration camp. There they saw seven thousand former SS soldiers, too weak to stand, rolling from side to side on the ground in misery. "We had to lie on bare concrete with no heat; we could not sleep; and the food was intolerable. On the first day two men died."

Then they were transferred to a second concentration camp, the infamous Dachau, where they spent Christmas Eve and were served a meager supper with no bread or water. "That was the worst time of my life." Then, on the first of January 1947, veteran Peter Marl, who had served his country for 825 harrowing days in three submarines and endured twenty months of prison, walked through the gates of Dachau to freedom and home.

Back in Austria, Peter started a new career, taking over his father's successful farm in Krungl. As well as farming, the former seaman became a famous member of the *Bergwacht,* a volunteer group who rescued injured mountain climbers and skiers in the Alps.

NOTES

Chapter 1: Jürgen Wattenberg

1. Jürgen Wattenberg, interview by author, Hamburg, Germany, 6 April 1995.
2. Sweetman, "Great Sea Battles," 10.
3. Dönitz, *The Drama of the Graf Spee,* 420.
4. Wattenberg interview.
5. Ibid.
6. Millington-Drake, *The Drama of the Graf Spee,* 345.
7. Ibid.
8. Sweetman, "Great Sea Battles," 11; Wattenberg interview.
9. Dönitz, *The Drama of the Graf Spee,* 385.
10. Wattenberg interview; Kreis, "Schweinejagd auf dem Atlantik."
11. Alfred Dietrich, interview by author, 3 April 1995; Royal Navy Submarine Museum, Portsmouth, England, "Narratives: (a) sinking of '162' by H.M. Ships *'Vimy,' 'Pathfinder'* and *'Quentin'* 50 miles northeast of Tobago on 3rd September, 1942."
12. Wattenberg interview.
13. Moore, *Faustball Tunnel,* 143.
14. Walter Kozur, Johann Kremer, interview by author, Köln, Germany, 3 April 1995.
15. Wattenberg interview; Wattenberg, "Amerikanischer Gedenkstein für Deutsche Tunnelflucht."
16. Moore, *Faustball Tunnel,* 205, 206; Wattenberg interview.
17. Wattenberg interview.
18. Wattenberg, "Deutsche Tunnelflucht."

Chapter 2: Georg Högel

1. Georg Högel, interview by author, München, Germany, 27 June, 1997; correspondence, 1995-1997; Högel, "Kein Tag wie jeder andere."

2. Georg Högel, telephone interview, 27 April 1998.
3. Roskill, *The Secret Capture*, 104–15.3.

Chapter 3: Otto Kretschmer

1. Robertson, *Night Raider*, 46, 47.
2. Ibid., 50, 51.
3. Ibid., 8; Otto Kretschmer, interview by author, Hinte, Germany, 20 June 1998.
4. Rohwer, *Axis Submarine Successes*, 41.
5. Kretschmer interview.

Chapter 4: Josef Erben

1. U.S. National Archives and Records Administration (hereafter NARA), "Report on the Interrogation of Survivors from U-128," 11.
2. Morison, *The Atlantic Battle Won*, 210.
3. Josef Erben, report and correspondence, 1993, 1997.

Chapter 5: Hans Burck

1. *New York Times*, 17 February 1942, 1; Rohwer, *Axis Submarine Successes*, 78, 79.
2. *New York Times*, 17 February 1942, 1.
3. Rohwer, *Axis Submarine Successes*, 79.
4. Dönitz, *Memoirs*, 202, 212.
5. Miller, *Submarines of the World*, 99; photograph archives at Koblenz, Germany.
6. Hans Burck, diary and correspondence, 1993–1997.

Chapter 6: Ernst Göthling

1. Ernst Göthling, interviews by author, Möltenort, Germany, 24 March 1995, and by telephone 17 November 1997; correspondence, 1997.

Chapter 7: Hermann Frubrich

1. Lamb, *The Corvette Navy*, 21, quoted in Terraine, *The U-Boat Wars*, 334.
2. Rohwer, *Axis Submarine Successes*, 177.
3. Erich Topp, *The Odyssey of a U-boat Commander*, 88.
4. Norris Jones, correspondence with Ferdinand Heger, 1994.

5. Hermann Frubrich, report on U-845, including correspondence with Ferdinand Heger; Frubrich correspondence with author, 1995–1997.

Chapter 8: Hermann Wien

1. Wolpert, *New History of India,* 333, 337; Hermann Wien, correspondence with author, 1996, 1998.
2. Hermann Wien, report on U-180; correspondence with author, 1996, 1998.

Chapter 9: Otto Dietz

1. Otto Dietz, tape recording of memoirs made by Dietz and interviews by author, 12 October 1990, 14 September 1992.

Chapter 10: Tom Poser

1. German mothers, instead of saying *Komm!* (come here) to a child, would say *Tomm,* in baby talk, because children could not pronounce a "k."
2. Sweetman, "Great Sea Battles," 18, 19.
3. Sommerville, *World War II Day by Day,* 153.
4. Solzhenitsyn, *Gulag Archipelago,* 21.
5. Tom Poser, interviews by author, 8 February 1993, 2 August 1993, and biographical writing by Poser. (N.B. Poser joined the U.S. Submarine Veterans of World War II in Galveston, Texas, as an honorary member, and became president in 1994. At his funeral two years later, in June 1996, the sub group attended, paying a final tribute to their German friend.)

Chapter 11: Wolfgang von Bartenwerffer

1. Hadley, *U-boats against Canada,* 175.
2. Ibid.
3. Wolfgang von Bartenwerffer, interview by author, Essen, Germany, 1 May 1994, and correspondence, 1994–1997.

Chapter 12: U-682 and U-735

1. NARA, Modern Military Division, RG 242, *Records Relating to U-boat Warfare,* Kriegstagebuch U-682, PG 30707/1–2, 3376, T-422, 17 April, 1944–4 January, 1945; NARA, *Records Relating to U-boat Warfare,* 52.
2. Report by Herbert Hermann on the sinking of U-735 at Horten,

Oslo Fjord, on the night of 28 December 1944 and correspondence, 12 January 1997.

3. R. E. N. Porrett, "Blind Bomber."

4. John Whiteley, correspondence, 1993–1997.

5. War diary of the *Köln*, courtesy of former crew member Fritz Lamprecht. (N.B. On 9 January 1945 the cruiser returned to Germany and was bombed and sunk at a Wilhelmshaven shipyard on 31 March of that year.)

Chapter 13: Oskar Kusch

1. Heinz Kuhlmann, correspondence, 17 October 1997.

2. Passages from *Konteradmiral* a.D. (Rear Admiral) Karl Peter, "Der Fall des Oberleutnants zur See Oskar Kusch," unpublished report, date unspecified, courtesy of Heinz Kuhlmann.

Chapter 14: Siegfried Koitschka

1. Morison, *The Atlantic Battle Won*, 252–61. (N.B. The eight U.S. destroyers were *Ellyson, Rodman, Hambledon, Emmons, Macomb, Hilary P. Jones, Nields,* and *Gleaves.*

2. Dr. Siegfried Koitschka, report and correspondence, 1992, 1997.

Chapter 15: Hans Georg Hess

1. Hans Georg Hess, interviews by author, 25 September 1992, 30 September 1995, and correspondence, 1995–1997; Hess, *Die Männer von U 995.*

Chapter 16: Walter Tegtmeier

1. Tarrant, *The U-Boat Offensive,* 138, 144.

2. Walter Tegtmeier, interview by author, 27 March 1995, report and correspondence, 1997.

Chapter 17: Josef Matthes

1. Josef Matthes, interview by author, 25 April 1994, Görlitz, Germany.

Chapter 18: Helmut Wehlte and Günther Thiemrodt

1. Dönitz, *Memoirs,* 433.

2. Ibid., 465, 466; Helmut Wehlte, interview by author, 25 April 1994,

Görlitz, Germany, and correspondence; Günther Thiemrodt, correspondence, 16 April 1993.

Chapter 19: Peter Petersen

1. Terraine, *The U-Boat Wars*, 648.
2. Peter Petersen, interviews by author 21 September 1992, Hamburg, Germany, and 12 July 1993, Chicago, Illinois.

Chapter 20: Wolfgang Heibges

1. Wolfgang Heibges, *U 999 auf "Kurs Regenbogen"*; correspondence and telephone interview, 8 October 1997.

Chapter 21: Peter Marl

1. Rohwer, *Axis Submarine Successes*, 42, n. 7. "The 10,516-ton *Arthur F. Corwin* was hit by two torpedoes fired by U-123 [should be U-103] and sunk by U-96 with two additional hits." Footnote corrected by Dr. Rohwer in correspondence to author, 10 December 1996.
2. Tarrant, *The U-boat Offensive*, 183.
3. Ibid., 124. U-197 was sunk 20 August 1943, depth charged by RAF aircraft (259 and 265 Sqns) south of Madagascar; NARA, *Records Relating to U-Boat Warfare*, 63. Kentrat wrote in his KTB that he attempted unsuccessfully to rescue survivors of U-197, 20–24 August.
4. Dönitz, *Memoirs*, 475. On 14 May 1945, a few days after Germany had surrendered, Wolfgang Lüth, one of only two commanders awarded the Knight's Cross with Oak Leaves and Swords and Diamonds, failed to answer a German sentry's challenge and was shot to death.
5. Weigley, *Eisenhower's Lieutenants*, 271–75, 414–19.

BIBLIOGRAPHY

Books

Boyd, Carl, and Akihiko Yoshida. *The Japanese Submarine Force and World War II*. Annapolis, Md.: Naval Institute Press, 1995.

Dönitz, Karl. *Admiral Dönitz Memoirs: Ten Years and Twenty Days*. Translated by R. H. Stevens, in collaboration with David Woodward. Cleveland, Ohio: World Publishing Company, 1959.

————. *The Drama of the Graf Spee and The Battle of the Plate: A Documentary Anthology 1914–1964*. Compiled by Sir Eugen Millington-Drake. Foreword by Admiral of the Fleet Earl Mountbatten of Burma. London: Peter Davies, 1964.

Gannon, Michael. *Operation Drumbeat*. New York: Harper & Row, 1990.

Hadley, Michael. *U-boats against Canada: German Submarines in Canadian Waters*. Kingston, Canada: McGill-Queen's University Press, 1985.

Hess, Hans Georg. *Die Männer von U 995*. Wunstorf-Idensen: Hess-Press, 1979.

Högel, Georg. *Embleme Wappen Malings Deutscher U-Boote 1939–1945*. Hamburg: Koehlers Verlagsgesellschaft mbH, 1996.

Kahn, David. *Seizing the Enigma*. Boston: Houghton Mifflin Company, 1991.

Krammer, Arnold. *Nazi Prisoners of War in America*. New York: Stein and Day Publishers, 1979.

Lamb, James B. *The Corvette Navy*. Macmillan of Canada, 1978. Quoted in John Terraine, *The U-Boat Wars 1916–1945*. New York: G. P. Putnam's Sons, 1989.

Miller, David. *Submarines of the World*. New York: Orion Books, 1991.

Moore, John Hammond. *German POWs in America and Their Great Escape: The Faustball Tunnel*. New York: Random House, 1978.

Morison, Samuel Eliot. *History of United States Naval Operations in World War II*. Boston: Little, Brown, 1956.

Pope, Dudley. *Graf Spee: The Life and Death of a Raider*. Philadelphia: J. P. Lippincott Company, 1957.

Robertson, Terence. *Night Raider of the Atlantic*. New York: E. P. Dutton & Co., Inc., 1956.

Rohwer, Dr. Jürgen. *Axis Submarine Successes 1939–1945*. Annapolis, Md.: Naval Institute Press, 1983. (N.B: Dr. Rohwer's book has been updated and will appear in a new edition entitled *Axis Submarine Successes of World War Two: German, Italian, and Japanese Submarine Successes in World War II, 1939–1945*. Annapolis, Md.: Naval Institute Press, forthcoming 1999.)

Rohwer, J., and J. G. Hummelchen. *Chronology of the War at Sea 1939–1945*. Annapolis, Md.: Naval Institute Press, 1983, 1998.

Roskill, Captain S. W. *The Secret Capture*. St. James Place, London: Collins, 1959.

Rössler, Eberhard. *The U-boat: The evolution and technical history of German submarines*. Translated into English by Harold Erenberg. Annapolis, Md.: Naval Institute Press, 1989.

Shirer, William L. *The Rise and Fall of the Third Reich*. New York: Simon and Schuster, 1960.

Showell, Jak P. Mallmann. *U-boats under the Swastika*. Annapolis, Md.: Naval Institute Press, 1973.

Solzhenitsyn, Aleksandr. *The Gulag Archipelago*. New York: Harper & Row, 1974–1975.

Sommerville, Donald. *World War II Day by Day*. New York: Barnes & Noble, 1989.

———. *The Story of the U-505*. Chicago: Museum of Science and Industry, 1955.

Tarrant, V. E. *The U-Boat Offensive 1914–1945*. Annapolis, Md.: Naval Institute Press, 1989.

Terraine, John. *The U-Boat Wars, 1916–1945*. New York: G. P. Putnam's Sons, 1989.

Thomas, Lowell. *Raiders of the Deep*. Garden City, N.Y.: Garden City Publishing Company, 1928.

Topp, Erich. *The Odyssey of a U-Boat Commander*. Westport, Conn.: Praeger, 1992.

Weigley, Russell F. *Eisenhower's Lieutenants: The Campaign of France and Germany 1944–1945*. Bloomington: Indiana University Press, 1981.

Werner, Herbert. *Iron Coffins: A personal account of the German U-boat battles of World War II*. New York: Holt, Rinehart and Winston, 1969.

Wiggins, Melanie. *Torpedoes in the Gulf: Galveston and the U-boats, 1942–1943.* College Station, Texas: Texas A & M University Press, 1995.

Wolpert, Stanley. *A New History of India.* Oxford: Oxford University Press, 1977.

Articles, Published

Clark, Lloyd. "Escape." *Arizona Highways* (December 1993): 36–41.

———. "Denn wir fuhren." *Kristall* Nr. 5–10 (1956), Hamburg.

Fincher, Jack. "By Convention, the enemy within never did without." *Smithsonian* (June 1995): 126–43.

———. "German Prisoners Recall America's Great Escape." Associated Press, publisher and date unspecified.

Heibges, Wolfgang. "U 999 mit Kurs 'Regenbogen.'" *Schleswig-Holsteinischer* (6 May 1945).

Kreis, Hans. "Schweinejagd auf dem Atlantik." German newspaper, title and date unspecified.

Prager, Karsten. "Flight to Freedom." *Time* (15 May 1995): 53–56.

Schriefer, Von Roland. "Der 'Faustball-Tunnel' ging in die Geschichte der USA ein." *Kölner Stadt-Anzeiger* Nr. 194 (22 August 1995).

Sweetman, Jack. "Great Sea Battles of World War II: River Plate; Exercise Rhine." *Naval History* (May-June 1995): 10, 11, 18, 19.

Articles, Unpublished

Högel, Georg. "Kein Tag wie jeder andere, Erlebt auf U-30."

Porrett, R. E. N. "Blind Bomber."

Wattenberg, Jürgen. "Amerikanischer Gedenkstein für Deutsche Tunnelflucht."

Archival Sources

Bundesarchiv, Koblenz, Germany.

National Archives and Records Administration (NARA), *Guides to the Microfilmed Records of the German Navy, 1850–1945. No. 2: Records Relating to U-Boat Warfare, 1939–1945.* Compiled by Timothy Mulligan. Washington, D. C.: U.S. National Archives, 1985.

Royal Navy Submarine Museum, Portsmouth, England.

U-Boot Archiv, Cuxhaven, Germany.

INDEX

Abel, Ulrich, 148, 149, 150, 152
Achilles, 3
acoustic torpedoes, 156, 158
Adams, Bill, 143
Admiral Graf Spee, 3–5, 210
Admiral Scheer, 210
aground: U-128, 38–40; U-845, 75;
  U-995, 165
Ajax, 3
Allied Control Commission, 152
Andrews, Frank, 55–56
Angler POW camp, Canada, 64–65
Ark Royal (British aircraft carrier), 20
Aruba, U-boats attack, 55, 56
Athenia, 14, 23, 24, 25

Baddenberg, Karl, 181
Baker-Cresswell, *Bulldog* commander,
  23–24
Banff POW camp, Scotland, 64
Bänsch, U-195 seaman, 226
Bartels, Robert, 220, 222
*Bayou Stalags: German Prisoners of War
  in Louisiana* (Schott), 109
Behnert, U-845 petty officer, 78–79
Behrens, Udo, 68, 70
Bergwacht, 233
Biscay Cross, 41–42, 219
Bismarck, 111–13
Black Watch, 176
Blairlogie, 14
Böhme, U-845 petty officer, 78–79
Boost, U-196 torpedo mechanic, 222
Bopst, Eberhard, 170, 172
Bordeaux, Allied attacks on, 224
Börner, Hans-Joachim, 137, 139
Bose, Subhas Chandra, 92–94, 95, 98,
  102–3
Brady, Gilbert, 11

breathing devices, 61, 69, 214, 225. *See
  also* schnorkel devices
Broadway, 23, 24
Brown, (British) captain, 44
Bruskin, Robert, 56
Buck (U.S. destroyer), 156
Bulldog, 23–24
Burck, Hans, 49–59; Gulf of Mexico
  mission diary by, 49–55; on Japanese
  I-30 visit to Lorient, 58–59
Burghagen, U-195 group leader, 230
Büsgen, U-30 chief petty officer, 18

Camp Bowmanville for POWs, Canada,
  36, 125–26
Camp Harford Grange for POWs, Eng-
  land, 109
Camp Hearne for POWs, Texas, 107
Camp McCain for POWs, Mississippi,
  88
Camp Mexia for POWs, Texas, 106–7
Camp Sheffield for POWs, England, 109
Canadian navy, 126–27
Carter, 197
Charlotte Schliemann, 216, 220
Chatelain, 104
Cherry, Charles, 11
Cities Service Empire, 40
Clark, Lloyd, 11
Cockfosters (POW) Camp, England, 36
code, military communications, 222;
  British seize German books/machine,
  24–25; British use of, 46; Canadians
  break Ireland code, 126
Corbis, 97
Creasy, George, 31–32, 36
Curaçao, U-67 attacks, 52–54, 56

Dachau, 233

Hitler, Adolf, 204, 209, 210, 228; demand for obedience to, 148–49; on foreign radio broadcasts, 148, 150, 195; Legion of Free India and, 93–94, 102–3; Poser and, 111; salute to, 70–71
Hoffmann, Rudolf, 70–71
Högel, Georg, 13–25; art show at Thunder Bay of, 25; on attacks on U-30, 17–19, 20–21; *Fanad Head* and, 14–17, 19–20; Lemp asks to alter war diary, 23; as POW, 25; Schnurzl and, 13; on U-30, 13–14; on U-110, 23–25
Hood, 113
Hoppe, Joachim, 228
Horace Bushnell, 166
horseshoes as ship/submarine emblem, 30–31, 35
Horst, Friedrich, 7
Huber, Frau, 230, 231
Hungerhausen, Heinz, 46
Hurst, John, 143

I-29, Japanese submarine, 93, 97–98, 103
I-30, Japanese submarine, 57–59
Iceland, 22
Idefjord, 165
Ile de France, 153–54
Indonesia, Republic of, 228–29
insignia/emblems, U-boat, 13, 30–31, 35, 167–68, 181
Ireland code, 126

J. N. Pew, 54
Japanese submarine, 192. *See also* I-29; I-30
Jenks, 104
Jones, Freddie, 143
Jones, Norris, 87–88
Jouett, USS, 47
Joughin, Jock, 143
Junker, Ottoheinrich, 227

Kandeler, Batavia (Java) base commander, 226
Karlsruhe, 3
Kaura, 166
Kelmscott, 76
Kentrat, Eitel-Friedrich, 219, 220, 221, 222, 223
Kieler Sailing Week (1914), 1–2
Kitchitai, 228–29
Klaasen, *Bootsmaat,* 209
Klapf, Josef, 164
Klein, Hannes, 225

Kling, Herbert, 78
Koitschka, Siegfried, 153–59
Köln, 28, 141–42, 145
Königsberg, 170
Kozur, Walter, 7, 8, 9, 10
Kraus, Hans-Werner, 7
Kremer, Johann, 7–8, 9
Kretschmer, Louise-Charlotte, 26, 37
Kretschmer, Otto, 26–37; attacking convoys, 31–32; early life of, 26–28; medals for, 30, 36; as POW, 35–37, 125–26, 132; on U-23, 30; on U-35, 28–30; on U-99, 30–35
Kuhlmann, Heinz, 151–52
Kusch, Heinz, 151, 152
Kusch, Oskar, 46, 147–52; court-martial of, 148–51

Lamb, James B., 73
Lange, Harald, 102, 103, 104, 106, 107
Langsdorff, Hans, 3, 4, 5
Legion of Free India, 94
Lehmann, U-997 commander, 175, 176–77
Lehmann-Willenbrock, U-96 commander, 215
Leigh Light system, 81
Leipzig, 39
Lemp, Fritz-Julius, 14; on *Athenia* sinking, 23; escaping attacks on U-30, 21–22; *Fanad Head* and, 14–17, 19–21; Schnurzl and, 13; on U-110, 23–24
Lethbridge POW camp, Canada, 66
Leucht, U-845 navigator, 83
Longobardo, Italian submarine lieutenant commander, 32
Lorient, 45–46, 213, 215
Lorient Espionage Unit, 125–26
Lüdemann, Heinrich, 147
Lüth, Wolfgang, 220, 222, 223

Macintyre, Donald, 35, 37
Mai, U-845 navigator, 73
Maliikii Island, 164–65
Manchester POW camp, England, 64
Marl, Peter, 208–33; in Indonesia after WWII, 229–32; in training, 208–11; on U-103, 211–19; on U-195, 223–29; on U-196, 219–23
Matthes, Josef, 181–84
Mediterranean, U-616 in, 154–59
Meier, Heinz, 139
Meinert, J. A., 151
Meteor (Kaiser's yacht), 2–3

ABOUT THE AUTHOR

Managing family marshlands in a remote area of the Texas coast prompted Wiggins to write her first book, *They Made Their Own Law: Stories of Bolivar Peninsula,* in 1990. Her interest in local history and a visit to the site of the former Hitchcock Naval Air Station (for blimps) inspired her second work, *Torpedoes in the Gulf: Galveston and the U-boats, 1942–1943,* concerning the attacks of German submarines in the Gulf of Mexico during World War II as seen from a Galveston perspective. While interviewing U-boat veterans in Germany for *Torpedoes,* she met a number of men who offered records, diaries, and photographs of their submarine patrols in western oceans outside the Gulf of Mexico, and her fascination with their stories led to the present collection.

Born in Fort Smith, Arkansas, Melanie Wiggins graduated from Hollins College in Virginia and worked in art and photography before her entry into the literary realm. Since then she has undertaken to bring to light exciting historical events as told by the individuals who participated in them.

The Naval Institute Press is the book-publishing arm of the U.S. Naval Institute, a private, nonprofit, membership society for sea service professionals and others who share an interest in naval and maritime affairs. Established in 1873 at the U.S. Naval Academy in Annapolis, Maryland, where its offices remain today, the Naval Institute has members worldwide.

Members of the Naval Institute support the education programs of the society and receive the influential monthly magazine *Proceedings* and discounts on fine nautical prints and on ship and aircraft photos. They also have access to the transcripts of the Institute's Oral History Program and get discounted admission to any of the Institute-sponsored seminars offered around the country.

The Naval Institute also publishes *Naval History* magazine. This colorful bimonthly is filled with entertaining and thought-provoking articles, first-person reminiscences, and dramatic art and photography. Members receive a discount on *Naval History* subscriptions.

The Naval Institute's book-publishing program, begun in 1898 with basic guides to naval practices, has broadened its scope in recent years to include books of more general interest. Now the Naval Institute Press publishes about one hundred titles each year, ranging from how-to books on boating and navigation to battle histories, biographies, ship and aircraft guides, and novels. Institute members receive discounts of 20 to 50 percent on the Press's more than eight hundred books in print.

Full-time students are eligible for special half-price membership rates. Life memberships are also available.

For a free catalog describing Naval Institute Press books currently available, and for further information about subscribing to *Naval History* magazine or about joining the U.S. Naval Institute, please write to:

Membership Department
U.S. Naval Institute
291 Wood Road
Annapolis, MD 21402-5034
Telephone: (800) 233-8764
Fax: (410) 269-7940
Web address: www.usni.org